D0431582

THE EXPORT OF MEANING

THE EXPORT OF MEANING

CROSS-CULTURAL READINGS OF *DALLAS*

TAMAR LIEBES

ELIHU KATZ

Polity Press

Copyright © Tamar Liebes and Elihu Katz 1993

The right of Tamar Liebes and Elihu Katz to be identified as authors of
this work has been asserted in accordance with the Copyright, Designs and Patents Act
1988.

First published by Oxford University Press Inc. 1990.
Second edition first published 1993 by Polity Press in association with Blackwell
Publishers.

Editorial office:
Polity Press
65 Bridge Street
Cambridge CB2 1UR, UK

Marketing and production:
Blackwell Publishers
108 Cowley Road
Oxford OX4 1JF, UK

238 Main Street
Cambridge, MA 02142, USA

All rights reserved. Except for the quotation of
short passages for the purposes of criticism and
review, no part of this publication may be
reproduced, stored in a retrieval system, or
transmitted, in any form or by any means,
electronic, mechanical, photocopying, recording or
otherwise, without the prior permission of the publisher.

Except in the United States of America, this book is
sold subject to the condition that it shall not, by
way of trade or otherwise, be lent, re-sold, hired
out, or otherwise circulated without the publisher's
prior consent in any form of binding or cover
other than that in which it is published and without a
similar condition including this condition being
imposed on the subsequent puchaser.

ISBN 0-7456 1295-4 (pbk)

A CIP catalogue record for this book is available
from the British Library and from the Library of
Congress.

Typeset in 9½ on 11½ pt Palatino
by TecSet Ltd, Wallington, Surrey
Printed in Great Britain by Page Bros, Norwich

This book is printed on acid-free paper.

CONTENTS

INTRODUCTION TO THE 1993
EDITION

This new Polity edition provides a welcome opportunity to explain how the book originated, and why. It also provides the advantage of hindsight in that we are able to see how others, coming from elsewhere—literary studies, sociolinguistics, cinema studies, feminist theory, critical studies, and cultural studies—have arrived at more or less the same place. It seems to us a good time to cut through the several jargons to take note of the common interest. We are well aware that the idea of "convergence" or reconciliation is unpopular, by definition, among those who believe that the truth emerges only from struggle among paradigms. Maybe so, but there is no use locking oneself into one's paradigm and throwing away the key.

To contextualize ourselves, let us begin by saying that we sit in a place called Israel, which, like every other country in the non-Western world, introduced television with the rhetoric of social integration and cultural authenticity and found itself broadcasting *Dallas* (Katz and Wedell, 1977; Katz, 1971). Indeed, the introduction of television in Israel was postponed for fear that it might interfere with several central social values: books and reading, issue-oriented politics, renewal of the Hebrew language, anti-materialism. It took the war of 1967 (when the Arab countries tried to reach Israelis via television) and the occupation that followed (when Israelis tried to reach Palestinians in the territories) to push the Government to take the final step. In its first two decades, Israel television, on the BBC model, has established a first-rate news and current affairs division, but drama and entertainment are notably weak. The reasons usually given are that drama is too expensive to produce, that talent is sparse, that the language is too literary to adapt, and—perhaps more than a joke—that no melodrama can hope to compete with the drama of the news!

Like the rest of the world, therefore, we find ourselves asking whether the high proportion of fiction imported from American television is, in fact, doing damage to the goals of national integration and renaissance of culture. The question is all the more acute for Israel as it has now begun to install competing channels—a national commercial network and a cable system—that threaten the community of shared viewing of the 9 p.m. news.

So we began to think about cultural imperialism and what that connotes. As a continuation of economic imperialism "by other means" it implies that an outside power exploits a weaker power for its own gain (and at the expense of the self-interest of the other). The rhetoric of "global village" tends to understate this aspect of power. We asked ourselves, therefore, whether *Dallas* and programs like it are not merely culture-for-sale but also agents of subversion of indigenous values. A good place to look for answers, we thought, would be to observe the reception of the program in Israeli homes.

We also realized that Israel, like the rest of the non-Western world, is not homogeneous at all, otherwise there would not be so much concern about its integration. It consists of immigrants from dozens of cultures who arrived before and after the founding of the State, and who are classified, also by themselves, as Western (of European origin) and Eastern (Asian or African in origin). In class terms—defined by time of arrival, education, and occupation—the Western groups and their descendents are considered dominant, even though the economic and political map is changing with the rise of a second-generation of Eastern immigrants. In addition to these, there are the Arab citizens of Israel (17 percent of the population) who can be classified (also by themselves) as a national minority, and the newly arrived immigrants from Russia and Ethiopia. Each of these groups is continually jockeying for position *vis-à-vis* the others, not so much in terms of class, but in terms of cultural politics in a society that tends now towards pluralism, now towards homogenization.

We asked ourselves a second question, therefore: whether these different ethnicities might not "use" even the alien culture delineated by programs like *Dallas* to explore and redefine their own identities and to compare themselves not just with Americans but with the other Israelis. We therefore decided to give representation to specific sub-cultural groups in Israel, rather than to Israelis in general. We chose Israeli Arabs, Moroccan Jews, new immigrants from Russia, and veteran kibbutz members of Western origin. Each sub-culture is represented by ten focus groups, to which were added, for further comparison, Americans in Los Angeles, the original target audience, and Japanese in Tokyo, where the program failed.

The focus groups were anything but decontextualized. Each group, comprising three couples, consisted of friends or extended family, invited to their home by the host couple, and sharing age, education, sub-cultural identity, and loyalty to the program. The group discussions took place before, during, and after the real transmission time, with ourselves as quasi-ethnographers to view the viewing, and an interviewer to animate the conversation after the program ended. The fact is that much of the talk was spontaneous, certainly during the program itself, and the interviewers—recruited from the same ethnic backgrounds as the focus-groups they led—were almost forgotten. Group members talked to each other much more than they talked to, or for, us.

The sub-cultural differences in Israeli society—the extent of their centrality/ marginality, the ways in which they differ on the continuum of orality/literacy, their position on the scale of patriarchy—are well reflected in the ways each type of community discusses the program. The Russians in our study, for example, look down on Israelis who view *Dallas*, but nevertheless view it themselves as an entry into everyday conversation. "I view *Dallas*" said a Russian woman, "in order to become an Israeli!" Nevertheless, the Russians proved by far the most "oppositional" of viewers, believing that the program is, indeed, a capitalist manipulation, and that children should be forcibly prevented from viewing it.

The Arabs, for their part, are so embarrassed by *Dallas* that they prefer to view it in sexually homogeneous groups. "We don't let our women do things like that," said one of them. Speaking not only of culture but of domination, Arabs see J. R. -like figures in the Israeli establishment. On the other hand, the more dominant groups are more likely to assert that an Israeli J. R. would not go unpunished—either in business or in politics.

While presentation of self as Israelis (*vis-à-vis* American culture) and members of sub-cultures (*vis-à-vis* Israeli culture) dominated the "official" discourse, the more spontaneous interaction emerged from family and gender roles played *vis-à-vis* the program and the others in the group. In this sense, we were viewing families viewing families on television. What we observed was the process of family and friendship dynamics in action, triggered by the viewing and the relationships on the screen. As in Morley (1987), there were arguments about whose program it was and about who was doing whom a favor by watching. The fact is that the entire nation was watching religiously, household by household, kibbutz by kibbutz, making comparisons between the operation of power in families. Oldtimer couples of Moroccan origin, for example, squabbled over whether babies belong equally to both parents, or whether husbands in *Dallas* would dare ask their wives to interrupt their viewing in order to serve coffee to focus-group guests. (The text of this great conversation appears in chapter 4.)

Thus, having begun with the problem of the authenticity of culture, we found ourselves observing three sorts of struggle—between national cultures, between sub-cultures within a nation, and between the sexes within families. These concentric circles of power contextualize the hundreds of millions of viewers of *Kojak, Dallas, Dynasty, L. A. Law,* and *Married, With Children*. Of course, there is endless variety in the ways these contexts take shape: the relation between Japanese and American cultures is different from that between Israeli and American cultures; tribal Nigeria is different from ethnic Israel; family cultures among Israeli Arabs and Jews are different, and changing at different rates. Even the viewing situation varies considerably between societies in which there are television sets in every room and hardly any family and those in which the television's dream-family is still intact and sprawled in front of the set.

One analysis is based on interactions, or chunks of conversation such that we can distinguish, first of all, the several types of role that are invoked. These correspond, largely, to the three types of power relations; thus one might be speaking as an Israeli, as an Arab in Israel, or as a wife and mother. Secondly, we classify the chunks of conversation according to whether they frame the characters as if they were real ("referential"), or as raw material with which to fantasize ("ludic"), or as manipulations by the producer ("ideological") or as formulaic constructions ("aesthetic"). We then take note of the fact that the same groups, and the very same people, commute among the different identities and among the different types of framing.

We demonstrate the diversities of response to *Dallas* but we do not treat the program as a projective test. We show how open it is to different readings, but our study leaves no doubt that the text constrains its decodings. Decoding is an interaction between the culture of the viewer and the culture of the producer.

Rather than be satisfied with the idiosyncracies of this case study our object is to address the issues that arise in similar situations. We want to generalize to other societies that import American popular culture, to the ways viewers employ television texts to map their social relations within a nation or a family, to the abilities of viewers to decode such material critically, to the vulnerabilities that are the flip side of each type of decoding.

One can argue, without shame, that this approach derives ultimately from a functional tradition that, however poorly conceptualized and even more poorly operationalized, tried to assess the balance of power between the media and their audiences (Blumler, Gurevitch and Katz, 1986). We differ from most work in this paradigm, however, (1) by regarding entertainment as genres that open gates to the public sphere and politicize the private; (2) by placing more weight on the text, identifying its hegemonic ambitions, and the extent of its openness; (3) by contextualizing the viewer sociologically rather than psychologically; (4) by observing the patterns of viewers' decodings, and the involvements and vulnerabilities that accompany them; (5) by observing the manufacture of shared meanings through group interaction; (6) by paying attention to the way reflexive readings may sometimes lead to social change; (7) by examining the extent of viewers' consciousness of the content and structure of the text, interpreting the interpretations rather than relying only on viewers' self-assessments; (8) by being aware that this is an endless game; (9) by using quasi-ethnographic methods.

It is important to remember, finally, that our generalizations apply to near-universal reading and viewing situations, where everybody can assume that everybody else is familiar with the text. This meets Carey's (1989) definition of communication as culture, i.e. as ritual occasions on which societies gather together and as a reservoir of ideas to think with and debate (Katz, 1986).

With the present accelerated decline of public broadcasting systems and the concomitant rise of an infinity of channels, these conditions are increasingly unlikely. We are unsure, therefore, whether the future will provide many more "Dallases." The segmentation of television viewing and its frenetic pursuit of the spectator threaten the community of experience, universal and variant, that was sustained by long-standing classics like the Bible and, *mutatis mutandis, Dallas*.

Jerusalem   T. L.
May 1993   E. K.

PREFACE

Theorists of cultural imperialism assume that hegemony is prepackaged in Los Angeles, shipped out to the global village, and unwrapped in innocent minds. We wanted to see for ourselves; and thanks to grants from the trustees of the Annenberg Schools and the Hoso Bunka Foundation, we were able to do so — in the U.S., Israel, and Japan.

Israel itself is something of a global village, and *Dallas* was a big hit. In the environs of Jerusalem, we watched the weekly episode in the homes of Arabs, veteran settlers from Morocco, recent arrivals from Russia, and second-generation Israelis in kibbutzim — *Dallas* fans all. Following the viewing, we triggered a conversation about the program among the gathered family and friends. We compared these conversations with parallel conversations in Los Angeles (the real Southfork) and in Tokyo, where *Dallas* failed.

Each cultural group found its own way to "negotiate" with the program — different types of readings, different forms of involvement, different mechanisms of self-defense, each with its own kind of vulnerability. We found only very few innocent minds and a variety of "villages."

We are grateful, first of all, to Peter Clarke, dean of the Annenberg School at the University of Southern California, for believing in the study. We also thank Dr. Susan Evans for nursing the research team in Los Angeles: Lili Berko, Debby Ross-Christiansen, Vicki Owens, Eric Rothenbuhler. Lili Berko was also co-author of our first working paper. Other members of the Annenberg community helped in various phases of the production of the final manuscript: Agnes Uy, Rachel Osborn and Carolyn Spicer.

In Jerusalem, the organizer of field work was Gaby Daus, assisted by Ilan Nahum. Interviewing and coding — in Hebrew, Russian, and Arabic — was done by Anat Cohen, Adi Malul, Gil Feigelman, Ariela Lazar, Liora Hiamson, Yoav Shanzer, Zoya Tsidkin, Abd al-Salam Najar, Ahmed Natur, Nahum

Gelbar, Naomi Levav, Amnon Levav, Gali Gold. Word processing was done by Naomi Miller, Nira Raveh, and Yael Wyant. Andre Goodfriend helped with translation. Shosh Zilberberg and Rivka Ribak helped throughout.

Professor Sumiko Iwao joined us for the Japanese portion, and she is co-author of Chapter 9 of this book. In the field work she was assisted by Professor Koichi Ogawa. Translations from Japanese into Hebrew and English were expertly done by Hirokazu Oikawa in Jerusalem. Dorit Meier wrote a master's thesis on part of the Japanese data.

We consulted colleagues at many points in the design and analysis. Our greatest debt is to Daniel Dayan. Don Handelman and Michael Wade served as co-advisers to the Ph.D. dissertation which was a first draft of the book, and we had the advice of Dmitri Segal on the responses of the Russian groups. The late Beverle Houston, Horace Newcomb, Ron Gottesman, Muriel Cantor, Kim Schroeder all contributed of their experience and ideas in the analysis of media texts. William Gamson shared his experience with focus-group methodology. David Jacobs and Andre Guttfreund treated our team to a day on the *Dallas* set.

Some chapters and parts of chapters were published, in earlier versions, in collections and academic journals, and we wish to thank their editors and publishers: *Studies in Visual Communication; European Journal of Communication; Critical Studies in Mass Communication; Inter-Media* (published by the International Institute of Communication, London); *Television: The Critical View*, ed. Horace Newcomb, New York: Oxford University Press; *Myths, Media and Narratives*, ed. James Carey, Newbury Park, Calif.: Sage; *La Physique des sciences de l'homme: Mélanges offerts à Abraham Moles*, eds. M. Mathien et al., Strasbourg: Oberlin; *Remote Control: Television, Audiences and Cultural Power*, eds. Ellen Seiter, Hans Borchers, et al., London: Routledge; *International Dissemination of Television Drama*, ed. P. Larsen, Paris: UNESCO; *Television in Transition*, eds. A. Drummond and R. Patterson, London: BFI; *Intermedia*, eds. G. Gumpert and T. Cathcart, 2nd edition, New York: Oxford University Press.

Jerusalem
February 1989

E. K.
T. L.

THE EXPORT OF MEANING

1

ON VIEWING *DALLAS* OVERSEAS: INTRODUCTION TO THE STUDY

American popular culture travels the world with ease. Films, pop music, musicals, fast food, jeans, and American advertising have taken hold almost everywhere, in spite of the objections of patriots of the indigenous heritage. Television stations everywhere have the same stories to tell, partly because the stories *are* the same—imported, as they are, from New York, Hollywood, and London—and partly because the formulae for the stories are the same—imported, as they are, from New York, Hollywood, and London. Jeremy Tunstall (1977) and others have documented in scholarly fashion what jetsetters know from experience—namely, that the television set in the hotel room will not help you decide whether you are in Lagos or Los Angeles.

Others have tried to answer *why* American television programs have turned the world into a global village. That is not the purpose here, although our study of *Dallas* overseas will offer suggestions to explain the universal appeal of so ostensibly parochial a program. Our purpose, rather, is to answer even more elementary questions: How in the world is a program like *Dallas* so universally understandable, or is it? Is it understood in the same way in different places? Does it evoke different kinds of involvement and response? Mesmerized by the pervasiveness of American television programs, media professionals, including researchers, assume blithely that everybody understands them in the same way. It is equally plausible that a program so essentially American as *Dallas* might not be understood at all, especially after dubbing or with subtitles. It is not enough to argue that the story is so simpleminded or so visual that anybody in the world can readily comprehend it. In fact, the story is *not* understandable without dialogue; and in some ways—in kinship structure, for example, and in the number of interwoven subplots—it is quite complex.

3

Cultural Imperialism

Critical studies of the diffusion of American television programs overseas have labeled this process "cultural imperialism" as if there were no question but that the hegemonic message the analyst discerns in the text is transferred to the defenseless minds of viewers the world over for the self-serving interests of the economy and ideology of the exporting country (Dorfman and Matelart, 1975). Perhaps so. But labeling something imperialistic is not the same as proving it is. To prove that *Dallas* is an imperialistic imposition, one would have to show (1) that there is a message incorporated in the program that is designed to profit American interests overseas, (2) that the message is decoded by the receiver in the way it was encoded by the sender, and (3) that it is accepted uncritically by the viewers and allowed to seep into their culture.[1] Let us assume that a critical reading of *Dallas* would, in fact, reveal to the analyst that a central message is that "the rich are unhappy." Is this a self-interested message from the point of view of the encoders? Perhaps so, if one assumes that the producers are working in the cause of class or country to create content-ment among the disadvantaged of the world rather than to encourage enter-prise and initiative and risk frustration and revolution. It may be, of course, that the program *both* encourages enterprise and consoles those who are unable to succeed (Thomas and Callahan, 1982). Whatever the message in the text—if there is one—*our* interest is in what message reaches the viewers. We argue that ideology is not produced through a process of stimulus and response but rather through a process of negotiation between various types of senders and receivers. To understand the messages perceived by viewers of a television program, one cannot be satisfied with abstract generalizations derived from content analysis, however sophisticated. The actual interaction between the program and its viewers must be studied. In the case of *Dallas*, the challenge is to observe how the melodrama of a fictional family in Texas is viewed, in-terpreted, and discussed by real families throughout the world, in the light of the drama of their own lives and of those of the fictional and real others whom they have come to know through symbolic culture and actual community.

Indeed, a clue to the pervasiveness of American television programs over-seas may lie in their "openness" to negotiation, raising the possibility that they are not so culture-bound as they seem. Arlen (1980) makes the point that markers of place are not very evident in *Dallas*—that Southfork could be any-where. (The Children's Television Workshop thinks that an installment of *Sesame Street* can be made value-free for export.) The openness that we discern in *Dallas*, however, is more than just anonymity; it is an invitation to guessing games, ludic fantasies, self-reflection, moral outrage, critical disdain, and more.

Vigorous marketing is certainly a second answer. An ample supply of American television programs—assembly-line series and serials—is available to fill the gap created by the overcommitment of television systems almost everywhere to broadcast many more hours than they can hope to produce. If this was the rule for the Third World of the 1950s and 1960s (Katz and

Wedell, 1977), it is becoming no less a rule for the Europe of today, as cable and satellite channels multiply the number of broadcast hours that must be programmed.

We propose three reasons for the worldwide success of American television: (1) the universality, or primordiality, of some of its themes and formulae, which makes programs psychologically accessible (see Chapter 10); (2) the polyvalent or open potential of many of the stories, and thus their value as projective mechanisms and as material for negotiation and play in the families of man; and (3) the sheer availability of American programs in a marketplace where national producers—however zealous—cannot fill more than a fraction of the hours they feel they must provide.

On the Worldwide Popularity of *Dallas*

The name *Dallas* in the 1980s became a metaphor for the conquest of the world by an American television serial. *Dallas* signifies an international congregation of viewers (one of the largest in history), gathered once weekly to follow the saga of the Ewing dynasty—its interpersonal relations and business affairs. That the name *Dallas* evoked the memory of an earlier congregation gathered to attend one of the most dramatic of all television events is probably no coincidence, echoed as it is in the names John (J. R.) and Bobby.

Because *Dallas* became the most popular program in the world, students of the media also treated the program paradigmatically. Researchers in the United States and elsewhere, in unusually large numbers, gave their attention to the program, and it is likely by now that it is the most studied of all television texts. Researchers also found interest in the pioneering role played by *Dallas* as a prime-time variant of the soap opera—what might be called a "Grand Soap Opera." While nighttime soaps have long been a staple of South American and British television, they were altogether new for the United States and most of mainland Europe. It seems appropriate to say that the American studies focus on the ideological content of the program as an expression of changing American values (Mander, 1983; Arlen, 1980; Newcomb, 1982), while the overseas studies are concerned with the attraction of this kind of American product for foreign viewers (Bianchi, 1984; Silj, 1988; Herzog-Massing, 1986; Ang, 1985; Stolz, 1983; Livingstone, 1987a).

Ang (1985) counted ninety countries in which *Dallas* succeeded, complete with proverbially empty streets while the program was in progress and overstrained telephone and water systems during breaks. *Dallas* became a lingua franca, providing shared characters and situations to strangers without a common language. Tracey (1985, 1988) reminds us that locally produced soap operas compete well with the imported product despite the vast difference in production costs. Depending on the episode and year of production, an episode of *Dallas* costs somewhere between $500,000 and $1 million.

Dallas failed in only a few places. One hears of its irrelevance in Brazil, which is itself a center for the manufacture of soap operas. Japan is another country that rejected *Dallas*—after little more than six months it was removed from the commercial station that imported and dubbed it (see Chapter 9).

Our starting point, however, is *Dallas* in Israel. As it did the Germans, English, Danes, and Algerians, *Dallas* fascinated the Israelis. It gained as close to total viewership as any program ever has on Israel's single channel (even including the must-viewing of *Mabat*, the nightly news magazine). Kibbutzim rescheduled their well entrenched, Sunday-night town meetings because of the program, and cinema owners offered special Sunday-night prices to lure people away from their TV sets (without success).

The ethnic composition of Israel provided an opportunity to examine our assumption that meaning emerges from negotiation, that is, that understanding, interpretation, and involvement vary as a function of the interaction between the symbolic resources of the viewer and the symbolic offerings of the text. We wanted to observe this process in action and, insofar as possible, in normal viewing circumstances.

Accordingly, we assembled small groups of family and friends, each group consisting of three married couples of like age, education, and ethnicity. Forty-four such groups were chosen from among Israeli Arabs, newly arrived Russian Jews, veteran Moroccan settlers, and members of kibbutzim (typically second-generation Israelis). Each group met in the home of one of the couples on the Sunday night of the *Dallas* broadcast, together with a trained interviewer who, following the broadcast, led a discussion based on a standardized set of guidelines (see Appendix One). In addition, during the viewing, observations were made of interactions among group members and between group members and the screen.

The Israeli groups were matched with ten groups of second-generation Americans in the Los Angeles area in order to compare the Israeli readings not only among themselves but also with those of viewers who share the producers' culture. At a later date, eleven Japanese groups were selected and interviewed in the same way. Because *Dallas* failed in Japan, the Japanese were shown a videotape of the first episode of the program, and because the Americans were seeing programs two seasons ahead of the Israelis, they were shown videotapes of the same episodes that were on the air in Israel to ensure comparability. In all, there were sixty-five groups of six persons each, approximately ten from each of the six cultures. Groups were interviewed in their own languages.

Outline of the Book

This book is a record of our research experience. Chapter 2 presents the program, first through the eyes of academics and professional critics and then through the eyes of pioneering researchers, on viewers in different cultures. The chapter illustrates the fruitfulness of asking viewers to be critics and responds to the questions, Why do we know so little about the variability of readings (both among critics and among viewers) and Why has the study of viewer decodings been so neglected?

Chapter 3 elaborates on the design of the research. This chapter also portrays typical reactions of the various cultural groups to the interview situation. The protocol of a Moroccan group discussion is presented in Chapter 4 to illustrate the richness and the naturalness of the conversation in the sessions.

The discussion group as a simulation of the social mechanisms which contribute to viewers' understandings, interpretations, and evaluations is the subject of Chapter 5. The chapter also examines the uses of *Dallas* as a conversational resource. Chapter 6 exemplifies the process of cumulative storytelling. It is based on the groups' responses to our opening request to retell in their own words the episode just seen. The groups differ in their inclinations to tell the episode as a sociological story of family, as a psychological story of personality, or as an ideological paradigm.

Chapters 7 and 8 examine the groups' discussions from the points of view of the two major types of viewer involvement. In one type, the viewers relate the program to reality. When considering a character, a problem, or a situation, they are led into a discussion of real life, especially their own situations. In the other type of involvement, viewers see a program as a dramatic construction, and their pleasure is based on applying a variety of critical mechanisms to the program. Most viewers commute between these two types of involvement (the referential and the critical), but some specialize in the referential (Chapter 7). Chapter 8 analyzes the various forms of critical ability used by average TV viewers.

In Chapter 9, we try to explain why the Japanese did *not* get involved in *Dallas*. They reject the story's bid for acceptance as reality, perceiving it as incongruous with the models of society they know—American or Japanese, traditional or modern. But even as critical readers, for which they show themselves to be better qualified than any of the other groups—the Japanese viewers cannot enjoy the program as art because it violates their expectations of the genre to which it claims to belong. It is "neither here nor there," they say, both referentially and critically.

Chapter 10 argues that *Dallas* refers in both theme and form to the elementary myths of our civilization—the tales in Genesis, for example. The primordial content—such as sibling rivalry and a family that fills the world—and the serial structure of repeated variations on the same narrative make *Dallas* intuitively recognizable. Referential readers enjoy the program naively, living their lives in the echoes of these myths and reading the myths in the echo of their lives. Critical readers join in the "writing" of the program and are aware of its intertextual references to primordial myth.

In Chapter 11, we discuss the further research that is needed to substantiate our conclusions and to open some new doors. We also consider the unlikely sounding idea of "applied *Dallas*," that is, how popular fiction of this sort might be enlisted in the service of social and psychological change—how the Devil might be made to do God's work.

2

READING TELEVISION:
TELEVISION AS TEXT
AND VIEWERS AS DECODERS

The study of television is the study of effect. Research on ownership patterns, ratings research, and content analysis are all oriented primarily to assessment of the influence of senders on receivers in indirect ways. Owners are assumed to be selling their ideologies and products; audiences are assumed by their mere presence to be mesmerized; texts are *assumed* to imprint the messages perceived by content analysts. These are substitutes for the study of actual effects on audiences, because proving effects is so difficult. It is much easier to count heads or to count acts of violence or to identify the power structure which controls the media than to make certain that the audience is awake, that the owners actually have a message, and that the message is getting through. However, what possible justification can there be for studying the corporate deals between American and overseas broadcasters or the patterns of flow of American programs in the world without trying to ascertain whether the overseas audiences of these programs *are* getting the message that the text allegedly carries?

As long as one focuses on the influence of television within a particular society, it may be reasonable to assume that the message perceived by professional critics and content analysts is the message that gets through to the audience; perhaps one knows intuitively—as a member of society—what the powerholders really want. *Verstehen* has a chance, perhaps, *within* a society in which both researchers and subjects are members. Even then, the case is not strong. Domestic audiences are not homogenous entities. The ethnic and cultural communities that make up most societies, not to speak of the aggregates of age, education, gender, and class, are all different enough to raise the possibility that decodings and effects vary widely within any given society.

Content Analysis and the Study of Effect

But content analysis is clearly an essential prerequisite for defining what's on television. Such analysis constitutes a basis for the construction of hypotheses about viewer decodings and effects, thus making it possible to compare readings within the community of analysts and between the community of analysts and the communities of audiences. While we would argue strongly against the possibility of inferring effects from content analysis alone, we do not wish to belittle the role of the content analyst. In this, we dissociate ourselves from the empiricism of mass-media research, which too often assumed that any text was simply projective and could serve to gratify any social or psychological need. This is the counterpart of the no less arrogant position of certain critical theorists who assumed that their text was the one that imposed itself unequivocably on the audience (Fejes, 1984; Liebes, 1989; Schroder, 1987).

Though content analysis is a central concern, communications research is by no means of one piece. There are several different methodological strands. The critical theorists, and more recently structuralists and semiologists with humanistic and philosophical orientations, obviously lean to the qualitative and the latent. Mainline communications researchers—as social scientists—have focused on manifest content in a quantitative way. But the more important difference is in the definition of the unit of analysis. Compared with qualitative analyses, studies employing quantitative methods tend to be much more microscopic, focusing on small units. Ironically, this microscopic orientation leads to less interest in the boundaries of a program or a genre and more interest in the supertext of television as a tantalizing medium which delivers incidents of violence, messages about the ethnic types that qualify as heroes and villains, rankings of different occupations, instructions about the behavior expected of the several sex and class roles, and toutings of the values of consumerism and success (Browne, 1984; Houston, 1985; Gerbner, Gross et al., 1979). The qualitative orientation, by contrast, stresses genre, sometimes individual programs, emphasizing themes and their interrelations, such as the relationship between civilization and wilderness in the Western. The two types of analysis do converge, at least to a certain extent, on the study of genre. Two genres, in particular, have occupied communications research almost from the beginning: the news and family drama.

The news, of course, has long been the subject of students of political communication (Galtung and Ruge, 1970), although it has recently attracted the interest of students of the sociology of rhetoric and narrative structure as well (Tuchman, 1973; Molotch and Lester, 1974; Gitlin, 1980; Glasgow University Media Group, 1976; Dahlgren, 1985; Gans, 1979; Graber, 1984; Hartley, 1982; Robinson and Levy, 1986). Analysis of daytime family serials dates to the early days of radio (Herzog, 1941; Arnheim, 1942–43; Warner and Henry, 1948) and has experienced a major revival in the television era (Katzman, 1972; Greenberg, 1982; Cassata and Skill, 1983; Cantor and Pingree, 1983; Newcomb, 1974; Braudy, 1982; Cavell, 1982; Booth, 1982; Eco, 1985; Allen, 1985), gradually widening the circle to include sociologists, literary scholars, semiologists, film scholars, etc. The fact that television resides in the bosom of the family and that it was long considered the daytime companion of housewives (now joined by students and professors) makes the soap opera an obvious object of fascination for the study of involvement, decoding, gratifications, and effects. The recent upsurge of feminism has added further interest, inasmuch as these daytime programs are thought to be relevant for, and to provoke, reflection and debate over the issue of family roles (Modleski, 1984).

With expansion of the American daytime serial into prime time and its subsequent export to other countries, new dimensions were added to the fascination with the television soap opera. The allegation of cultural imperialism was made, and students of international communication began to take interest. Looking at the soap opera in this new comparative context, scholars took note of the indigenous development of prime-time family stories in many countries. In line with the earliest communications research, these recent studies also assert that the soap is a conservative agent of socialization to familistic values, disconnecting viewers from the political arena while reassuring them that the world will continue to turn. Some studies have begun to rethink the soap opera as a locus for the discussion of social issues and the focusing of social conflict. Internationally, soap operas are seen as mobilizing ethnic and national identities and as capable of promoting social and economic change (Bombardier, 1985).

On the Content Analysis of *Dallas*

Dallas is surely one of the most studied texts in the history of television. This is probably due to its worldwide status as a best-seller and perhaps because it is perceived as the beginning of a new genre in American television, combining the afternoon soap with other prime-time forms. The analysts are literary scholars and professional critics of various ideological inclinations. Integrating their very different versions of the themes and messages of *Dallas* will give us a base from which to proceed. The diversity of critical readings will immediately reveal how farfetched it is to assume that there is one dominant reading that will produce a single, monolithic effect. And if the critics treat the narrative so polysemically, why not the viewers?

The debate centers on whether *Dallas* is anomic and unprincipled or conservative and patriarchal. Thus, Michael Arlen (1980), the critic, treats *Dallas* as an expression of our modern anarchic era. For him—speaking, presumably, for cosmopolitan readers—it is a chaotic comedy of manners. We enjoy the Ewings, says Arlen, because, like us, they improvise both morals and actions as they go along. There are no fixed values to guide behavior, and there is no knowing what anybody will do next.

Unlike Arlen, Gillian Swanson (1982), a feminist critic of *Dallas*, is not amused. For her, the story is about the failure of women's liberation. Far from being unpredictable and creative, Swanson sees the Ewings operating within a patriarchal system in which reward or punishment can be expected for the woman who conforms to or deviates from the stereotypical role assigned to her. Inevitably, women who strive to achieve professional independence or emotional fulfillment outside their roles as wives and mothers have to pay. For Swanson, there are no surprises here, only the one hegemonic principle lurking everywhere.

Mander (1983) couples this family principle with modern lawlessness. She sees the program as reflecting a change in American society in which the myth of mobility is sacrificed to the *Godfather* myth of corrupt, self-contained family networks that hold the key to success. Modern life may seem anarchic and unexpected, but, in fact, it is governed by the oldest rules, which Banfield (1958) calls "amoral familism." It is the family against the world, where particularism and ascription dictate who is in and who is out, and no institutional restraints bridle family imperialism. This formulation shifts the *Dallas* narrative generically from Arlen's anomic anti-soap to the gangster or Mafia genres in which crime—that is, the breaking of norms—is a central theme. This new focus can be well illustrated by the issues that arouse most public interest, ranging from "Who killed Kristen?" to "Who shot J. R.?" to "Who set Southfork on fire?"

In yet another look at *Dallas*, Newcomb (1982) reads the story nostalgically as a modern Western in which shootouts take place not in the bar on Main Street but over the telephone and in the boardrooms of Dallas skyscrapers. Elaborating on this notion, Y. Nir (1984) points to the title sequence that juxtaposes the big-city office buildings with the open fields and oil rigs of the old Wild West where the unions are still weak, income tax is low, and oil millionaires are thriving. For Newcomb, Dallas is a place where national monopolies and bureaucratic rules have not yet stamped out the original American values of initiative and individuality.

Our reading is different still, based on kinship relations among the Ewings and between the Ewings and their rival dynasties (see Fig. 2.1). Clearly these relations involve two competing principles. The vertical line from generation to generation (grandfather-father-son) is based on loyalty and harmony; it is a sacrosanct structure. Horizontal relations within generations, however, are based on treachery, where everybody is fair game for everybody else: siblings, spouses, friends, business partners, etc. We disagree with Michael Arlen's proposal that *Dallas* is anomic and unpredictable. It *is* based on contradiction, but it is systematic contradiction in that one principle (loyalty) inheres in the vertical strand of the kinship system, and another principle (treachery) inheres in the horizontal. Moreover, it is impossible to understand the story without taking account of both principles, since the justification for the back-stabbing on the horizontal line is continually rationalized in terms of the loyalty on the vertical line. The source of women's strength can also be derived from a glance at the chart. Women derive their power from their joint affiliation in rival dynasties, that is, in being intermediaries, spies, or double agents between their families of orientation and families of procreation. Only Sue Ellen is powerless in this sense.

A second theme in our content analysis has to do with the permeability of

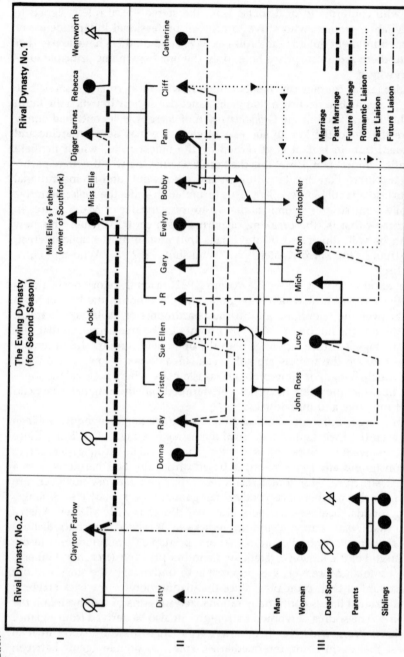

N.B. *The parentage of John Ross and Christopher is problematic. The father of John Ross is either J R or Cliff. Christopher — later adopted by Bobby and Pam — is probably J R and Kristen's biological son.*

Fig. 2.1. The *Dallas* Family Tree

the institution of the family to the norms of business, and vice versa. The insulation between these institutions that allows family to function as relief from economics is altogether absent in *Dallas*. The success of marriage is dependent almost wholly on exchange (Liebes and Katz, 1988); true love is either absent or without sexual consummation. Self-interest prevails at the most intimate moments, as is evident throughout the horizontal line. And the opposite is true as well. Emotion is exported from primary relations into the world of business, transforming fair business practice into a total war with no holds barred. Economic power is wielded in the name of private passion, as when J. R. buys up all the oil in Texas in order to destroy father and son of a rival dynasty at whose ranch Sue Ellen and baby John Ross have sought refuge.

This diversity of interpretations makes clear that professional readers are hardly of one mind. Classical content analysis (Berelson, 1952) could not tolerate such unreliability, but the new literary theory is quite hospitable to such diversity (Fish, 1980). Depending on the mood and the theoretical perspective of the analyst, J. R. becomes a metaphor for a chauvinist patriarch, a modern swinger, a city gangster, a lone rider of the Wild West, and a dutiful son and treacherous brother.

But it would be equally wrong to conclude that the text is so open that the range of headings is infinite. In fact, these readings have the text in common. All of these analysts note the breakdown of society into an earlier (or later) state in which the family is the central (remaining) institution, incorporating economic and political functions, and is at war with other families. The readings differ, perhaps, concerning the stability of the family; Mander and Swanson see it as strongly paternalistic while Arlen sees it as an experimental laboratory. The point is that the text evokes certain shared perceptions—at least among members of the same culture—which are then assimilated and evaluated within the analysts' different frames of reference. Arlen's frame is ironic, Newcomb's is nostalgic, Swanson's and Mander's are serious and even angry, ours is primordial. It is obvious that the effect implied in Swanson's analysis is different from Arlen's; the former is hegemonic, aimed at keeping women down, while the latter invites play and experimentation.

We have found that viewers' decodings also vary, but within the limits of the text. If professional critics and scholars do not tell the same story, even among themselves, why should we expect viewers to see a single story or to be affected by a monolithic message about which even the experts disagree? The absurdity of this expectation is all the more clear when some of the viewers concerned are not even members of the analysts' culture and not even of the so-called modern world.

The Export of American Television

It follows, therefore, that the study of audience decodings of American television programs is even more acutely needed overseas than it is domestically.

What *do* Zairians make of the Ewings? Until very recently nothing at all was known about meaning perceived by overseas viewers of American television programs. The emphasis of intercultural communications research was almost exclusively on institutional aspects, on audience ratings, and on occasional studies of effect (particularly in the area of economic development), but nothing at all was known about the meanings perceived in imported programming.

A number of studies (e.g., Tunstall, 1977; Head, 1974; Dorfman and Matelart, 1975) deal with the transfer of the technology, the organizational forms, the ideologies, and the programs of Western broadcasting to the capitals of the new nations of Asia, Africa, and South America. *Broadcasting in the Third World* (Katz and Wedell, 1977) deals at some length with the irony of a process whereby television is introduced, in part, to promote culturally authentic self-expression but rather quickly digresses to transmitting what then was called *Kojak*, what today is called *Dallas*. The process begins from the moment the prime minister announces that the great day of the first broadcast is near at hand (thanks to the combined efforts of the Treasury, Western technical assistance, and local talent). Then follows the realization that most of the promised four to five hours per day must be purchased abroad; the odyssey of the director of programs charged with purchasing material that will "open a window on the world"; the realization that the only programs available to fill the voracious appetite of a television broadcasting station as internationally defined are mass-produced, long-running American series and serials. At about the time of the study, British broadcasters were waking up to the idea that one-off programs or short series of four or five episodes, the pride of British television, could not hope to compete in the export market. The director of programs needs as much time to preview a one-off program as to preview the whole of *I Love Lucy*. The one-off solves his problem for a single Monday evening; *I Love Lucy* solves his problem forever.

Like Tunstall, the authors of *Broadcasting in the Third World* noted the patterns of international flow of American programs and analyzed the outcry against this new brand of alleged imperialism. The book focused on the transplantation of ideas and practices at the level of the organization. Extensive studies of the audience, apart from collecting simple surveys of the popularity of programs, were not attempted. These surveys, however, suggested that local productions often outdraw much more elegant imports, but no thought was given to the possibility that local programs might be better. It was *assumed* that the programs conceived in the capitals of the West were equally well understood and that their messages were getting through. Indeed, the book speculates at some length on the functions and dysfunctions of such programs for political integration, for modernization, and for cultural continuity. However, "What, for example, are the gratifications derived from viewing *Ironside* in Bangkok or from listening to American pop music in Nigeria? What is understood of *Peyton Place* or *Mission Impossible* in rural areas where electricity has only just arrived? Is the idealization of the American way of life really perceived by the viewers in a conscious way? What picture of the world does the imported staccato-style news format of radio and television bulletins present to the peasant farmer?" (Katz and Wedell, 1977, p. ix)

These questions are equally valid for Europe. In Europe, as in the Third World, very little was known about how imported programs are decoded. Dutch or French readings of *Dallas* should be as interesting as those of Thailand or Nigeria—so should American readings. But on the whole, prior to *Dallas*, little thought had been given to perceived meanings. In the best case this was because no adequate research method was available for doing so and certainly no adequate supply of funds; in the worse case, it was because it did not occur to anybody to ask. Both the best and the worst reasons leave unchallenged the assumption that the presumed message of the foreign producers is getting through.[1]

Decodings of *Dallas* Overseas

Curiously, *Dallas* changed all this. Researchers in a number of different countries decided, quite independently, to study the meaning of the program for foreign audiences. It is not so difficult to explain how this happened. For one thing, there was the striking fact that *Dallas* had captured the world: scholars, no less than journalists, asked themselves why. They also seized upon the opportunity to come to grips with what might be a good test of cultural imperialism. Unlike *Kojak* and other previous best-sellers, *Dallas* is the undisguised story of a family. However remote its cultural setting, viewers were invited to examine their own interpersonal relations and values in the light of those on the screen. When they did so, researchers thought that something might be happening.

Ang (1985) in Holland and Herzog-Massing (1986) in Germany explain the pleasure of viewing *Dallas* in terms of psychological needs whose origins are in social structure. While Dutch viewers are said by Ang to suffer from a lack of inherent meaning in a life that modern society has rendered meaningless, German fans of *Dallas* are perceived by Herzog as repressed by a patriarchal family structure. It is interesting that the two studies explain the attraction of the program in opposite ways: one as an antidote to the absence of structure, the other as an antidote to too much of it.

Herzog analyzes fans of the program in terms of both interviews and projective tests to reveal fantasies about the glamor of richness, corruption, and adultery which are taboo in the conservative German society. For Ang, in her analysis of forty letters from fans responding to the advertisement she placed in a women's magazine, the pleasure of viewing is generated by the need to be reassured that life has a meaning after all. She describes viewing as a rebellion against the superficiality and rootlessness of a life cut off from tradition and lacking in any integrating values. For Dutch fans, *Dallas* does not serve as escapist fantasy but transmits the sense of the tragedy in life. Admittedly, says Ang, it is not very feminist to identify with the masochism of Sue Ellen and

Pamela, but it is not altogether antifeminist either. Inasmuch as feminist politics can only promise a utopian future at the expense of pain and unease in the present, such identification supplies a way to endure the present.

This interim solution wherein the unfortunate social role of women leads women to find comfort in the troubles of the soap opera echoes the early radio studies of Herzog (1941) and Warner and Henry (1948). In her new study, however, Herzog-Massing (1986) finds viewers using the program subversively. German viewers of *Dallas* show great admiration for J. R.—what Gitlin (1983) calls "the id unbound." But they can do so, says Herzog, only after declaring that their allegiance is with Miss Ellie, the virtuous mother. Miss Ellie's function, according to Herzog, is to reinforce the superego and set boundaries to her son's mischief. Identifying with her legitimizes German viewers' admiration for J. R.

The type of involvement generated by *Dallas* may result, paradoxically, from the fact that it is not considered serious artistically and, perhaps, also because of its perceived distance from viewers' reality. In her study of women viewers in Denmark from the middle and working classes, Hjort (1986) found that *Dallas* allows the expression of emotions like love and hate in a liminal context, removed from one's life to neutral ground. The Danish series *Daughters of the War*, on the other hand, is regarded by viewers as more realistic and, therefore, is more likely to invoke critical evaluation both about the accuracy of its reality and about its artistic quality. In their critical statements, Danish viewers articulate their aesthetic pleasure by comparing the slower tempo and more profound images of *Daughters* with the speed and superficiality of *Dallas*. Attention to an element such as tempo is a good illustration of the metalinguistic or attributional aspect of viewers' critical abilities and implies awareness of possibly more subtle elements of cultural imperialism. The staccato tempo of American advertising, adopted as a formula for *Sesame Street* and then exported worldwide, has been debated at the BBC and elsewhere for the hidden message of its form.

An increasing number of countries are producing their own serials (Tracey, 1985), and it is, therefore, of interest that such local productions may be more likely to be judged in terms of their reality than imported programs from which viewers feel more culturally distant. This does not mean that the local program is necessarily perceived as more real, even though this seems to be the case for Danish viewers of *Daughters*. It is certainly not the case for American viewers in our study, who insisted that *Dallas* was not real because they compared it with the reality they know first-hand.[2] This is unlike both Hjort's Danish viewers, who seem to enjoy the nowhere-no-time unreality of the program, and the more traditional Israeli viewers in our study, who take for granted that *Dallas* reveals America or the rich or the modern world. In other words, cultural distance reduces the preoccupation with the question of reality, and proximity causes viewers to measure critically how real it really is.

Another example of this phenomenon is reported by Stolz (1983) about *Dallas* viewers in Algeria. Again, the reality of the Ewings is unquestioned and, therefore, invites translation into local terms. Rather than a reflection of modern capitalism, for Algerians *Dallas* is a reminder of the reality they are fast losing. It is reminiscent of the traditional values of a world where one's basic allegiance is to the extended family, where it is normal for three generations to live under the same roof, where the pater familias is king, where a cousin would do all he can to help, and where a state bureaucracy is regarded suspiciously as an enemy to be fought by family solidarity. Thus, what Mander (1983) considers a postmodern story of a Mafia family is recognized by Algerians as a premodern family tale where universalistic principles of fairness, of equality, of opportunity do not obstruct the showing of favoritism to a relative, showing hostility to another clan, or cheating the alien bureaucracy. *Protektzia* is not labeled as corruption but taken for granted as the way society operates.

Even if *Dallas* may be read as compatible with the values of a society based on principles of ascription rather than the modern ones of achievement, Stolz (1983) believes that it contributes, nevertheless, to the erosion of traditional cultures by changing the leisure-time agenda. In Algeria, viewing *Dallas* became everybody's favorite entertainment, displacing such a popular pastime as gathering to listen to grandmother's folktales.

An altogether original approach to viewers' perception of *Dallas*—indeed, almost a formal ethnosemiotics of the program—is proposed by Livingstone (1987a). A small sample of British viewers was asked to indicate the extent of similarity among characters in *Dallas*, and the same procedure was followed for viewers of *Coronation Street*, the British serial about daily life in a working-class neighborhood. Employing a multidimensional scaling method, Livingstone measured (and then validated) the "goodness of fit" between the resultant ranking of the characters in *Dallas* and a number of value dimensions, of which morality and power were the best fits. Moreover, these two dimensions were found to be orthogonal, that is, good and bad were *not* correlated with strong and weak. It was different in *Coronation Street* where the good tended to be weak and the bad tended to be strong. Moreover, Livingstone found that viewers perceive the *Dallas* women as divided among strong and weak (although they concentrate on the weak side), whereas *Coronation Street* women are perceived as more matriarchal in character, not the mix of irrationality, softness, or weakness usually attributed to television women. From the orthogonal relationship between power and morality in *Dallas*, Livingstone was also able to suggest that the dramatic tension in the story is not between strong-and-weak and good-and-bad but between all four combinations of morality and power. This, of course, makes for a greater number of possibilities and surprises.

Convergence on the Study of Decoding

There is yet another reason explaining the flurry of studies on the decoding of *Dallas:* this has to do with the coincidence in time of certain developments within communications research and the appearance of the program. The division of labor in communications research was such that some had been study-ing the texts of popular culture while others were studying their effects on audiences, including popularity ratings, uses, and gratifications. The former ascribed influence to the text without knowing anything about the audience, while the latter, more surprisingly perhaps, did not know anything about the text. Blumler et al. (1986) have pronounced this anomaly "a dialogue of the deaf." The students of texts believed that the reader role and reader reaction were determined by the text, while the gratificationists believed that the text existed only in the eye of the beholder; therefore, why look to the text at all?

In recent years these extreme positions are being abandoned, and there is a growing convergence of interest among theoretical traditions on the process of interaction between readers and texts. This convergence makes bedfellows not only of functionally oriented audience research and Marxist-oriented critical studies but also, even more surprisingly, of so-called reader-response theory in literature studies. It is of some interest to trace the ways in which the three traditions transformed themselves—each in its own way—after finding them-selves at dead ends.

The clearest case is that of critical studies. Having long assumed that the texts of popular culture inscribe themselves hegemonically in the defenseless minds of their readers, critical theorists realized that their theory left no room at all for social change. How to explain feminism, for example, if culture is totally mobilized to maintain the status quo? In recent years, therefore, critical theorists—such as the Cultural Studies group in England—have made room for alternate readings, thus acknowledging that the ordinary viewer, not only the theorist, may know how to read oppositionally. This realization led critical theorists to the empirical study of reader decodings (Morley, 1980).

As critical theorists became aware that they were studying texts without readers, gratifications researchers came to realize that they were studying read-ers without texts. The idea that readers, listeners, and viewers can bend the mass media to serve their own needs had gone so far that almost any text—or, indeed, no text at all—was found to serve functions such as social learning, reinforcing identity, lubricating interaction, providing escape, etc. But it gradu-ally became clear that these functions were too unspecified: these studies did not say *what* was learned, which aspect of identity was reinforced, what was talked about, where one went for escape, etc. This more specific set of ques-tions reopened the larger issue of which kinds of communications serve these more substantive purposes.

It is more than trivial to differentiate between viewers who use *Dallas* as a guide to reality and those who use it as an aesthetic game. Such concerns did, in fact, characterize the early days of gratifications research when the radio soap opera, the quiz program, or Kate Smith's war-bond marathon were stud-ied for the specifics of the interaction between listeners of particular social backgrounds and very specific attributes of the program. The study of decod-ing by gratifications researchers is as much a return to an earlier formulation as something new. The reinstatement of text in mainline communications research also speaks to the long-standing anxiety of gratifications theorists that the receiver, more than the sender, is responsible for the message.

It is striking that literary theorists began to take interest in reader decodings more or less at the same time. Unconnected with either of the other branches of communications research, literary theorists moved from the idea that qualified readers are defined and positioned by authors to the idea that readers, no less than authors, create the text. Like gratifications theory, literary theory of this brand also went through the throes of asking whether there is a text, any text, that constrains the reader's reading (Fish, 1980) and reemerged with the idea of interaction between types of readers and types of texts, even to the point of conducting empirical studies of readers (Radway, 1985).

The new convergence on reader decodings clearly implies an active reader—selecting, negotiating, interpreting, discussing, or, in short, being involved. But this image of the reader—and, a fortiori, this image of the television viewer—does not sit well with those theories of communications research that emphasize the passivity of the viewer. Researchers such as Csikzentmihalyi and Kubey (1981) insist—based on a method which signals respondents to jot down what they are doing and feeling when the beeper sounds—that television is consumed in a semi-dazed state, and unlike other activities, dazes its participants even more. The psychoanalytically oriented film theorists seem to be saying something similar in proposing that the television viewer regresses to an infantile state in which the teasing flow of the supertext stimulates and frustrates. Gerbner et al. (1979), too, approaches the viewer as a passive recipient, not so much because he is anesthetized by television, but because he is its victim; shut in and nurtured by the medium to the exclusion of other sources of influence, heavy viewers learn the television message ritualistically and hegemonically, not by negotiation.

The convergence on the study of decoding is, therefore, a challenge to these theories. Perhaps the viewers are more active and more independent than these researchers suggest—more like gratificationists have assumed. Perhaps this activity characterizes only certain sorts of programs—such as *Dallas* and the moon landings. The empirical study of viewer decodings should help us find out.

We have tried to point out in this chapter that the flurry of research on the decoding of *Dallas* overseas has roots both in the text itself—the phenomenon of *Dallas*—and in new or newly revived theories of the active viewer. What follows should be seen, therefore, as an exercise in the study of viewer involvement in the process of consuming television. It will contribute, we hope, to a clearer conceptualization of the different types of decodings and their connections with different types of involvement on the one hand, and different types of uses and effects on the other.

3
THE RESEARCH DESIGN

Ideally, we should like to have empirical data on how people interact with their television sets under natural conditions: how they arrange themselves before it; how they decode what they see and hear; how they help each other to do so; how they talk about it; whether they refer to the medium or to specific programs; whether they have categories for classifying programs and criticizing them, and if so, what they are; whether and how they weave the experience of viewing into their social and political roles. But such data are hardly available, suggesting to some that it is not worthwhile to go into depth about the experience of viewing. We think otherwise.

One set of studies of viewer involvement in television denigrates the experience. To refer again to an important, recent example, Csikzentmihalyi and Kubey (1981) conclude that among daily activities television is a sort of last resort—a resource that rewards its enervated practitioners by emptying their energy levels even further. Based on the synchronous self-reports of viewers, these conclusions are supported by other observations of viewers in their living rooms as recorded by video cameras mounted on television sets (Bechtel et al., 1971). While Csikzentmihalyi and Kubey suggest, at least, that television is a soporific, the pioneering videotape studies of viewing behavior found that television is ignored altogether; family members enter and exit, go about their other activities, and pay only fleeting attention to the "moving wallpaper." These studies are inadequate from our point of view, however, because they tend to average the viewing experience over all sorts of hours and programs and because they are behavioristic; they do not even try to explore the possibility that something is getting through even at the low moments and, a fortiori, at the high moments of active involvement. In any case, it is clear to us that these data cannot explain the ways in which *Dallas* viewers use the program to comment upon life and upon art.

There exists another small group of studies that is more in keeping with our approach. Some of these are also observational; others are based more on challenging viewers—in interviews and focus groups—to exhibit what they learned from television, however inadvertently. Thus, we get some insights into how television is interwoven into family life from quasi-anthropological observations in several cultures (Bryce and Leichter, 1983; Lull, 1980) and from Morley's (1987) interviews with families. There is more data on the interweaving of broadcasting and other institutions in gratifications tradition (Rosengren et al., 1986), beginning with Herzog's studies (1941) in the early days of radio. Research on media events also provides examples of how individuals seat themselves at attention before their television sets, assuming the roles of citizens at presidential debates, mourners for an assassinated leader, loyal subjects of the Royal Family, Olympic sports fans (Rothenbuhler, 1989), and so on; the earliest of such studies was Merton's (1946) study of the Kate Smith warbond campaign and the Langs' (1968) study of the return of General MacArthur from the Pacific. There are, in addition, at least two interview studies that attempt to clarify the critical abilities and vocabulary of television audiences (Neuman, 1982; Himmelweit et al., 1983). Altogether, the implication of these studies is that there are at least certain kinds of programs that cause viewers to "sit down and be counted." It may be that the key to this kind of involvement is in the process of role-taking, whereby the viewer assumes a role in another institutional realm—sports, politics, religion, family circle, etc.—or the broadcasting realm, assuming one or another of the critical roles we shall propose (see Chapter 8).

Theorists like Newcomb (1984), Meyrowitz (1985), and Gerbner et al. (1979)—however different from one another—also share the idea that attention is invested in the viewing experience and that the meanings so obtained make their way into viewers' personal and social lives. Even if the units employed in their analyses may be larger or smaller than the program, these researchers argue that the themes that punctuate and recur in television discourse shape identities, affect social relations, set agendas for discussion, and shape consciousness (Gerbner would say, false consciousness).

Proceeding from this latter perspective, we assumed and hoped to verify that viewing a program like *Dallas* is, indeed, an active and involving experience. More than that, we hoped to be able to demonstrate that the nature of involvement varies with the cultural background one brings to the viewing. Thus, we chose four widely different groups within Israeli society to compare with each other, with second-generation Americans in Los Angeles (as representatives of the audience for whom the original program was intended), and with Japanese in Japan (where the program failed). In the choice of the Israeli groups, in particular, we hoped to be able to demonstrate that the nature of involvement in the program, in spite of its universal popularity, nevertheless varies with the social and cultural backgrounds of the viewers.

We chose to include Israeli Russians in our study as one of four ethnic communities because we had reason to expect that their images of America and of American capitalism would be activated by viewing *Dallas* and because we expected the rich literary tradition in which Russian Jews specialize to lead them to view the program critically. We found Russian immigrants to Israel to be critical not only of American materialism and culture but also of the Israeli culture which forced *Dallas* upon them, or so they said. To be integrated in Israel, they complained, one must view *Dallas*, but *Dallas* is a program to be feared—because it is no less manipulative than Soviet propaganda and therefore requires serious surveillance. Their suspicions were expressed towards media research as well, leading them to wonder about the hidden intentions of the researchers and the possible misuse of the tape recorder. Thus, the Russians—not yet integrated in the new society and with a history of dissent in the old—demean *Dallas* as unworthy (even while enjoying it) and take pains to carefully decode it for possible mental dangers to themselves and their children.

We know something of each of the six groups and had reason to believe— as in the case of the Russian immigrants to Israel—that their cultural and social values would lead them to negotiate with the program in different ways and, thus, to incorporate the program differently into their roles as members of a broadcast audience, a family, a subgroup within Israel, and within Israeli society as a whole. We not only found what we assumed but also a much richer mosaic of intergroup differences that lead to variations in decodings, involvements, enjoyments, uses, and effects.

The Sample

In addition to the Russians, the Israeli communities included in the study were Arab citizens of Israel, Moroccan Jews of long standing in the country, and kibbutz members who are mostly Israeli-born. We could, of course, have chosen to differentiate among viewing groups by education, gender, or age rather than ethnicity. There is every reason to expect important differences along such dimensions as well. Our preference for ethnicity, however, stems from the desire to observe the process of exporting meaning to other cultures. Since the object of the study was to simulate the reception of *Dallas* in the world, we took advantage of the Israeli situation to choose an assortment of subcultures that could be expected to vary as other foreign cultures might.

We are not proposing that multiple cultures within Israel are a fair replication of the world. Even if Russian immigrants to Israel might once have been representative of other Russians, after their migration one cannot allow this kind of assumption. By the same token, Israeli Arabs may not be representative of Arabs elsewhere, given their minority status. Similarly, Moroccan Jews in Israel are likely to be different from Moroccans in Morocco or even Moroccan Jews in France. Kibbutz members, on the other hand, are probably representative of second-generation Israelis of European origin. Nevertheless, a case can be made that the variety of these groups, and the differences in their reactions to *Dallas*, may illuminate the diversity of reactions elsewhere in the world. Israel may not be a microcosm of the world in a technical sense, but it may offer a basis for generalizing.

To understand foreign decodings of *Dallas*, it was necessary, of course, to obtain American decodings. We did so by including American viewers as well, chosen from among native-born residents of Los Angeles. It also seemed valuable to include representatives of a culture—one of the few—in which *Dallas* failed, and, thus, our study includes Japanese viewers.

Altogether, then, the study refers to the ways in which *Dallas* is read in six very different cultural communities. We must now add something that will displease methodological purists, namely, that the number of individuals chosen from each community averaged "only" between forty and eighty people and that the sampling design was unorthodox. We could say in our defense that this is, nevertheless, a very large number of decodings for the study of a text of popular culture.

The sampling is problematic because, first of all, there are no ethnic rosters from which to sample; at best, one can enter a community where there is an assumed concentration of residents of a given ethnicity. Moreover, we were less interested in random selections of a sample of each community than we were in clusters of community members who are in close contact and among whom television programs are likely to be discussed.

Given our belief that television programs such as *Dallas* are the subject of both shared viewing and discussion, random sampling—whereby sample members are as distant from each other as possible—would hardly have achieved our purpose. The ideal solution, if money and ethnic rosters had been readily available, would have been to choose an initial sample on a random basis and then to assemble social "molecules" of the "atoms" in the original sample. But we could not afford this nor were such rosters available.

Instead, we chose to assemble small groups of friends and neighbors more informally, approaching approximately ten couples in each of the communities and asking them to invite two other couples to their homes on the evening of the weekly *Dallas* broadcast. The initial couples were chosen from areas of known ethnic concentration—Moroccan *moshavim*, housing estates populated by Russians, Arab villages—and from the personal connections of our field supervisor and interviewers who were recruited, in part, because of their own ethnic affiliations. The initial couples also were screened for age (thirty to fifty years of age), education (secondary school and less than full college), and regular viewing of the program. In the process, about fifteen groups were disqualifed (six of them Arab groups) for reasons of too few participants, lack of ethnic homogeneity, overcrowding by uninvited family members, failure to collect background data, and incoherent or incorrectly guided conversations.

In general, we are satisfied with the naturalness of the result. Host couples invited others of like ethnicity, and the groups assembled were, therefore, homogeneous. In our instructions to the host couple, we tried to constrain the choice of guests by indicating the age and education range which we wished to hold constant. We were largely successful, with the exception of the Russians, who were of somewhat higher education due to the higher average education in the Russian immigrant community.[1] But even the range in these groups was not too far off. The American and Japanese groups were similarly assembled, except that the Japanese groups do not all consist of mixed couples since the viewing situation in Japan tends to be sexually segregated, especially in the middle classes.

All told, the sample consisted of sixty-six groups of (usually) six persons of like ethnicity, age, and education (three closely acquainted married couples— the Japanese groups were an exception) for a total of some 400 participants. The analysis involved ten groups of Israeli Arabs, sixteen groups of Israelis of Moroccan origin, ten groups of recent immigrants from Russia to Israel, six groups from kibbutzim, ten groups from the Los Angeles area, and eleven groups from greater Tokyo. Each group, meeting in the living room of one of the couples, viewed an episode from the second season of *Dallas*,[2] filled in a background questionnaire, and participated in a focus-group discussion immediately following the program. This discussion lasted about one hour and was led by a trained interviewer in the dominant language of the group.

Obviously, we cannot make a strong claim for statistical representativeness. The sample population is too small, the sampling method too casual, and, as we have said, the population parameters too uncontrolled. Indeed, the claim that these groups are representative at all is based on an assumption—which may legitimately be challenged—that these ethnic and communal labels (Israelis of Moroccan origin, kibbutzim, native-born Americans in Los Angeles) share a definable set of attitudes, values, and social relations which can legitimately be called culture or subculture. The study, therefore, is based on an assumption that these groupings are, indeed, subcultures, and that the subcultures differ from each other in ways that will be projected in their readings of an American television melodrama.[3]

The Viewing Sessions: Establishing the Research Situation

The study was initiated during the second season of the broadcasting of *Dallas* on Israel's one-channel television station. To ensure the most natural viewing conditions and to minimize researcher intervention, we arranged for the groups not only to meet in homes but also to view the programs during their actual time of transmission.

Ideally, we would have liked all groups to see the same episode, but this would have involved a one-time field operation which was beyond our ability. We chose, instead, to spread the study over four consecutive Sunday evenings, so that ten to twelve groups from all the ethnic communities would see the same episode. Even this compromise put very high pressure on the organization of field work, since it meant recruiting a large number of groups each week, as well as supervising the work of the interviewers and the assistants who operated the audiotapes and made field notes during the viewing and subsequent discussion. Obviously, we were heavily dependent on the goodwill and initiative of the host couple, the faithfulness of the guest couples who accepted the invitation, and the split-second timing required of interviewers and field assistants who had to be in the right living room at the right moment. The field-work staff and the interviewers sometimes acted to repair groups whose members failed to report on time or to show up altogether. Despite our best efforts, several groups did not meet the requisite standards and were disqualified.

The American and Japanese groups were less problematic. Although assembling these groups was even more difficult than it was in Israel[4] there was no problem of timing the meetings to the broadcasts. In the United States, this was due to our decision that the American groups would see the same episodes as the Israelis. We decided that this was preferable to the more natural alternative of seeing a current episode on the air which would, necessarily, be different from the ones shown in Israel (inasmuch as *Dallas* in Israel was two seasons behind). This meant in practice that the Americans saw on video a program that they had seen two seasons before and which returned them to an earlier stage in the program's development.

This decision permitted us to compare viewer decodings of the same episodes, but it deprived the Americans of the spontaneity of responding to a new episode.

The Japanese groups presented yet another problem. Since *Dallas* survived in Japan for only six months and was already long off the air, there was no possibility of showing the same episodes as were shown in Israel or the U.S. (not to mention the fact that these second-season episodes did not even exist with Japanese dubbing). Instead, we chose to show them the episode that introduced the series.

All groups—given that they were previously acquainted—gathered around the TV set—or the video monitor in the case of the Americans and Japanese—and, after being reintroduced to the purpose of the study, were asked by the interviewer to fill in a background questionnaire. The set was then switched on, and the full episode was viewed. The Japanese groups saw a version dubbed in Japanese and the Israeli groups a version subtitled in both Hebrew and Arabic.

Dubbing and subtitling presented another methodological problem that complicated the making of comparisons between American and foreign viewers. One might wonder whether it is not unfair to compare native viewers with those who are dependent on subtitles, if only because of the difficulty of keeping up with the printed words or for the necessarily abbreviated version that the subtitles provide. It should not be surprising, therefore, to find overseas viewers less learned in the nuances of the story. Even dubbing does not erase the possibility that the translator has missed something of the original and that understanding by viewers is thereby affected. More generally, one might wonder if the immediacy of the viewing experience is not compromised by the intermediacy of subtitling and dubbing: surely, dissonance must be created between the familiarity of the speech and the unfamiliarity of the pictures.

In spite of the reasonableness of these concerns, available evidence is, nevertheless, reassuring. A study by R. Nir (1984) of the reliability of subtitles on Israeli television strongly suggests that both story and dialogue are faithfully transmitted. Our own work will make clear that a basic understanding of *Dallas* characterizes all of the groups we have studied, and that intergroup differences cannot be attributed to subtitling. We have not tested the adequacy of the Japanese dubbing, of course, but there is good evidence that Japanese participants understood what was going on as well as, maybe better than, anybody else.

All of the Israeli viewers were dependent on the subtitles, at least to a certain extent. Occasional viewers were at a greater loss, given their difficulties with literacy, and others sometimes became confused. Chapter 4 will point out some of the ways in which group members helped each other over the obstacles, a process which we presume takes place regularly within family and community.

Differences among ethnic communities abound. Some of them are evident in the very organization of the viewing situation. We have already noted that the Japanese couple is not the typical viewing unit; this is the result of the well-known itinerary of white-collar workers in Japan who unwind from the tensions of the corporate workday by reaffirming solidarity with peers and bosses on the long way home. One would expect, therefore, rather different kinds of decodings by men and women. Arabs, too, have a gender sensitivity. Men seem to be uneasy about viewing with women, and there is some reason to believe that more traditional men would prefer that the women not view at all. Quite opposite to these segregated tendencies, some of the male Russians and kibbutzniks found it necessary to explain that they viewed the program *because* of their wives. These differences in husband-wife relations, as well as communal attitudes towards the legitimacy or desirability of viewing the program by anybody or by certain subgroups such as women or children, manifested themselves both in the viewing situation and in the discussion that followed.

Validating Some Hypotheses: The Background Questionnaire

After the group settled down and before the program began, each member was asked to fill in a questionnaire calling for demographic data and for patterns of viewing behavior. A first object of the questionnaire was to validate the composition of the groups—to make certain that members fit the criteria of age, ethnicity, and fanship. This was of particular concern in Israel because of the high pressure to maximize the number of groups that would be exposed to the same episode on the evening of its actual broadcast. We compared statistics on

Table 3.1. With Whom Do Viewers View *Dallas* and With Whom Do they Discuss It? (in percent)*

	Americans		Moroccans		Arabs		Russians		Kibbutz	
	View	Talk	View	Talk	View	Talk	View	Talk	View	Talk
With nobody	13	3	4	5	16	2	8	34	0	49
With spouse	53	43	41	27	35	34	62	27	61	27
With family in residence	22	21	36	22	28	15	19	9	24	3
With family from outside	2	11	5	13	7	0	6	3	6	3
With friends	11	23	14	33	14	49	3	27	9	18
Number of replies	(64)	(65)	(116)	(117)	(43)	(43)	(65)	(67)	(33)	(33)

*Sometimes more than one answer was given.

the educational level of each of the ethnic communities participating in the study with those of the Israeli census (see Appendix Three). The real-life distribution of education by ethnicity imposed itself on our effort to hold education constant across all groups—which was somewhat higher for the Russians, somewhat lower for the Moroccans. We will examine whether this is or is not the explanation for the ethnic differences we observe. A few groups that were assembled were so much out of line that we found it easier to disqualify them; for example, if a host couple invited guests of incorrect ethnicity, we disqualified the group. But this was a rare occurrence.

A further object of the background questionnaire was to attempt to validate our assumptions (1) that people watch programs, not only moving wallpaper; (2) that viewing is a social affair; and (3) that programs like *Dallas* become conversational pieces during the viewing, immediately after viewing, and even the next day. The responses to the questionnaires gave strong support to these assumptions.

Thus, viewers indicated on the questionnaires that they made a point of watching *Dallas* regularly; that they viewed together with spouses, children, other family members, and friends; and that they often discussed it with co-viewers and with others. Kibbutz members and Russians were least likely to admit that the program was talked about. In the Russian case, at least, this reflects—perhaps accurately, perhaps not—their superior attitude towards the program which we encountered in the focus-group discussions.[5] Table 3.1 presents these data.

The Focus-Group Discussions

Following the viewing of the program, the interviewer turned to the group members and guided them through a focus-group discussion of a series of questions. The early questions were open-ended. ("Could you retell the story you have just seen as if you were reporting it to somebody who had not seen it with us?" "Who are the three leading characters?" "What goals motivate them, and what obstacles get in their way?") The later ones were somewhat more closed. ("Is *Dallas* real?" "What are they trying to tell us?" "What does it say about America?" "Why all the fuss about babies?" etc.) The full text of the questionnaire appears in Appendix 1.

Questions were not necessarily presented in a precise order; rather, each interviewer was instructed to employ the questionnaire as a guideline, making certain that each area of the questionnaire was covered in the discussion, and that the time frame allotted to a particular question was not exceeded. Often, the questions were anticipated by the group and answered spontaneously without guidance from the interviewer.

Questions were put to the group as a whole, rather than to specific individuals, although at times reticent participants were prodded by the interviewers. The discussions engaged the interest of all groups—we do not know of any exceptions—even if some of the openings encountered resistance on the part of participants, such as some of the Russians, who thought the subject too trivial for their attention. The length of the discussions averaged one hour.

Why groups? By choosing the method of focus-group interviews (Merton and Kendall, 1946; Kaboolian and Gamson, 1983; Morgan and Spanish, 1984) we were, in effect, operationalizing the assumption that the small-group discussion following the broadcast is a key to understanding the mediating process via which a program such as this enters into the culture. That such discussions take place—albeit casually and sporadically—we now know from the evidence in the background questionnaires. Further confirmation comes from the discussions themselves, during which participants refer to prior conversations about the program and its characters. An introduction such as "How can you feel sorry for her (Sue Ellen) when just last week you still despised her?"— directed by one kibbutz discussant to another—illustrates this point, as does the Russian complaint already alluded to that one cannot become integrated into Israel without being able to discuss *Dallas*!

Focus groups impel participants to think about and stay with the subject being discussed in a way which is surely *not* natural. The analytic abilities revealed in some of these discussions is probably far beyond the level of everyday discussion of television and is probably inspired by the seriousness with which participants' opinions are solicited. Group members were asked to generalize about themes, messages, and characters, as well as about the functions of such programs for the viewer, at levels of abstraction which are unusual in gossip. Thus, the focus group was a catalyst for the individual expression of latent opinion, for the generation of group consensus, for free-associating to life, and for analytic statements about art. But even these more formal discussions have an informal thrust; in fact, a major part of our analysis is devoted to the casual commuting in the focus groups between the story and real life, where the story serves as a basis for interpreting and evaluating life and vice versa. The group context induces the expression of such latent thoughts.[6]

Negotiation within the group then produces an awareness of others' thoughts. The result is an incremental input into the worldview of the community. This is the reason we opted for the constructed conversations (the focus-group method) over individual interviews, even in-depth interviews. We are aware that the method does not give equal weight to every individual's reactions to the program. Nor do we *wish* to give equal weight to every individual. Group dynamics are such that opinion and participation are *not* equally weighted; some people have disproportionate influence. But real life is like that: opinions are not as much the property of individuals as public-opinion polling would have us think. Opinions arise out of interaction, and "opinion leaders" have disproportionate influence.

The open character of the early questions—beginning with the request to retell the episode—also gives insight into variations among groups in their definition of the research situation and in their image of the role of the researchers. Thus, there appear to be differences in the perceptions of the status of the interviewers as representatives of academia; there are differences, too, in the degree to which the subject of the research—television, *Dallas*, etc.—was treated earnestly. Impressionistically, the Moroccan groups looked up to the interviewers and treated the questions as if they were an examination; some were concerned to the point of asking whether or not their answers were correct or even adequate. The Russians, by contrast, appeared to feel superior to the subject of study, were not awed by the interviewers, and acted almost as if *they* were conducting the test. Some Russians resisted joining the conversation in assumed protest over the unworthiness of the subject (in fact, one Russian couple actually walked out after delivering an impassioned speech against American culture); others worried about the tape recorder and what might be held against them. Nevertheless, the Russians, too, in the sense that they were soberly occupied by thought of the possible dangers of hegemonic trivia, treated the discussion seriously.

The American and kibbutz group members, on the other hand, were much more relaxed. They saw the interviewers as equals, neither acting deferential like the Moroccans nor patronizing like the Russians. Rather, they incorporated the interviewers into the discussion, and treated the focus group as a ludic happening. They roamed freely into personal and political gossip and into fantasy games. The Japanese had no need to apologize for viewing because they had, in fact, rejected the program and were being asked why.

In a sense, each of the groups assumed some distance from the subject—but in different ways—as if applying for a permit to enter into the liminal forum (Turner, 1985; Newcomb and Hirsch, 1983). The Moroccans may be said to have taken a moral stance; the Russians, an ideological stance; the Americans, kibbutzniks, and Japanese, an aesthetic stance.

An ideal design, perhaps, would have had three stages in which individuals would have been interviewed separately before and after the group discussion, and the group discussion would then have intervened as the catalyst.[7] But there was a limit to our resources, and having to choose between individual interviews and group discussions, we chose the latter. Moreover, the objection that focus groups are unnatural applies no less to the individual interview; it can be argued, in fact, that the focus group of intimate acquaintances is more natural than a face-to-face interview between strangers.[8] Indeed, some of our discussion groups took off on their own almost from the initial question and virtually ignored the interviewers who had a hard time intervening with the subsequent questions. The focus-group method has been found useful in advertising, marketing, and broadcasting research as a tool for the semiotic assessment of messages, products, and programs and as a method of psychotherapy in which a soap opera, for example, is used as a trigger to group interaction. Academic research has used this method only rarely (Morley, 1980; and Kaboolian and Gamson, 1983, are the most recent examples), elaborating on the focus-interview method introduced by Merton (1987) and Merton and Kendall (1946).

This study does not pay close attention to the particular group dynamics, although at various points in the analysis we note the relevance of cultural differences in interaction. Some groups, for example, may be characterized as societies of couples where husbands and wives interacted frequently, alluding to their relationships, while others inclined to more sex-segregated interactions. Arab men, for example, invited women to join in only when they required their expertise. Unfortunately, we could not explore this aspect in the depth that it deserves. We do make note of our impressions about the group-specific roles that emerge in the viewing and in the discussions (see Chapters 4, 5, and 6).

The Coding Scheme

One should not be misled by our resurrection of the focus-group method into thinking that the data thus generated lend themselves easily to systematic analysis. In fact, most users of this method are quite satisfied to extract the themes which emerge from the discussions without even trying to be rigorous. For the same reason, conveners of focus groups—such as advertisers, marketers, broadcasters, psychotherapists—are satisfied to base their conclusions on far fewer groups. We recorded sixty-six groups.

We were interested in more than just impressions, although we, too, report impressions in areas where we did not carry out systematic and reliable coding. We wished not only to propose hypotheses about community differences in patterns of decoding and involvement but also to prove them. More, we wished to comb these readings microscopically in search of the social and psychological mechanisms which redirect attention from story to life or from story to art. We treated each discussion as a text to be subjected to both quantitative and qualitative analyses.

The tape recordings of the discussions were transcribed and, in the case of the Arabs, Russians, and Japanese, were translated into Hebrew or English, our two working languages. We elected to risk loss of fidelity in the stage of translation rather than impose English or Hebrew on those participants who were more at home in another language. Whenever possible, the interviewers themselves transcribed and translated the material on the assumption that their recollection of the discussion would enhance the reliability of the written text. There was much difficulty in this process because the turn-taking that makes tapes audible is often lost in informal discussion, especially when the discussion becomes heated. In the transcript of a Moroccan group (see Chapter 4), for example, there were sections that we had to hear several times before we felt reasonably satisfied that we had transcribed them correctly. This problem is further exacerbated in those sections of the conversation that took place during the viewing and prior to the focus-group discussion because of the added television sound.

The translation presented an even more serious problem. We spot-checked, and when we had doubt, we commissioned more than one translation. We had particular difficulty with translations from the Arabic and are still unhappy with the result. In the case of the Japanese groups, the recordings that were made in Tokyo were translated in Jerusalem and double-checked by our collaborators in Japan.

Our first analytic step was to repeatedly read through a subsample of the discussions, typically choosing one from each ethnic community. We did these preliminary readings first to refine our method of analysis; second, to understand the ways in which group members defined the research situations and their developing roles within it; and third, to identify the parameters which would allow us to characterize differences among the groups. We noticed in these early readings how group members turned to each other for mutual aid in decoding and evaluation, and we noticed how easily all groups moved back and forth from the story to real life throughout the course of the discussion. We also noticed that the freer opening sections of the discussion evoked more playful responses, while the latter questions ("What is the program trying to tell us?" "Is *Dallas* real?" etc.) evoked more normative responses.

Through these readings we gradually developed a set of coding categories—both quantitative and impressionistic—that we employed in the analysis. We also decided to which coding units the categories would be applied. The coding unit was, in some cases, that portion of the discussion that related to a specific issue—"Why all the fuss about babies?" or "How would you end the story if you were the writer?"—or, in other cases, the narrative styles that might be said to characterize responses to the opening invitation to retell the story. Indicators of other codes were sought throughout the entire discussion such that we noted every instance within the group when the conversation switched from the story to real life and every instance when the conversation switched from the story to television (or other) art. In some cases, therefore, a coding unit might be as large as ten pages (styles of retelling); in other cases, two or three sentences (commuting to real life or to art); and in some cases, only a sentence or even less ("Why all the fuss about babies?"). Chapter 4 will make this inductive procedure clear; we will pinpoint—within the context of a Moroccan discussion—where we noticed interesting analytic dimensions.

Instead of leaping into superficial study of effects or focusing on viewer gratifications, we thought it appropriate to address more basic questions, particularly with respect to overseas viewers of American programs. Do they understand the story at all? *What* story do they understand? (Do they, for example, give equal weight to the two realms—family and business—which figure in the plot? Do they perceive the story as traditional or revolutionary from the point of view of relations between the sexes? Are the women dependent or liberated? Is J. R. the hero or the villain or both?) Do all groups perceive the story in the same way? What critical categories do they employ? Do they evaluate it in moral or aesthetic terms? Do they discuss it playfully or moralistically? Equipped with these questions and armed with some theoretical orientation from students of decoding (Worth and Gross, 1974; Hall, 1985; Morley, 1980; Allen, 1985; Thomas and Callahan, 1982), we entered into the subsample of group discussions to construct codes that would answer our questions.

The basic distinction we employed is between what we labeled referential and critical passages in the flow of the discussions. These passages consist of free associations which frame the program for some moments as either real or art. Referential framings treat the characters as if they were real, suspending disbelief so that attention is redirected to the viewers' lives or to the lives of other real people, whether intimate acquaintances or of various social categories such as businessmen, women, etc. Critical framings, on the other hand, discuss the program as an aesthetic project, comparable to other projects and programs within the same or different genres. This distinction is also central in Jakobson (1972) who uses the terms "referential" and "metalinguistic" (our critical).

We further subdivided referential passages in terms of the subject of these associations (the viewers themselves, their families, their ethnic community, their country, etc.), whether the associations are treated as playful fantasy or as serious, whether they are spoken moralistically or without passing judgment. Thus, if talk of J. R. and Sue Ellen led a couple to joke about their own marital tensions, we coded this passage as referential framing, ludic keying, primary-group referent, and nonevaluational.

We also divided the critical framings into subtypes. Here, too, we found it useful to invoke linguistic terms and coded the critical passages as relating to discussion of the story syntactically, semantically, or pragmatically. All these were based on a manifest awareness on the parts of the viewers of the constructedness of the program and the audience experience of it. To dwell on the theme of sibling rivalry, for example, or the message that ruthlessness is a prerequisite to success, relates to the semantic aspect of the text; defining *Dallas* as a family melodrama or a prime-time soap qualifies as syntactic criticism; and reflexive observation on the ways in which aspects of the text evoke patterns of viewer involvement—"Babies grab everybody"—was coded as pragmatic.

A code that is applicable to the discussions from beginning to end, rather than to specific areas of the questionnaire, deals with the processes of mutual aid among viewers. In a qualitative discussion of this kind of technical and normative assistance, we distinguish among interactions that deal with elementary understanding of the picture and the text, with the interpretations of the motives and causal relations of and between characters, and with evaluations which bring normative or aesthetic criteria to bear on communal attitudes towards the program and its characters. In these processes, one can observe the ways in which consensus about the program arises from the interaction with community norms and how the program enters the culture via agenda setting, identification, para-social interaction, and the like (Curran et al., 1977; Horton and Wohl, 1956).

Yet another code that flags passages throughout the discussion parses the messages that viewers perceive in the program. These messages are coded in terms of several dominant themes and in terms of viewers' attitudes to these messages.[9] In the matter of messages, we also made a distinction between messages that were volunteered spontaneously by group members and those which were offered in response to our specific questioning about messages.

Two codes that are specific to particular areas of the questionnaire concern "the fuss about babies" and "retellings." These also represent, respectively, the smallest and the largest coding units in our study. Replies to the question, Why does *Dallas* make so much of babies? are often quite brief—a sentence or so—and are coded first as referential or critical. Relying on Barthes (1975a), we also coded viewers' styles of retelling of the episode. Retellings can be primarily linear or sociological, emphasizing the sequence of the story; they can emphasize the psychological motives of the characters; or they can emphasize the ideological, to the neglect of both social sequences and characters' motives.

Except for retellings, all coding was done in two steps—first, by marking passages relevant to the code in question, and second, by categorizing the passage in terms of the coding categories. Coder reliability was checked at each step, and only after a satisfactory level of intercoder reliability was achieved (averaging 80 percent) was a coder permitted to work alone. Coded passages were extracted from the text and filed in order to permit the researchers to go back and forth between the statistical results of the coding and the tangible examples from the conversations.

The initial coding of the referential and critical passages gave a ratio of approximately three to one in favor of the referential. When we received the Japanese data, however, we were impressed by the high proportion and richness of their critical statements, and we decided to return to the original protocols of the Americans, Russians, and kibbutzniks—who also had a high proportion of critical to referential statements—in order to compare subtypes of these statements with those of the Japanese. A recoding of critical statements in smaller units and in more subdivisions produced a much larger number of critical statements than before. The earlier coding is biased toward the referential, since the coders searched for subtypes of the referential and did not subdivide the critical. It is for this reason that we report both sets of data (see Chapters 7 and 8) without attempting to reconcile them beyond what is explained here.

4
ONE MOROCCAN GROUP: A TRANSCRIPT AND COMMENTARY

Before attempting analysis and generalization across the sixty-six focus-group discussions, we present here most of the transcript of one discussion in order to share our conviction that focus-group discussions resembled the kind of day-to-day conversation that is otherwise unavailable to the researcher.

The participants in the conversation were three Jewish couples of Moroccan origin who are well integrated into Israeli society and all good friends. With one exception, the participants can all read the subtitles: they do not understand English. Adi, the interviewer, came to the home of Zehava and Yossi; two other couples—Cecile and Itzchak, and Massudi and Machluf—joined them. Even before the episode went on the air, spontaneous conversation on *Dallas* began and, therefore, taping was started early. The discussion continued during the viewing, and characters and events on the screen were sometimes incorporated into the conversation. By the time the focus discussion was due to begin, the conversation flowed quite naturally. By that time, Adi was comfortably integrated into the group, making it difficult for her to stick to her moderator's role, and some of the points of discussion had already been covered. There is no question but that the following transcript is a record of the way these people normally talk to one another, even if it is unlikely that they talk in such a sustained way about a television program. In any case, it is a rare documentation of television talk.

The episode discussed was entitled "Little Boy Lost," in which J. R. loses custody of his son to Sue Ellen, who has left him and is living with her (impotent) lover, Dusty, the scion of a competing oil dynasty. The episode is from the second season of the American television serial, broadcast in Israel during the winter of 1983 with subtitles in Hebrew and Arabic.

To illustrate how the material was coded and analyzed—the dimensions within which we worked—we have annotated the protocol of the conversation and flagged each of the notes with one or more subheads (that may help to clarify what is going on; that illustrate the coding categories which are employed in our analysis; and that raise questions of interest, theoretical and methodological, that deserve attention): (1) *understanding*, for coherent perception of the story line; (2) *interpretation*, on making sense of the story or *interpretation (attribution)*, on making sense of the motives of characters; (3) *moral evaluation*, on the acceptance and rejection of perceived values in the story; (4) *interaction*, on the social dynamics and roles within the group; (5) *parasocial interaction* (Horton and Wohl, 1956), on relating to the characters as if they were real; (6) *identification*, both positive and negative, with characters; (7) *acculturation*, on bringing communal or traditional sources to bear on interpretation; (8) *mutual aid*, group interaction with respect to understanding, interpretation, or evaluation; (9) *referential*, on spontaneous use of the text as a springboard for relating to personal, interpersonal, or communal problems, or *referential forum*, when the referential constitutes the basis for group discussion; (10) *critical*, for statements that reveal understanding of the genre or of dramatic requirements of television fiction; (11) *narrative*, for ethnic or personal patterns of retelling the story; (12) *gratifications*, for self-defined uses of the program in connection with social and personal needs; (13) *definition of the (interview) situation*; and (14) *methodology*.

In addition to the three couples and Adi, the observers Gil and Elihu were present, operating the tape recorders and making notes. Some preliminary conclusions may be suggested on the basis of this case study (which served as part of the subsample of preliminary readings):

1. The group clearly understood the basic narrative, unimpeded by subtitles and cultural differences. Their focus on primordial passions and the patterns of interpersonal relations may conceal a lesser understanding of the intricate machinations of a particular subplot (cf. note 21, where the meaning of the secretary's phone call to the restaurant is misunderstood). The universality of these elemental relationships seems to be a key to the ease with which the program is understood.

2. Retelling of the narrative by group members was in an interpretative and evaluative mode. They edited the story as if it were more linear than it is on the screen, stringing together the segments of only one of the main themes, and they treated it as if it were leading to a final resolution rather than to a never-ending and potentially reversible serial. They were certainly closer to Tannen's (1982) Greek storytellers, who defined their task as telling an interesting story, than to her Americans, who tried to be as detailed and precise as possible, even at the expense of being boring.

3. Their reediting of the story invokes a moral frame, whereby the plot rewards and punishes characters according to the moral or immoral motives that are attributed to them. Approval of a character entails attribution of an intrinsic moral motive to explain action. Our Moroccan viewers would surely disagree with Arlen's (1980) proposal that the fascination of *Dallas* is its moral improvisation and equivocation and its consequent unpredictability. Their

reading is more lawful, their characters less ambiguous. That Sue Ellen discovers true love with Dusty (note 61) may not be in the text; it is in the reading.
The story may be anomic: this reading is not.

4. It is likely, therefore, that the program serves as more of a forum (Newcomb and Hirsch, 1983) for Israeli Moroccans than for Americans. The constant
negotiation between their own values and those of the program leads the group
to commute between discussion of the program and discussion of life. The
conversation is replete with referential allusions to issues of family, sex roles,
justice, standards of living, and the like. On the basis of issues raised in the
discussion of the program, reference is made to social relations within the
immediate group itself, to personal relations in the community of group members, to problems of Israeli society, to American society (where Dallas is often
treated as equivalent to America), and to philosophical issues more generally.
Interchanges of this kind are another of the keys to the process whereby
American television programs penetrate linguistic and cultural frontiers. People
help one another to decode them. The same interchanges constitute the filters
through which the story—as hero, metaphor, message—makes its way into the
culture. This group is of particular interest because it illustrates vividly how
community members negotiate meanings by confronting the text with their own
tradition and their own experience. The conversation suggests that the program
serves viewers as a forum for discussion of personal, interpersonal, and social
issues such as justice (our notes 41, 52); whether or not fathers have equal rights
in their children (note 73); child-rearing problems (note 59); gender-role differences (notes 27, 73); attitudes toward adultery and divorce (notes 13, 40, 84,
85); the problem of cramped quarters (note 86); religious demands (note 20); and
the harsh reality of prolonged war in Lebanon (note 89). Consider also the
references to other texts—especially religious ones (notes 12, 28, 83, 85).

5. The reciprocal of referential allusion is critical distance, that is, discussion
of the program as genre, as formula, as a story governed by aesthetic and
business constraints and not necessarily related to life. Not so much of this sort
of distancing is displayed in the present discussion. Occasionally, however,
there is a flash of critical insight, as when the Mafia is alluded to (note 80),
echoing the critical analysis by Mander (1983), who argues that Dallas is a
version of the newly prevalent Godfather myth in America. The group is
strongly aware of escapist gratifications of the program—in giving relief from
the structures of religious observance, the constriction of living quarters, and
the terrible strain of the war in Lebanon.

6. The group, of course, had dynamics of its own, and if certain roles
emerged during the course of the conversation, and even if certain members
were more dominant than others, this may well be an accurate simulation of
everyday television talk. If Machluf prevails in his view, the group may well
refuse entry of the values of the program into their lives as traditional Jews; if
Yossi prevails, the program is altogether unworthy of serving as a forum for
discussion of real problems. Among the roles engendered by the discussion,
one can discern that of commuter (triggering transitions between the story and

real life) and resource person (providing details from past programs). Note also the ways in which knowledge of the program is used as a source of status (Cecile at note 38), just as knowledge of traditional texts conferred status.

iscussion Before Viewing Begins

MACHLUF: Even when I look at it and I know it's an actor, that it's only cinema, but they act so much theater, they play it so much from their gut, especially J. R.; he's great.

Methodology. Following completion of the background questionnaire and before the viewing of the episode, an informal chat began, and the tape recorder was turned on. Machluf is teetering on the borderline of what we code as *critical* in the sense of betraying a clear awareness of the story as a construction in spite of being carried away by its reality. This is not explicit enough, however, for us to apply the *critical* subcode, "mimetic." We wish to point out that we are not here coding the discussion systematically but illustrating the several codes and explicating their use. We urge attention to the ways in which context functions to influence our own understanding and, thus, the coding.

ADI: Do you understand what he says, or do you read the subtitles?
MACHLUF: I understand what he says and what he acts, and I understand him.
YOSSI: She (the interviewer) means the translation (subtitles). Do you read the translation?
MACHLUF: Of course, the translation.
ADI: Anybody here understand English?
MACHLUF: Well, unfortunately, we studied French in our town, only French.
YOSSI: Yes, we all read the translation.
CECILE: I was in France a month ago, and I saw a few episodes. In French it was simply a pleasure. Here I enjoy it less, that is, there I discovered I enjoyed it more. Because I saw it here all the while without knowing whether I enjoy it more or less. I don't read Hebrew 100 percent, and it takes me time to read, it's a pity.
ADI: (to Massudi) What do you think?

Referring to the background questionnaire, Adi discusses the extent of dependence on the subtitles.

. MASSUDI: I don't see *Dallas* at all.
MACHLUF: I see it for her—and in the middle of the night, I tell her everything. (general laughter)
CECILE: I always see it even though I get fed up. I anticipate what's going to happen,

Understanding: Unlike the other participants, Massudi does not know Hebrew and is, therefore, reluctant to answer questions. There are indications that she does watch *Dallas* and comprehend it, such as her remark during the viewing of

and sometimes I think, well, what did I sit for? But anyway, I do sit and watch . . .

4. CECILE: The landscape.
   ITZCHAK: The landscape.
   CECILE: It's rich . . .
   ITZCHAK: It's rich like all American movies.

5. MACHLUF: The beach, the pool, the colors, the apartment.
   ZEHAVA: The house.
   ITZCHAK: But after a while the subject becomes a little tiring because there are unacceptable things.
   MACHLUF: For example?
   ITZCHAK: Things that don't happen in life, let's say things that happen in a family, all the stories. . .
   CECILE: They exaggerate sometimes.
   ITZCHAK: It's exaggerated that they all give in to somebody like that. It's simply not real. It doesn't seem as true to life as it was at the beginning (of the serial). After

the program regarding J. R.'s unsuitably informal dress in court (cf. note 34) which shows that she can both understand and criticize the basic plot. This would explain why her husband fills her in at night on the more detailed *Dallas* gossip.

Interaction: Cecile's repeatedly breaking into her husband's sentences should not necessarily be looked at as interruption. In certain cultural settings, this constitutes what sociolinguists call "corporate sentence building" (Bennet, 1978). This form of conversation characterizes cultures in which there is need for reassurance and encouragement—being polite, therefore, means cooperating in presenting oneself and the other. This does not exist in cultures where the need for privacy and autonomy is considered crucial and, therefore, being polite consists of respecting the boundaries of each individual (Brown and Levinson, 1979). Conversations in which there are frequent pauses and strict turn-taking belong to the second type of politeness, as it is concerned with respect for the distance among people. The discussion of the Moroccan group under consideration here, characterized by frequent overlaps, is associated with the first type of politeness, which creates an atmosphere of intimacy. Thus, Cecile's overlapping with Itzchak is probably (1) an indication of intimacy and consensus between husband and wife and (2) her particular way of joining the conversation and adding to the discussion rather than interrupting it.

Interpretation: Since most Israelis live in apartments, Machluf slips into calling the Ewing mansion "the apartment." He is immediately corrected by Zehava who, as we later discovered, was just in the process of trying to find a way to move her own family from a two-room apartment to a slightly larger one.

a while it starts to become boring. Even annoying.

ADI: But you see it faithfully?

CECILE: Yes, yes.

ITZCHAK: I see it for two reasons. The first reason to our regret, is that we don't . . .

CECILE: We don't have programs here.

Israel has one television channel. About half of the programs are imported from abroad, mostly from the United States. Subtitles are in Hebrew and Arabic.

ITZCHAK: We don't have very good programs. The second reason is that it's done so well—the setting and all—it attracts one; simply that. But I think it's good they stopped showing it for a time because we became almost slaves to this subject (the serial), even though I'm sure everybody knew what was going to happen.

ZEHAVA: There are also books (about Dallas).

Gratifications: Itzchak's comment suggests that viewing *Dallas* provides a different kind of experience than, say, viewing *Kojak*. He is, in effect, saying that the pleasure of watching does not arise from being curious about *what* the characters are going to do but about *how* they do it. Not having to worry about the technicalities of the plot, viewers can relax and enjoy following the Ewings, whose idiosyncracies are anticipated. For the viewers, the pleasure of seeking out and discovering all the intricate details of the TV program may be similar to the pleasure of a reader in reading a novel for the second time (Barthes, 1975a).

CECILE: And people see it in Jordan, and it's more advanced.

ITZCHAK: It's something that almost repeats itself. The same mistakes that J. R. made repeat themselves, and it's no longer a subject for study.

ELIHU: What mistakes?

ITZCHAK: For example, when the father capitulates to J. R.'s mistakes in business.

MACHLUF: Which cost many millions . . .

One source of information on future developments in the story is Jordanian television, which is one season ahead of Israeli television.

ITZCHAK: And he always makes sure that he will succeed at any cost, and the women fall into his arms like I don't know what, and this is something in the story which is not really normal ("normal" = normative) in life.

Moral evaluation: Itzchak is raising a central moral and philosophical issue concerning the viewing of *Dallas*. Describing it in terms of the celebration of the success of ruthless power over moral values, of the victory of id over superego, leads him to consider whether this is a reflection of what happens in real life. Itzchak's answer is negative because normal to him means normative. This means a better interpretation of Itzchak's meaning than the mimetic concern with the relation between the program and life. Throughout this discussion *normali* and *lo normali* mean normative and deviant.

10. MACHLUF: Don't forget that J. R. is very
    good-looking and very rich.
    ZEHAVA: And what do people like? Money.
    MACHLUF: Good-looking and rich is some-
    thing which attracts many women.

Referential forum: This leads to a discussion about social norms in interpreting
the story. Machluf and Zehava draw on
knowledge of life—and vice versa. They
generalize about life, and this provides an
interpretation of the story. Either way,
they talk about *Dallas* as if it were real.

These generalizations about what
"people" like contradict what the group
members say they themselves like and
identify with. *They* select and evaluate
characters on a strictly moral basis. When
they are asked to name the central characters in the episode, J. R. is not included.
The difference between talking about
what "they" (people, most women) like
and what "we" (Jews, Moroccans) like
shows that normative rules are invoked
when speakers feel personally responsible for their statements. In Newcomb's
(1984) terms, they might be employing
different or even conflicting discourse
systems in the two cases. Whereas here
they talk as if they were participant observers in informal chatting about *Dallas,*
later, in answering the interviewer's
question, they define themselves with
the voice of a particular social and cultural community.

11. CECILE: Everybody, more or less, also in the
    film, knows what he's worth.
    ADI: What does that mean?
    MACHLUF: His character, his character . . .
    CECILE: That he is not honest in business,
    with women, in everything. But never-
    theless, women continually . . .
    MACHLUF: . . . go after him.
    CECILE: Anybody he wants . . .
    MACHLUF: . . . gets caught in his net.
    CECILE: . . . fall very fast.
    YOSSI: . . . are attracted to him.

The group regularly refers to the serial as
a film; we have retained this usage. It
seems to connote a festive involvement to
which one looks forward, etc.

12. MACHLUF: Are attracted to him. Kristen,
    zichrona livracha ("her memory be
    blessed"), was also attracted.
    YOSSI: The truth is, he's attractive; he's a
    good-looking fellow.
    CECILE: They don't want to believe what
    they hear. They love him, and they don't
    want to accept the complaints against
    him. What one hears.

Acculturation: Zichrona livracha, the traditional Jewish way of alluding to someone
who has died, is used ironically in this
case. The term still gives a sense of how
the participants chat about *Dallas*'s characters as real people who live or, as in this
case, die.

13. MACHLUF: You see, I'm a Jew wearing a
    skullcap, and I learned from this film to

Moral evaluation: This is just one instance
in which Machluf invokes quotations

say (quoting from Psalms), "Happy is our lot" that we're Jewish. Everything about J. R. and his baby, who has maybe four or five fathers. I don't know. The mother is Sue Ellen of course, and the brother of Pam left; maybe he's the father . . . I see that they're all bastards. Isn't that true Doctor Katz?

ELIHU: Really bastards or bastards in character?

MACHLUF: According to the movie, this son is literally a bastard. She was pregnant from Pam's brother.

CECILE: . . . but the tests show that J. R. is the father . . .

MACHLUF: . . . and J. R. recognizes this himself. She told him the truth. She says: "I am pregnant from Pamela's brother." What's his name . . .

ITZCHAK: Bobby.

MACHLUF: No, no. Bobby is Pam's husband.

CECILE: Cliff. Cliff.

ITZCHAK: But, in fact he (J. R.) saw that it was his *son*.

GIL: OK, we're beginning. The program is starting.

from religious sources as a way of relating to the invading world of television. Here a quotation is used to contrast and express the mores of *Dallas* with those of Jewish culture; thus, he reinforces traditional values.

Mutual aid: The debate over J. R.'s paternity points to the kind of involvement through speculation that *Dallas* arouses: the "facts" of the story turn out to be a matter of interpretation. Different, sometimes contradictory bits of information are brought forth as evidence for various ways of understanding the story. Machluf knows the baby is *not* J. R.'s and proves it with Sue Ellen's words: "She *told* him the truth." Cecile brings up the laboratory test as proof of the opposite.

iscussion While Viewing—From Observers Notes, Not Recorded

MACHLUF: There's Miss Ellie.

ITZCHAK: Miss Ellie is wonderful, but the queen is Pam.

YOSSI: It's only the second time I'm seeing *Dallas*. It looks like an Arabic film, begins with an accident (*te'una*) and ends with a wedding (*hatuna*).

ZEHAVA: The men see the film because of the beautiful girls.

Methodology: Taping was discontinued here on the assumption that there would be little or no conversation during the viewing. Fortunately, the observers took notes verbatim until the recording resumed.

Critical: Yossi places *Dallas* within the genre of Arab melodrama. These shows are popular on Israeli television. His use of the rhyming words *te'una* and *hatuna* accentuates his awareness of the repetitive, formulaic nature of the succession of crises that lead, à la Propp (1968), from a "lack" to a "coronation." (Compare our analysis in Chapter 5 of the linear style used by Arabs and Moroccans in their retellings of the episode.) Parenthetically, there is reason to doubt Yossi's declaration that he is not a *Dallas* regular on the basis of his other statements.

17. CECILE: And there's a good mother. (on screen: Miss Ellie is reprimanding J. R. because he intends to buy off the judge.) Bravo. Bobby is too good and J. R. too bad, both extremes.
    YOSSI: J. R. looks like Tony Curtis.

Interaction, mutual aid, critical: Cecile is here making her bid for the role of moral pedagogue or authoritative interpreter on the *Dallas* goings-on. There is also a parasocial note in the "Bravo" she awards Miss Ellie. Also note the exaggerated polarization of Bobby and J. R., which has overtones of both the moral and the critical (in the sense of identifying the nexus of the dramatic tension). Our own analysis of the episode in Chapter 5 will argue that this polarization of the two men is unwarranted, as is the group's tendency to overdetermine other characters as well, such as Sue Ellen (see note 60).

18. CECILE: There's Rebecca, Cliff's mother. Suddenly she's here again.
    YOSSI: What business are they talking about?
    MACHLUF: Oil. These are the actors who were in Israel.
    YOSSI: Who's the boss; who decides things.
    MACHLUF: J. R.
    CECILE: Jock.

Mutual aid: Continuing her expertise, Cecile's surprised comments on seeing Cliff's mother sound like those of someone meeting an almost-forgotten old acquaintance. Characters are typically identified in terms of their family relations, "Cliff's mother," especially in the more traditional groups.

19. ITZCHAK: Look at how money corrupts things, corrupts people.
    CECILE: A little money doesn't hurt; a lot does. The money simply pours out in this film.

Moral evaluation, forum: An illustration of how Dallas becomes a *forum* for the articulation of social issues (Newcomb and Hirsch, 1983) can be found in this discussion which starts with Itzchak pointing to the message of *Dallas*. Itzchak chooses to apply a moral criterion for judging characters, which is psychologically gratifying for the group because although they cannot be as successful as the Ewings, they can be more honest.

Machluf introduces an academic or spiritual standard of measuring success, alluding to tradition and to a type of success where the children of the poor may outdo the others. Thus, Itzchak and Machluf suggest two ways of using *Dallas* as a morality play, useful in defining success in ways that provide "substitute frames for self-judgment" (Merton, 1946).

20. MACHLUF: I've seen how well poor children do at school and how rich children are just spoiled and fail. (referring to the women on screen) They're like Hanukkah lights, only there to be seen.
    CECILE: My child sees swimming pools on TV and says how good it is to be rich.

Acculturation: Machluf's metaphor again refers to a traditional source (cf. note 12) by drawing an analogy between the women in the program and Hanukkah candles, which are forbidden for practical use but are there to be admired. Use of this traditional Jewish allusion for defin-

YOSSI: (referring to a car on screen) What a Mercedes!

CECILE: Afton knows what J. R. is asking her to do is not kosher. She said as much to her brother. But, nevertheless, she goes on being with him. They choose beautiful women, one after the other. We see one beautiful girl, and after her appears another even more beautiful girl. (on screen: J. R.'s secretary calls to give him an excuse to leave Afton alone with the judge.) She is waiting to be next in line. (general laughter)

ITZCHAK: J. R. is a bastard.

ZEHAVA: Would you like to be in his place? I don't think there are many people in the world like him as far as trickery goes. That's why it's not real.

MACHLUF: J. R. is the perfect man. J. R. only loves himself. Couldn't care less about the others.

CECILE: In real life Sue Ellen is better than Pam. They say that Pam in real life is not good; she takes drugs.

MACHLUF: (shakes his head unbelievingly)

YOSSI: There is too much cinema here. You know what movies are? Business, money. (on screen: J. R. is trying to set the judge up with Afton.)

MACHLUF: Filth, that's what we're seeing.

. MACHLUF: (on screen: Afton sings in a nightclub.) Moroccans are drinkers; what can we do? It causes us to forget about kosher rules, about our tiny flats. Thank God for that . . . Look at how she sings.

ZEHAVA: He is simply a good-looking man (J. R.). (turning to the others) We are always talking about good-looking women—talk a bit about men.

CECILE: (referring to Mitch on screen) Voilà. le plus beau.

ZERHAVA: Who?

. CECILE: Mitch. mitz.

MASSUDI: Not mitz tapuzim.

CECILE: (referring to the woman who was choking on screen) Mitch will help her. He studied medicine.

. MACHLUF: Something like that happened to us at work; do you remember?

ing the pleasures of TV is intended to be funny and serves to contribute to the group's cohesion versus the screen.

Understanding: This is a rare example of a viewer who may be said not to understand the plot. Trapped in her theory, according to which all women are attracted to J. R., Cecile misses the point of the secretary's call, prearranged by J. R. in order to carry out his scheme.

In Israel, as elsewhere, much is known about the well-publicized private lives of the stars. As Machluf has already noted, some of the *Dallas* stars made a royal visit to Israel, and Prime Minister Begin received them.

Forum: Watching the bar scene on screen triggers a comment on the reasons for the prevalence of drinking in Machluf's own milieu. The function of drinking as a means of escape from sordid reality is talked about in the group in the same way they talk about the function for them of *Dallas* (cf. note 89).

Interaction, acculturation: Cecile and Massudi make a play on words in Hebrew in saying that "Mitch" is not *mitz*—the Hebrew word for fruit juice.

Referential: Machluf and Zehava by association, are reminded of two similar chok-

ZEHAVA: My friend almost died because of this. She swallowed a piece of meat.

MACHLUF: One woman actually fasted two days because there was a wedding reception.

CECILE: (referring to Mitch on screen) That's it. They got it out.

MACHLUF: . . . and she came and fell over a tray of turkey meat and put it into her mouth and choked. Thank God, among the guests, there was a doctor; he gave her a stroke on the back, pah, got it all out, very very hard. And she returned to life.

CECILE: That's it. He's saved her.

ZEHAVA: This girlfriend of mine practically choked to death. They took her in an ambulance to the operating theater, and the fear, when she saw everything, made her spit it up all at once. And they took it out: the doctor couldn't believe it. He saw this meat and said: "How could she do such a thing?" A friend of mine told her . . .

MACHLUF: It's a whole cow's tongue she swallowed in one breath.

ing instances they have witnessed. Both give parallel, competing dramatic scenarios resembling the one taking place on the screen, which does not in the least disturb Cecile, who is absorbed in the program and maintains her own dialogue with the screen.

26. ZEHAVA: She should eat like a human being. (asked by her husband to serve tea) Sorry, I'm watching (the program). Otherwise, afterwards, when they (the interviewers) ask me, what shall I answer?

Definition of the situation: Zehava defends herself against her husband's request that she serve tea by referring to the role of focus-group members.

27. YOSSI: With us, it's not like with J. R. With J. R. the woman looks after everything. He's got a servant girl. (Zehava and Cecile laugh)

ZEHAVA: Why, do you mean to say I am your servant?

Interaction, gratifications (uses): TV here provides shared associations, which are activated, as it were, for expressing negative feelings in a subtle way, thus preventing a direct confrontation.

This is only one of the ways in which the program is used to comment on present problems that occupy viewers in their personal or social lives. Whereas this switch to talking about life deals with gender roles in marriages (cf. note 59), the next transition to real life (note 31) deals with the norms of Israeli society in contrast to the presumed norms of *Dallas*.

28. MACHLUF: No, this is your house. You will be given "up to half the kingdom"—it is Purim.

ZEHAVA: (reacting to coffee offered to Mitch in the film) Coffee, Cecile?

This is a quote from the biblical book of Esther associated with the carnivalesque holiday of Purim, which was being celebrated at the time of the interview session.

CECILE: (*on screen: The doctor examines Pamela.*) What a show-off.
MACHLUF: Who's the old man?

CECILE: A doctor.
YOSSI: I thought they have some private doctor.
CECILE: (in French, offering her diagnosis) *Depression.*
MACHLUF: Why?
CECILE: *Elle veut un bébé,* and they ask her to wait too long. She wants it too much.

Cecile continues her pedagogic leadership.

YOSSI: The same story all the time. He (J. R.) feels himself strong with his money. I'm telling you, who in Israel could get away with that?

Critical: Recognition of the formulaic character of the plot by Yossi is continued also in Yossi's next intervention.

MACHLUF: Akiva Nof, the member of Knesset, had a similar story with his wife. The journalists have shaken the whole country with Akiva Nof until now. In Israel he (J. R.) could not possibly behave in such a way.

Referential: By comparing J. R. to a member of the Israeli Parliament who went through a well-publicized divorce case, Machluf is assuming (1) that *Dallas* reflects American society, (2) that America is corrupt, and (3) that Israel is not. Thus, he again uses *Dallas* to reinforce his own values.

ZEHAVA: "The taste of life."

Critical: In order to support Yossi's argument, Zehava quotes Coca-Cola's frequently broadcast commercial (in Hebrew). She chooses an example par excellence of America inundating the world with its idea of taste—the equivalent of *Dallas* in the area of material consumption—where (1) both represent American (consumer) hegemony, (2) both are relentlessly repetitive, and maybe (3) both add flavor to ordinary life.

CECILE: (*on screen: Mitch is having breakfast with a plastic surgeon and his wife whom he saved from choking.*) But (please) without the bones.

Para-social interaction: In conducting a conversation directly with the characters, Cecile brings them into the living room, so to speak, so that she can joke with them, give them advice, and even criticize their actions. In rebuking the doctor, she introduces her own social norms, implying that his invitation to Mitch to come for a meal defines their conversation as something personal, so that offering money seems in bad taste.

MASSUDI: (*on screen: J. R. enters the court.*) He came without a jacket.
ZEHAVA: (asked again to bring some tea)

Understanding: Massudi, who cannot read the subtitles and claims she does not understand what is occurring on the screen

Well, I got an order from the captain, so I have to bring it.
CECILE: (*on screen: J. R. insults Pamela at the breakfast table.*) Now there's violence.

35. MACHLUF: Why does Pam go to work? Her husband is so rich.
CECILE: But they have no satisfaction in life. So they search . . .
YOSSI: Satisfaction in life.
CECILE: What does it mean, why does she go to work? What will she do? Wait until Bobby comes home?
YOSSI: Does she lack anything? Of course, she does not have to wait that much for her salary. She couldn't care less. I stand in queue at the bank on the first of the month.
CECILE: Too much money.
YOSSI: (*on screen: Another glamorous woman appears in a car.*) She doesn't work. (everybody laughs)

36. CECILE: (*Cliff is introduced to his new sister.*) Suddenly he discovers a half-sister. It's lucky that she said to him she's a sister, otherwise, he could have fallen in love with her.
YOSSI: They all have blue eyes.
CECILE: Now, please. (quiet) That's the trial for the child.
ZEHAVA AND YOSSI: Moroccans want only food.
YOSSI: Not *Dallas.*
CECILE: (responding to the general noise) You've no heart; this is a trial about the child.

37. ZEHAVA: (If) it was a *Beit Din* (rabbinical court), this would be a trial. Of course, the child will go back to his mother.
YOSSI: Is this Sue Ellen's lawyer?
ZEHAVA: (when Gil gestures her to stay in her seat rather than get the tea) I get up— immediately he looks at me. (to the interviewer) Don't worry. You will ask me, I will answer you.

38. CECILE: (*on screen: Sue Ellen's lawyer discloses he has a doctor's certificate about Dusty.*) Oh, what they're going to discover now. It's not nice, in public like that.
GIL: What is not nice?

(cf. note 3), nevertheless criticizes J. R. for not showing more respect to the court by dressing more formally.

Forum: Although the group's discussion overtly deals with what is happening on the screen, they are, in effect, making use of *Dallas* to enter into a debate on the roles of the sexes. Machluf and Yossi voice the traditional position in this debate, while Cecile brings up the concept of the right of women to self-realization. (This discussion happens to follow closely after Zehava's joking remark about getting an order from "the captain.")

Referential: Cecile's relief upon hearing the formal definition of family relationship is a sign of her awareness that *Dallas* scripts hover on the borderline of kinship taboos, which the characters constantly threaten to—and sometimes do— break (cf. note 13, 78). We would have coded this as *critical* had Cecile betrayed awareness that this policy of brinkmanship is caused by (1) the need to produce new entanglements within the rather closed *Dallas* circle (a new relative has to provide a new twist in the plot) and (2) the need to provide new excitement to viewers who, due to the socializing influences of television, become more and more immunized against shock.

Acculturation: It is not clear whether Zehava considers the *Dallas* custody trial real or not when she compares it to the *Beit Din,* which deals with cases of marriage and divorce in Israel.

Referential: The same norm that is behind participants' embarrassment over public discussions of sex (see discussion of Dusty "not (being) a man," below) may also underlie Cecile's reluctance to see

CECILE: (shaking her head) What they're going to discover . . .
GIL: Do you know what they'll discover?
CECILE: I know.
GIL: How do you know?

CECILE: For some time he's not been a man.
GIL: From former episodes?
ZEHAVA: Yes.
CECILE: Since the accident.

ZEHAVA: And he told her beforehand: "It's a pity for you to go on with me, I don't want to go on." And it was because of her. He was in the airplane because of her.
CECILE: (*Sue Ellen's lawyer calls her "the girl he (Dusty) intends to marry—his future wife."*) "His future wife." Here, at least, there's a nice contrast. The second family she's falling into—people . . . not just . . . people with heart, people—not just money.
ITZCHAK: Just for that, she will get the child now.
CECILE: Yes, sure. It's people . . . not just the money.
MACHLUF: After the accident he is not a man anymore.
CECILE: But she wants to be with him. Also he had the accident because of her.
ITZCHAK: So they shouldn't think as if she wanted.
MACHLUF: (to lawyer on screen) Because of love—that's right.
CECILE: J. R.'s lawyer is not pleased.
ZEHAVA: (repeating lawyer's words) "True love."

CECILE: (*on screen: Sue Ellen's lawyer says, "How can we deprive her of the only child she'll ever have?"*) J. R. already has Kristen's son. It's enough.
ITZCHAK: (*Sue Ellen's lawyer wins.*) She beat him.
CECILE: He (J. R.) killed her (Kristen), and the child remains.
YOSSI: But the judge is corrupt. He talked to J. R. in the cafe. He is corrupt.
ITZCHAK: They didn't show a bribe.

Dusty's impotence made public in the show. Another, less conscious reason might be that one of the sources of enjoyment of the series is in the arid, viewers' "privileged" position over that of other characters in the show and over less knowledgeable viewers.

Interaction: Cecile's tactful way of describing Dusty's impotence is indicative of the way group members tend to use euphemisms and literary or biblical expressions—or may even leave sentences unfinished—when sex is being discussed. Note how Cecile continues her expertise.

Mutual aid in interpretation: The discussion provides a running commentary on what is happening on the TV screen, beginning with definitions of the conflict (Cecile sees it from Sue Ellen's point of view—money versus heir; Itzchak sees it from the court's point of view—sex versus love), moving on to predictions about the outcome of the trial and speculation about Sue Ellen's motives. Note that the implicit question in Machluf's statement that Dusty is "not a man" is understood by Cecile to mean, "Why should Sue Ellen want to stay with Dusty?" and is answered accordingly. For her, not having sex is proof of true love.

Forum: Cecile introduces here a new concept of distributive justice, equal allocation of babies. The basic facts of the story—that J. R. has had a baby from Kristen—serve only as the basis for an argument over whether or not J. R. has a right to another baby. The total destruction of the institution of the family passes by unnoticed and uncriticized.

CECILE: In the former . . . she was pregnant, and she came to get money out of him . . . to blackmail (J. R.) . . . if not, she would tell her sister the truth.
YOSSI: The judge . . . he talked to him in the cafe . . . he's corrupt.
MACHLUF: It looks like the end.
CECILE: And Cliff came in at that moment and accused him of murder.

42. MACHLUF: I don't understand one thing. J. R. knows; he heard from his wife that the child (John Ross) is not his, and in spite of that, he wants to *take* him.
CECILE: But it's his name. His . . . how do you say, his *nom propre*, his name in the world.
ZEHAVA: That's right.
CECILE: His name. It's the principle. It's his wife. It has to be his son. If not, his whole name collapses; his whole honor in the world rises and falls with this.
MASSUDI: I never see it (the program).

Mutual aid in interpretation: Machluf calls attention to the improbability of some of the dynamics of family relations in *Dallas*. How can babies be bought, sold, and transferred? In their answers, Cecile and Zehava avoid the issue of how J. R. can accept the fact that the baby has another father.

43. MACHLUF: (*The judge's decision about the money Sue Ellen gets for maintenance is announced.*) $5,000 a month times 360.
ZEHAVA: It will increase. Until then it's linked.
CECILE: (anticipating the announcement on the screen) It was given to his mother. (*on screen: ". . . to Sue Ellen Ewing . . ."*) Marvelous.
ZEHAVA: I knew.
YOSSI: $1,000 a month (for the baby).
CECILE: Oh, no. (*J. R.'s smile at the end of the show.*) What a marvelous look.

Acculturation: The award is immediately translated into Israeli currency and Zehava remarks that with the rate of inflation in Israel, this amount of money will increase considerably within a short amount of time.

44. ZEHAVA: Finished. Now the examination (the interview session).
GIL: So she got $1,000 for the child as well?
CECILE: It's nothing to him.
ZEHAVA: It's nothing to him.
ITZCHAK: $5,000 maintenance and $1,000 for clothes.
ADI: $5,000 goes straight into the fuel for the car.
ITZCHAK: Nonsense. What is $1,000? It's like 1,000 *lirot* here. (comparing it to Israeli money)
MACHLUF: $6,000 times 360 *lirot*.
ZEHAVA: He talks in millions, not, not in thousands.
ITZCHAK: (repeats) There a thousand dollars is 1,000 *lirot* here.
ZEHAVA: It's nothing. Nothing.

Definition of the situation: The transition to the more formal part of the session is immediately announced by Zehava, the hostess, defining the interview situation as an "examination" (as noted in Chapter 3). Other groups define the situation quite differently.

MACHLUF: That's what we're condemned to: "We can but admire them."

Acculturation: Machluf alludes to his earlier joke about Hanukkah candles (cf. note 20). Just as the *Dallas* women, the amounts of money that are paraded on the show are only to be admired from a distance.

ram Ends, Focus Discussion Begins

CECILE: (to the interviewer) I think you got your answers within this—while we were watching the movie, right?
GIL: Let's start so we can all get some sleep.
ZEHAVA: If not you can (all) sleep here tonight, with the snow we've got here.
ELIHU: It's actually snowing?
ZEHAVA: Yes, wet snow.

Methodology: To a large extent, it is true that many of the questions to be brought up in the focus discussion were already touched on before the formal discussion took place. These questions focus on characters' kinship relations and their personalities as well as on how realistic they are as people, the extent to which *Dallas* reflects America, the concern with babies, and the gratifications of watching *Dallas*. Such anticipations of our questions reassured us in our conviction that the guidelines of the questionnaire were not intrusive.

ADI: I'm going to ask you something simple. I want each of you to tell me what was in the film. As if I hadn't seen it or as if you were coming to tell me tomorrow morning . . . Can somebody please tell me what happened in the film?
YOSSI: The same as last week. (everybody laughs) Believe me, the same faces. Only the judge is new. (laughter)

Methodology: Having the participants recount the story of the *Dallas* episode was intended to reveal (1) the extent to which people in various cultures, who depended more or less on subtitles, understood the basic plot, (2) the extent to which this understanding was shared or universal and the points at which it varied, and (3) differences in *styles* of narration that reflected variations in what may be called critical distance from the story as well as various traditions in storytelling.

ZEHAVA: Suzi (Cecile) always sounds as if she can explain things.

Interaction, definition of the situation: Zehava demurs, passing the task on to someone else, thus betraying a newly awkward feeling of the group in organized discussion. They soon forgot about this, however. Note how Zehava tries to put the group's best foot forward by cutting short her cynical husband and proposing Cecile as the group spokesperson.

YOSSI: In *Dallas* there's the law of Texas. (laughter)
ADI: What's on here? Tell me what happened in the film we've just seen.

Interpretation: By "the law of Texas," Yosi means the law of the jungle, where those with power do as they please (cf. Yossi's comments at note 52).

50. MACHLUF: To the point. The main thing in the movie was the trial, who'll get the child. Who'll get the child. This family, it has a lot of surprises.
ZEHAVA: (serving chicken) Have a taste. This is a surprise really.

51. MACHLUF: Last week the whole episode was based on J. R. wanting to kidnap his child. He came with a helicopter and tried to make use of his mother for kidnapping the son, and owing to his mother being honest and she understood what might happen to her and understood as a mother what a child and a baby means for his mother, she didn't want to follow him, and she returned the son to Sue Ellen. Here in this movie, I think the main thing is that: J. R. wanted to get back his son at any cost, and in the end the court decided what it decided, and we saw at the end that the child went back to his mother, and she also received alimony for her and child.
ADI: Anybody else want to tell what was in the film?

52. YOSSI: I will tell you. The law, the trial, you saw today in the film, is called dry law. Why is it dry law? It's law that doesn't have any law, does not have a *sujet;* how do you call it?
CECILE: Sue Ellen.
YOSSI: Not Sue Ellen. The basis of the law, the subject. This law is dry like . . . I don't know how to describe this. Who says that the court should have to decide that the child should stay with the woman? Whose fault is it that he had an accident? Was it J. R.?

Narrative: Dallas is almost impossible to relate in linear story form because it is actually a succession of segmented subplots. One way of recounting what goes on is by pointing out a main theme—which is what Machluf does here. In what follows immediately, Machluf invokes the linear form that is characteristic of the retellings of this community.

Narrative: It is useful to look at Machluf's linear version in light of Propp's scheme for analyzing folktales, according to which the basic narrative unit is called a "function"—an act of a character defined from the point of view of its significance to the course of the action (Berger, 1981). But it should be noted that *Dallas* is different from the classical folktale (1) in its cyclical, unending nature and (2) in J. R.'s alternating functions as villain and hero. Therefore, Sue Ellen's future wedding—which completes this sequence—is actually a remarriage to the villain-turned-hero.

In Machluf's version of the kidnapping attempt, Miss Ellie is the *hero,* "owing to his mother being honest . . . ." She fights the *villain,* J. R., "wanting to kidnap his child," (*struggle*) in order to repair the harm (*liquidation*) caused to a member of the family (*villainy*) because she understands what "a baby means to his mother." She returns the child to Sue Ellen, thereby repairing the harm caused to a family member. Thus, the "princess" gets what she lacked and wanted when "the child went back to his mother and she also received alimony."

Moral evaluation, narrative: Unlike Machluf's account Yossi's is paradigmatic rather than linear. The story theme according to Yossi involves the carrying out of "dry"—or legalistic—law, which contradicts his idea of justice. The romance between Sue Ellen and Dusty is a betrayal of J. R. Yossi believes that the child should not have been awarded to the unfaithful mother even if Dusty's impotence clears her, technically at least, for the moment.

CECILE: (correcting) No, her friend.
YOSSI: His friend.
MACHLUF: No, her friend.
YOSSI: Yes, her boyfriend, and he can't go to bed or make children with her, or something. Whose fault is it? She shouldn't have betrayed him, and the court should not have cleared her so that she can get the child.
ADI: But other things happened. Tell me as if I hadn't been here.
CECILE: Just a moment. Do you want us to tell the story or to analyze?
ADI: Tell us what happened as if I didn't know.

CECILE: Here the film starts after J. R. wanted to kidnap the child, and the mother did not agree to it. His mother, of course. Actually, that's what we saw in the beginning of the movie. It's also about Bobby and Pamela who passed through a difficult period that she wants a child as if she's in a depression . . .
MACHLUF: A child at any price.
CECILE: She wants to adopt a child, and they won't give it to her in the near future, and she's passing through a very difficult period, and J. R. tells her openly, he hurts her, that it's because of his son that she wants this, and I think that J. R. on every subject is trying to influence people with his opinion so much that Pam thinks he's right.
ADI: We'll soon get to J. R. Itzchak, you want to tell us a little?
YOSSI: He (Itzchak) was a lawyer in Morocco. Before he talks, tell me which party J. R. belongs to, Likud or Labor? (everybody laughs)
ITZCHAK: So he (J. R.) tried to bribe the judge and didn't manage, and he was also sure that in the court he would use all of her (Sue Ellen's) past in order to win and to get the child legally into a proper family, and this also didn't succeed. And very simply, the court did not have a choice because her lawyer actually proved that she's actually a decent woman, and that she didn't come (to Dusty) because of lust and because of . . .
MACHLUF: . . . pleasure.
ITZCHAK: Because of her own interests. She, after all, came to look after an invalid

Narrative: Cecile tells the story as two interconnected subplots in which J. R. is the villain. She describes him in the first subplot—as does Machluf—as acting in contradiction to his mother and in the second as a new cause of Pam's misfortune.

In terms of Proppian theory, Cecile describes Pam as lacking and wanting—"She wants to adopt a child and they won't give it to her." The functions Cecile elaborates on in her narrative about Pam are (1) trickery, where the villain (J. R.) uses information he receives (delivery) about his victim wanting a baby to try to trick her into changing her course of action—"He hurts her (by telling her) that it's because of his son that she wants a child"—and (2) complicity—J. R. influences her "so much that Pam thinks he's right," i.e., the victim submits to deception.

and to bring up her child in a family of
a . . .

CECILE: . . . decent sort.

54. MACHLUF: There are some points in the
film, which she hasn't told. There are
several points. Here it is not only about J.
R. and about the child. It's about Pam.
It's about her brother; how he succeeded
with his mother. It's about Pam. In my
opinion Pam loves the child (Sue Ellen's).
Why does she love the child?

ADI: Who do you think is the most important character today (in today's episode)?

CECILE: The trial.

Narrative: Following the segmented editing of the series itself Machluf mentions a
broader range of subplots according to
the characters involved: (1) J. R. and the
baby, (2) Pam and the child, and (3)
Pam's brother and his mother. It seems
that some events which created a lot of
excitement while the participants were
viewing the show—as did the incident
where Mitch saves the doctor's wife from
choking (cf. conversations at notes 24, 25,
33)—were forgotten when they re-
counted it later, perhaps because this
subplot is complete in itself and, therefore, does not remain unresolved and
troublesome in terms of the ongoing
story.

55. ZEHAVA: The child, the child.

ADI: No, the most important among the
actors.

Critical: The choice of the child who has
barely appeared on the screen indicates
that "central character" was understood
by the participants in terms of the character's dramatic function in the plot and
not in terms of his or her actual (speaking) role or length of appearance in the
show.

56. CECILE: Sue Ellen.

ZEHAVA: Yes.

Moral evaluation, identification: Two surprises emerge from the group's choice of
central characters: (1) all three of them are
women, of whom two are victims; and (2)
although it is stated right at the beginning
that everyone is attracted to J. R. (see
Itzchak's comment at note 9 and the conversation at note 10), he is not made one
of the central figures. This indicates that
the choice of main characters is based on
a *moral* criterion, that is, the group
chooses characters they can approve of or
identify with. According to Herzog-Massing (1986) who interviewed German
viewers, identifying with characters who
represent the superego (e.g., Miss Ellie)
legitimizes the viewer's pleasure in
watching the character who acts the id—
J. R. Our group's choice probably has a
similar meaning.

57. MACHLUF: I agree with her. In the trial today, we discovered that Sue Ellen went
with her boyfriend, begging your par-

Interpretation, evaluation: Machluf defines
Sue Ellen as the type of character who
commutes between the extremes of very

dons, without the sexual contact; that's what the judge says. Sue Ellen, in her role at the beginning of the films, in all the episodes, she always went after alcohol, after men—wanted to revenge herself against her husband. Her husband also always went with women; she also says, "I'll also go."

ZEHAVA: She wanted to compete with him.

MACHLUF: But today we say something special that we knew from the lawyer: that she went faithfully and that she went, like Cecile says, to look after an invalid and her own child.

ADI: Who's Sue Ellen? What are her connections? I haven't seen (the program) before.

CECILE: She's J. R.'s wife and was unfaithful in the beginning with Cliff, with Pam's brother.

MACHLUF: And from this the child was born.

CECILE: From this they say that this is the child. And afterwards there was an examination in the laboratory, and we saw that J. R. bribed the doctor, so we as spectators don't know exactly who the father is. Even if the result of the lab really says that it is J. R.'s, because we saw J. R. bribing the doctor in the lab, so we don't know.

MACHLUF: But Sue Ellen said to J. R. explicitly that it's not his son.

CECILE: She said but . . .

MACHLUF: . . . in the presence of his father.

CECILE: She actually could not know because at that time she went to bed both with her husband and with Cliff.

ADI: Do you all agree Sue Ellen is the main character today?

ITZCHAK: Sue Ellen.

YOSSI: The main character, that is.

ZEHAVA: It was all based on her. Because the child belongs to her.

ADI: What causes her to behave this way?

good and very bad (cf. note 17). Thus, from being under the influence of the villain (cf. note 51), who makes her into a promiscuous alcoholic, Sue Ellen has moved—through her contact with a child and an impotent lover—to being a nurturing mother and nurse.

Mutual aid in interpretation (attribution): Following Machluf's statement regarding the birth of Sue Ellen's baby, a debate resumes about how to interpret the information relating to the identity of the baby's father (note 14). While Machluf believes what Sue Ellen says, Cecile does not and argues that neither the viewers nor Sue Ellen possess enough information to know the truth.

Cecile talks about Sue Ellen as if she were a real person. Therefore, although her analysis is very persuasive, it excludes a more analytic or distanced kind of argument which might state that the program's writers themselves have not decided—or prefer to leave open—the identity of the baby's father. Such ambiguity might be useful in creating other twists in the *Dallas* plot.

Analyzing motives from the character's own point of view or from the point of view of other characters rather than using a critical frame (which would mean looking at the demands of the plot and the genre) is typical of this discussion. The group's way of relating to characters as if they were real often leads them to speculate on the moral of the story or to discuss life in general or their own lives.

This exchange provides an opportunity to clarify our use of the *referential* code. Even though the story characters are here discussed as if they were real, we reserve the use of *referential* for association of the characters' lives and the discussants' lives. This is an example of applying life to story (*interpretation, attribution*) rather than story to life (*referential*), as in the following note.

59. ZEHAVA: Because of the troubles her husband caused her. And her revenge . . . where does she take it out?
    YOSSI: The jealousy she has against her husband . . .
    MACHLUF: It's not jealousy.
    YOSSI: Jealousy and the principle of it.
    ZEHAVA: It's natural that when the husband and wife quarrel, where does all the tension go? Onto the children. The wife hasn't got anybody to unload it on. On the neighbor? No, she can't. On the children.

Referential, forum: Character analysis is sometimes used as a means for viewers to bring up their own problems. Zehava evokes a popular truism about unhappy wives taking it out on their children. Since at this point Sue Ellen is definitely not taking it out on her children, Zehava's interpretation suggests that she is voicing a problem of her own that is easier to express through discussing *Dallas*.

60. ITZCHAK: I think that actually she understood that she made a mistake when she married J. R. at all, and she came to the conclusion that the life she has lived with him until today was not a clean life. And she didn't find the love, the honesty, the normal life. All in all, according to what we understood from other scenes, she has an ambitious mother who pushed her onto J. R., to marry him because of the money, because of the economic situation, and today she has already understood she's happier with her boyfriend . . .
    MACHLUF: Don't forget, Itzchak, that he's also very rich.
    ITZCHAK: Not because of the money.

Interpretation (attribution), forum, gratifications: This very romantic image of Sue Ellen attributes the dubious aspects of her behavior to external forces (ambitious mother) and her so-called positive actions to her real will ("she understood," "she came to the conclusion"). Thus, the participants consistently cast her in a far more stereotyped role than does the script. (See the reactions to cast doubt on Sue Ellen's disdain for material things.) The group's normative approach makes it vital to idealize Sue Ellen in order to permit empathy with her.

61. ZEHAVA: She was looking for love.
    ITZCHAK: She already learned one thing from former episodes that it is not the money that makes her happy, and she came to the conclusion.
    YOSSI: If she has been considerate about J. R., that joker, until now, it's because of his mother.
    ZEHAVA: She (Miss Ellie) was good.
    YOSSI: She was considerate of his mother. It's a fact that in the last episode . . . it's the second time I've seen *Dallas*, and the first time was last week. Because of his mother, he did not kidnap the daughter.

Interpretation (attribution), moral evaluation: In the debate over Sue Ellen's motives, Zehava, Itzchak, Machluf, and Cecile reinforce each other in interpreting what Sue Ellen learned from former episodes: (1) Money does not equal happiness, (2) normal family life equals happiness, therefore, (3) Sue Ellen is looking for normal family life.

In the struggle between viewers' moral repudiation of *Dallas*'s worldly success and the notion that it is what everyone dreams of (see discussion of note 10) this one-sided description of Sue Ellen serves

MACHLUF: It's a son. He's a male. He's been circumcised.

YOSSI: And because of his mother, he didn't kidnap . . . that is, she (the mother) returned it.

ADI: Is there another way to hurt J. R. apart from the son?

YOSSI: Never. She can't hurt him because of the backing he's got in the law, and his money, and the bribe.

CECILE: Only the child.

YOSSI: The child is the one who might suffer.

ADI: Do you like her (Sue Ellen)?

CECILE: As a person, yes.

MACHLUF: As a mother.

to strengthen moral opposition. Describing Sue Ellen—who herself is rich and glamorous—as a character who rejects wealth, power, and prominence for the old-fashioned values of home and family makes it easier for the more disadvantaged viewers to do the same.

Sue Ellen's move from the ranch of one oil dynasty to another is, therefore, interpreted as a radical ideological change. Through her, material standards of success can more easily be superseded by moral standards.

The discussion treats Sue Ellen's current state as the happy end of a classical, closed narrative. This may be due to lesser experience with TV serials, or it may be explained functionally in the sense that Sue Ellen is being used for the rejection of the values of the program. Note that this pedagogic interpretation of Sue Ellen's behavior is not the only one possible. Indeed viewers in other groups (some of the American groups, for example) are aware that Sue Ellen's present mood, true to the genre, is bound to be reversed at any moment.

CECILE: Today as a mother, as a person, yes. Because she had no life. Then she had everything, and she didn't have anything. She had a husband, and she did not have a husband. She had money, and she could not enjoy it without a husband. She had a child at home, and she did not love it, and the maid looked after it. She had everything, and nothing worked. She went drinking, she tried everything. Today, she doesn't drink anymore; she looks after her son. And she does not want to cause harm to the family because, after all, they did not do her any harm apart from her husband. It hurts her that the grandmother cannot enjoy the child, but she has no other choice.

ADI: Who is the second most important person in the film?

MACHLUF: But one can still talk a lot about Sue Ellen.

Narrative: In describing Sue Ellen's past, Cecile acquires the rhetorical flair of a storyteller and uses parallel contrasting phrases that emphasize the conflict in their meanings. This accentuates the paradox of Sue Ellen's state—where she had everything, but had nothing; she was rich, but she was poor—and strengthens the group's stereotypical concept of Sue Ellen (cf. note 60).

ADI: But it can take all night. Who's second?

MACHLUF: Pam, too; she is the second person. She so much wants a child at any price, and she can have a child, but she is

Interpretation (attribution), gratifications: Pam provides gratifications similar to those provided by Sue Ellen, who is seen by this group as a spiritual saint. Assum-

afraid of this hereditary illness of the father.
CECILE: But I think you're making a mistake.
MACHLUF: It's this illness that she fears.
ADI: Which illness? I didn't see that film.
MACHLUF: Yes, in the earlier films. That was an illness from which a baby cannot live more than a year or two. Something like that, if I remember.

64. CECILE: But I think that you're making a mistake because you didn't see one chapter.
MACHLUF: Possibly, possibly.
CECILE: They've already come to the conclusion that she can have healthy children. There is no fear of that. By now she can have.
MACHLUF: Nevertheless, he always doubts.
CECILE: . . . once she did not want to have one because they told her such and such and such. But later they found out it was not true. Any child can be healthy, but the problem is now.
ITZCHAK: On the whole, Pam . . . her story . . .
MACHLUF: . . . is more painful than anybody's. She wants a child at any cost.
ITZCHAK: Her story . . .
ZEHAVA: God bless her.
MACHLUF: Wants to adopt it. And even in that, she has no luck. Even in adoption, she has no luck. She has to wait.
CECILE: Let's put it this way. I think that apart from the main story in this whole J. R. film, the problem of Pam with her husband is more (important) than anything. And this, I think, is the second character in this . . . (general noise)
ITZCHAK: This is the second character in the whole film. The most popular one. It's her story. She and her husband and all the problems she goes through—in order to adopt a child and in order to give birth to a child. And she objects, she very sim-

ing that the prevailing role models for women in American culture are those of homemaker-wife, career woman, or glamour girl, Pam clearly represents the last, whereas the image of mother is usually related to those qualities that suggest virtuousness and lack of glamour.

Glamorous, rich, and unhappy, Pam's longing for a child reassures the women in the group who are occasionally cramped as housewives and mothers. Thus, they are strengthened in their belief that their own lives are more rewarding than those of rich and glamorous women like Pam. She would like nothing better than to be a mother—hence, she is to be pitied and not envied.

Mutual aid in interpretation: The fact that Cecile updates Machluf on Pam's situation demonstrates the participants' willingness to play the game that Pam is real. This kind of involvement can be explained by (1) the illusion that TV serials carry on independently of whether people view them or not (Booth, 1982), (2) the ongoing narrative of TV serials that occupies viewers' minds between episodes, and (3) the slow pace of serials, where the same unsolvable problems are dragged out endlessly, with slight variations, giving them a life-like quality.

Arguments about the facts of the story can arise easily—even among regular viewers—because of the abundance of detail, the different importance each viewer attributes to various details, and the ambiguity of the plot, intentionally left open by the writers.

ply objects—as we have seen in the last episode—to go to a psychiatrist. Pam.

ADI: Why? Why does she object?

ITZCHAK: The doctor, the doctor . . . She did go through—here in this episode—go through a depression, and he suggested to her that it's not his specialty, the general practitioner's; that she can go to a psychiatrist who can help her, who can help her . . . in this, and she objects, quite simply she objects.

ZEHAVA: Her illness, her drinking.

MACHLUF: No, with Bobby she does not drink. We're talking about Pamela.

MACHLUF: Bobby's wife.

ZEHAVA: I just now . . . I just now thought about the glass you (Yossi) were drinking. (general laughter)

YOSSI: The glass I was drinking?

ZEHAVA: When you said, "One glass I had—"

YOSSI: Am I known to count?

ZEHAVA: I said to myself "How many glasses did he have?"

MACHLUF: He drinks; she went crazy. (everybody laughs)

YOSSI: It's finished, and I still don't feel anything.

ZEHAVA: Ah, he still didn't feel anything.

MACHLUF: It doesn't matter.

ADI: Why does she not want to go to a psychiatrist? Why . . . not?

CECILE: (assisting Adi) What prevents her?

MACHLUF: I think she's afraid of the illness—that she'll bring a baby into the world—and she can bring a baby—and later he will die.

ZEHAVA: If everybody were to think so, they'll never have babies.

ITZCHAK: I think that she is simply afraid to go to the psychiatrist, maybe because of what Sue Ellen went through, when she was . . .

MACHLUF: . . .was in treatment with a psychiatrist.

Narrative: Analysis of characters often turns into telling the story. In Proppian terms, Pam, as dramatis persona here, is the *princess* who *lacks* what she most wants. In Itzchak's words: "She did go through a depression." She goes to a *donor,* who suggests providing her with a *magical agent:* "The doctor . . . he suggested to her that it's not his specialty, the general practitioner's; that she can go to a *psychiatrist* who can help her." Here the plot comes to a halt because Pam refuses for the time being to take the next step.

Referential forum: After mistakenly saying that Pam has a drinking problem, Zehava goes on to discuss what appears to be her husband's, Yossi's, drinking problem. This is another good example of *referential,* moving from story to life. Further, it is an example of using the story projectively, whereby one reads into the story something of what one reads out of it. This is also an example, therefore, of reader as writer.

ITZCHAK: Was in treatment—maybe it can affect her—and also she believes in her incapacity to bring a child, and that surely stops her, prevents her from going to a psychiatrist. That's my opinion.

67. CECILE: Maybe the psychiatrist will discover some defect in her or something and will tell her she is not able to look after a child, and she wants it so much.
ADI: When Bobby told her to go to a psychiatrist, what did she tell him?
ITZCHAK: No psychiatrist.
CECILE: She did not agree. She did not agree. Maybe he'll discover something in her which will be against . . . (having a child), and she wants it so. Maybe she wants to escape from the truth? Maybe the psychiatrist will discover something in her . . .
MACHLUF: There's a difference between Sue Ellen and Pam.
ADI: Let's leave Pam now and tell me . . .

68. MACHLUF: No, just a moment. I'll say what I have to, the difference between Sue Ellen and Pam. Sue Ellen was a drunk, was an adulteress. Two things, very huge ones. Pam, according to the movie we saw, is not a drunk and is not an adulteress. Once she tried to be unfaithful, and one telephone call was sufficient to prevent it.
CECILE: She didn't try.
YOSSI: She was persuaded.
CECILE: No, it came by itself. She didn't try. It wasn't intended.
MACHLUF: It wasn't intended, but it came, and it had to be caught. The adultery had to be caught, and a ring from Bobby saved the whole situation.
ADI: Now, we left the two women, Pam and Sue Ellen. Who is the third person— and this is the last one we'll discuss—the third most important.
ITZCHAK: It's the mother. (common agreement in the group)
ZEHAVA: It's the mother really.
MACHLUF: Miss Ellie?
YOSSI: The mother in the last two programs started getting into things.
ZEHAVA: She didn't want any unpleasantness with her daughter-in-law, as if

Interpretation, narrative: Differences in meaning emerge clearly when the psychiatrist's function in Itzchak's version is compared to his *function* according to Cecile. Here his role tends to be one of a *villain* rather than of a *magical agent*. The psychiatrist may *trick* Pam by undermining her own will and convincing her to *comply* with him and abandon her goal: He'll ". . . tell her . . . (will advise her against having a child) and she wants it so." At this point both narratives are legitimate. Only in retrospect will it be possible to determine the psychiatrist's *function* in the story. But meanwhile, the pleasure participants derive from watching the weekly *Dallas* comes from their ability to interpret the story according to their inclinations and, thereby, to forecast various sequels to the plot.

Interpretation (attribution), mutual aid in moral evaluation: Group members blame Pam—to different degrees—for her slip, though all of them regard her as a victim. Cecile sticks to the definition of Pam as a good polar-type character (cf. note 17), absolving her of all blame in the seduction attempt—she did not try (to be unfaithful) " . . . it came by itself." Cecile seems to identify most with Pam in ascribing the incident to external factors, thus excusing Pam in the same way in which she would excuse herself. Machluf describes Pam as a shifty or changeable type, "Once she *tried* to be unfaithful," thus blaming the event on her own will, while Yossi remains undecided, "she was persuaded."

Analyzing this sequence in terms of *narrative building*, the context should be kept in mind. Up until now, Pam was described as the *princess* who *lacks* what she most desires. Therefore, she is easy prey for an interested villain—i.e., potential lover—who gathers information about her trouble (*reconnaissance*) and receives it (*delivery*). Within this context, Machluf and Cecile describe the seduc-

she wanted to take away her son. She promised her—she's only coming to visit him.

YOSSI: And on one hand, she also didn't want to put off her own son.

ITZCHAK: On the whole, in this whole family I think the mother is the most logical and honest, who doesn't get corrupted, not by business and not by money and looks for . . . behaves normally; let's call it that. And in the last scene, she really discovered what she didn't want to believe all the time about J. R., and she really understood that he's not honest, and the fact is she told him that "From today, I'm going to keep an eye on you, on everything you do."

CECILE: She always knew, but she looked the other way as if she didn't want to believe it herself.

ZEHAVA: (fervently) It's, after all, her son, and she didn't want to humiliate him all the time. She looked the other way. She knew everything he was doing . . .

tion attempt as (1) *trickery*—"Pam is not a drunk and not an adulteress", it came by itself"; (2) *complicity*—"it wasn't intended but it came and (the adulterer) had to be caught"; and (3) *victory*, where the *villain* is defeated by the hero—" . . . and one telephone call . . . a ring from Bobby saved the whole situation."

It is easy to see how the same pattern of plot can occur with different characters in the role of *villain*. Both J. R. and the psychiatrist were described as deceiving Pam into *not* wanting a baby (notes 53, 67), thus making her more desperate so that the potential lover could seduce her into betraying her husband.

Narrative, interpretation (attribution): Sue Ellen and Pam are both victims—Sue Ellen of her circumstances and Pam of her genetics—and participants sympathize with their misfortunes or their lacks rather than with any positive attributes (their main attribute, glamour, is never mentioned). Miss Ellie, however, being "the most logical and honest" "in this whole family," is as active as the Ewing men—not just as an equal, but also as the most virtuous. In relating the sequence of the story described here, group members deal with the problem of J. R. playing alternating roles, as *villain* and *hero* in Itzchak's view. Miss Ellie acts as the "father of the princess" who discovered that the person he thought was a hero was in fact a *false hero* who presented unfounded claims, and the false hero is exposed. "In the last scene, she really discovered " . . . that he's not honest . . .'" But unlike folktales, *Dallas* is an unending sequence of plots where nothing is irrevocable, and options always stay open. Therefore, the last kidnapping episode having ended, Miss Ellie goes on to propose a *difficult task* to the *hero*—who happens to be none other than the unmasked *false hero*. His task is a corrective version of his evil act: he has to bring back the princess with the baby. As in fairy tales, this sequence will end within a few more episodes in a wedding, but as in soap opera, it will be J. R. and Sue Ellen's second wedding and will hardly be happy ever after.

70. CECILE: And the grandson . . . in spite of the fact that she misses him and will miss him, she told her son, "If you want to bring back the child—only with his mother." In spite of missing the grandson, she said: "With mother."
    ADI: One can see the mother believes in her course of action. Does anybody get in her way?
    ZEHAVA: . . . because she feels it as a mother. If one takes away her son, what would she feel? So she feels that way herself and doesn't want others to suffer.

71. YOSSI: You speak like a mother.
    ADI: Not only about the child.
    ZEHAVA: I told you. I repeated it, and I repeat it again. If he would have loved his wife and child and if he had a little brains, he wouldn't do everything he did. He wouldn't!

72. CECILE: (laughs) Then there would be no *Dallas*.

73. ZEHAVA: No, if she asks, then I speak with my mind, and I explain to my husband. He says why should only the mother? As if one is only on the mother's side and not the father's. This is because the mother gave birth to him; the mother suffered for him, and she loves him more than the father because it's from her flesh and blood. And the father is not . . . He is a father. Okay, he loves his child.
    MACHLUF: It's not from his flesh?
    ZEHAVA: What's that?
    MACHLUF: What does it mean from his seed, not from his flesh?
    ZEHAVA: It's not the same thing. The mother, she suffered in birth and not the father.
    MACHLUF: They (fathers) haven't got 50-50 in the child?
    ZEHAVA: But the mother looked after the child when he was a baby.
    MACHLUF: Forget the looking after.

Narrative: It should be noted that Miss Ellie's instructions, the high points of the two scenes, are retold in direct quotation by Itzchak and Cecile in order to emphasize their dramatic power. In Chapter 5, on retellings of the story, we find this use of direct quotations at key points to be characteristic of the linear form, which presents the story as a sequence of dramatic actions.

Referential forum: The dominance Miss Ellie acquires, as she, in effect, takes over the role of both mother and father, is threatening to Yossi, who hastens to defend the father's role. This leads to a heated debate over the real-life aspects of this issue.

Critical: Here Cecile stops Zehava from attacking J. R. as if he were a real person by reminding everybody that they are talking about a TV show. It is one of the instances in which a member of the group has enough distance from the show to draw a clear distinction between real life and *Dallas* and, thereby, to relate to its qualities as dramatic genre.

Referential forum: The following is a debate between Zehava and Machluf, who is supported by Yossi, on the question of whether fathers have equal rights in their children. This is a version of the ancient conflict—between the matriarchal and the patriarchal principles—which is basic to culture and appears as a main theme in Greek tragedy (Fromm, 1958). Here it is prompted by Zehava who interprets Miss Ellie's special understanding of Sue Ellen's plight by saying that they both are mothers. Zehava's underlying argument is that the mother-child attachment is a primordial relationship that precedes the institution of the family. Her logic is founded in a prefeminist worldview. The mother has a special right to her baby precisely because of the *differences* between the sexes that express themselves (1) biologically and (2) in the specialization of tasks in the home. Zehava claims

YOSSI: . . . and thanks to whom was—(unclear). Thanks to the father.

MACHLUF: But the (in French) *fabrication* (production).

CECILE: The production.

MACHLUF: The production.

YOSSI: The production. Who produced it? Who produces this bottle? (holding in his hand the whiskey bottle) The machine. But who fabricated us? (laughter)

MACHLUF: (to Zehava) If you don't plant the seed in the earth . . .

ELIHU: This is another study.

ZEHAVA: (to Machluf) Look, I always gave you a lot of respect. I never said a word.

MACHLUF: Why, don't I respect you?

ZEHAVA: It's not nice . . . I'm only explaining the fact that you say to me . . .

YOSSI: What does he say to you?

MACHLUF: I didn't say anything to you. You said the mother, the mother deserves more in the child, more than the father. So I said . . .

ZEHAVA: Yes.

MACHLUF: So I said why? It's half-half.

ZEHAVA: The mother, she gave birth to him; she (carried) him for nine months.

MACHLUF: That's fine. In our government you (women) ask for equal rights. And you actually want 75 percent.

ADI: Later, it will be all in the tape, and they'll say, "What kind of talk went on there?" (laughter)

MACHLUF: I think that people who have a lot of money like this movie describes, everything can happen with them even more than that.

ADI: So you think there are such people in real life?

. MACHLUF: Of course there are, and there are even worse people.

ZEHAVA: Here in Israel there are people like that?

CECILE: No, there aren't.

MACHLUF: And all this because of the money. Too much. They have too much. So much so that they do things that we couldn't even imagine to ourselves that they could do. All this because of the money.

CECILE: People who have no problems look for problems.

MACHLUF: That's it exactly.

that productive effort gives the right to the product, and Machluf claims that capital investment does. Machluf's final joke is a total distortion of her point of view.

Moral evaluation: Some members of the group, without questioning the reality of the program, created a dichotomy between "them and us" in order not to be contaminated. In Israel, there are no such people (as those in *Dallas*) because if there were, they would constitute a part of the society, and that is regarded as a threat. They exist safely outside "our" norms, and because they are rich, they are (1) corrupt—"They do things that we couldn't even imagine to ourselves that they could do"—and (2) unhappy— "look for problems" (cf. note 61).

This condemnation of excess is related to the group's concept of the golden mean in Jewish tradition and is elaborated below (note 83). It acts as a buffer against admiring J. R. and accentuates the confrontation between the group's values and those represented by *Dallas*.

75. YOSSI: Yes. I say that the director who directed the whole series and this whole rubbish . . .
ZEHAVA: Don't blush, Yossi.
YOSSI: I don't blush. He (the director) has to be quite a genius. Because he engages here a population of 100 to 200 million people, a whole population in Jordan, in Egypt, in Israel, in the whole world.
ITZCHAK: You don't have it right.
YOSSI: I mean he got them hooked . . . he got it into them . . .
MACHLUF: He actually made the film with a very limited amount of people.
YOSSI: I repeat again, Max. Max, (Machluf) I'm not talking about Jordan and abroad. I'm talking about here in Israel. Do you notice every second Israeli says to you *Dallas, Dallas*, but nobody understands exactly what happens in this *Dallas*. Nobody.
MACHLUF: From what point of view?
YOSSI: From what point of view? Some people don't understand at all what I and you understand, about the (Ewing) family. Whoever didn't see it from the start.
ITZCHAK: Maybe he can get used to it.
YOSSI: It's not worth his while to see the second and third episode, do you see? But many people just drag along like I say to you, "I saw a good movie in the Eden Cinema," then you also go to see that good movie. But the director is very clever; he directed it very well. He did a lot of cinema here. Do you (Adi) know what it is? A lot of colors, a lot of tricks, a lot of bluffs, a lot of . . .
ADI: Do they play real parts or like Alice in Wonderland?

Critical: Here Yossi poses the elementary question of how it is that *Dallas* captivates the whole world, beginning with the Middle East, while doubting both that it is really understood and that it is worth understanding. This remark underlines the group's awareness of the program as a construction, even if most of their comments are referential.

76. YOSSI: Real characters. For instance, I read in the paper that they didn't find anybody to replace J. R.—"who killed J. R."—I read in the paper. They didn't find anybody to replace him.
THE WOMEN: No, the father.
YOSSI: The father, that's right.

Critical: In debating the difficulties of those who produce *Dallas*, group members show some knowledge of the TV industry. Unlike American viewers, Yossi, Cecile, and Zehava refer to the actors by their characters' names or by their screen roles, whereas Americans are familiar

CECILE: Jock, the father.
ZEHAVA: Jock, the father.
CECILE: Jock passed away and they wanted somebody to replace him.
ELIHU: But do you know such people?

'. CECILE: No, far, far, far from it. I've got something to add about the mother and the trial about the child. When J. R. asked the mother if she wants the grandchild back, she refused both as a mother and as a person who has been through the experience. She has already brought up a granddaughter without a mother, and nothing much came of that. She brought Lucy up already. J. R. has already caused problems to the brother, got him out of the ranch, and they accepted the daughter and brought her up, and what has become of that daughter?
GIL: Not good?

. CECILE: Of course, not good. What did she have? The whole time she suffered without a mother and a father in spite of having a ranch and a grandfather and grandmother and uncles. She always felt . . . who did she fall in love with, and who has she been with? True, today he is her uncle, but once he was the servant. Ray. She started the story with him. She was his lover. At the end when she got married, it was to someone without money. She wanted something, but nothing came out of this wedding as well. So she'll (Ellie) bring up a second grandchild without parents?

. ITZCHAK: On the whole, I think about this story of *Dallas*—there might be such cases, but I don't think there can be in the same family such great differences between the brothers, and one cannot imagine (them) in such a business because there are such differences; on one hand, one sees good-hearted, honest people in

with the stars' names. The confusion over two different newspaper stories (one about Larry Hagman's "J. R. style" financial demands and the other about Jock's death) leads to this ·rgument about the facts behind the scenes. This awareness of the "business behind the box" stands somewhere between a critical attentiveness to the constructedness of the program and a gossipy involvement in the lives of the characters.

Interaction: Two typical examples demonstrate how participants have no problems in systematically ignoring the interviewer's questions when they do not fit naturally into their conversation. Yossi brushes away Adi's question and goes on talking about the actors. Cecile here states that she is not going to answer Elihu's question elaborately by declaring "I've got something to add" and proceeding to analyze characters.

Acculturation: Cecile is consistent in promoting her rich-poor stereotype (cf. notes 61, 62). It is of great importance for a person's development to grow up in a proper family environment. Cecile's normative model of a family is made clear as the opposite to her non-normative description of Lucy's family. Lucy grew up "without a mother and a father" and, therefore, was not exposed to norms and, thus, cannot be normal, since nothing comes from nothing.

For Cecile, the outrageous aspect of Lucy's romance with Ray is *not* in the newly discovered incestuous connection—"true, today he is her uncle"—but in the fact that "once he was the servant."

Critical: This is a good place to say that the mimetic debate about the reality of the program does not interfere with the predominantly referential use of the program by the group. Itzchak here expresses doubt about the likelihood of the coexistence of two such brothers in the same family but stops short of indicating

the same family, and on the other hand, one sees people who cheat all the time, steal all the time, kill and do not get caught. These things are not real . . . It's not . . .

80. YOSSI: One could say Mafia.
    ITZCHAK: I don't think . . .
    YOSSI: One can say that it's a whole Mafia of J. R.'s. A whole Mafia built in . . .
    ITZCHAK: I don't believe it can be real . . . that it can happen in any country, in any place.

81. CECILE: I'll tell why. The father always thought that Bobby is *ne pas capable*, is not capable, and he wanted to show him that he *is*. The father always thought J. R., J. R., J. R. He always judged Bobby from the business point of view.

82. YOSSI: But who brought them up? Who is their boss? Who decides here for J. R.?
    CECILE: Nobody decides.
    YOSSI: Who has the biggest share of the money?
    CECILE: The father.
    YOSSI: The father. Why then doesn't he decide for them? Why? I'm asking you— why doesn't he decide for them?
    ADI: Explain to me why do they have so many problems in the family? What sort of relationships do they have?
    CECILE: They don't have any brotherly ties.
    ADI: Meaning?

an awareness of the dramatic function of this kind of opposition. (Moreover, his perception of the differences between the two is exaggerated, and probably derives from a desire to identify a good guy, even if one has to make him better in order to do so.)

Critical, interpretation: Yossi's attempt to elaborate on the idea that "it's a whole Mafia of J. R.'s"—which is unfortunately interrupted by Itzchak—recalls a theory put forward in an analysis of *Dallas* (Mander, 1983), according to which the show is a serialization of a new American mythology, expressed first in *The God- father*, which portrays America's social in- stitutions as corrupt. Success can no long- er be achieved by hard work but only by the power and the backing of the family. Individuals cannot be judged as immoral because the responsibility for immorality shifts to society as a whole.

Interpretation: In saying that the father's criterion for supporting one of his sons was the ability to do business, Cecile senses the conflict between family and business values underlying all *Dallas* epi- sodes.

The blatant domination of the busi- ness principle in J. R.'s case, which threatens to destroy the family al- together, is not remarked on explicitly in the discussion, but the surprising choice of the three women as central characters might be a clue to J. R.'s being conceived as a threat to the normal family order that hopefully will be overcome by the superi- or wisdom of the women.

Forum: It is evident that Yossi is bothered by the question of why the father of the family has lost his authority over his sons, because he keeps returning to it (see his comments at notes 18, 83). Yossi wants to know why there is not someone who reinstates order and prevents the chaos in which each family member fights the others, leading to total destruc- tion. It is worth noting that Yossi is from a generation of people whose immigrant fathers lost their standing in the family. Moroccan Jews who grew up in Israel were deprived of the orderly world of a

CECILE: It's not clean, the atmosphere is not clean.

CECILE: I think the father had not a little to do with it in the beginning, so J. R. follows in his footsteps.

traditional patriarchal family and were abandoned to a world of free-for-all competition, not subject to established norms or to fathers' final rulings.

Itzchak, Cecile, and Yossi have different approaches to the problems of anomie and the disintegration of the family. While Itzchak rejects or represses the issue by claiming that it is not the case in real life, Cecile and Yossi are not satisfied with this answer. Cecile looks for the reasons to explain the process, while Yossi gets very emotional in lamenting the loss of the father's authority. Although his statement does not formally qualify as saying, "it *is* real," the emphatic, recurring manner in which he brings this up indicates that it is relevant in his life.

3. MACHLUF: From everything I saw in *Dallas*, and I followed some sequences in *Dallas*, I came to the conclusion that a lot of money is no good for the soul. And a lot of women . . . Whoever has "a lot of property has a lot of worries," as it says in *Pirkei Avot*. A person should be in the middle, both in money, in honesty, in everything. We learn from the series that a lot of money—what does it cause? Even between brothers, one hates the other. (Zehava and Yossi agree)

YOSSI: But, Max . . . Why don't his father and his mother get into it? Aren't they the big shareholders?

MACHLUF: They get into it from time to time.

CECILE: The mother tries to fix as much as she can, but it's not enough.

MACHLUF: But sometimes they can't. J. R.'s influence is very great.

ADI: Does it say anything about the American society?

ITZCHAK: I don't believe.

Moral evaluation: In quoting the "Ethics of the Fathers" from the *Mishna*, Machluf makes an appeal for Jewish norms, defining himself again as Jewish in his reaction to *Dallas* (cf. note 13). The "middle" he refers to is the norm of the golden mean.

4. YOSSI: Yes, Americans usually live in this way. Especially where these people live in Texas, in Dallas. This is their life, and this is their way of life, and everything is natural. You can see worse things there. It's the life as it is—the adultery, the bribes, the cheating, all this goes on there in Texas.

ADI: I'll ask you two more questions—then you can go to bed. The first one is—if you were the director and were told that

Moral evaluation: This presentation of an alternative normative structure—which is "theirs" and not "ours"—might suggest that *Dallas* is a vehicle for projection. All sorts of impulses that contradict lower-middle-class and Jewish norms can be projected outside of the viewers' society and onto *Dallas*. This psychoanalytic approach to gratifications—where viewers exorcise their guilt feelings by attaching them to the alien program—suggests

there's no money and you had to do the
last episode, what would you do to tie it
together?

YOSSI: We would fix J. R. so that he is put in
prison. (everybody agrees) So that he di-
gests it properly.

ZEHAVA: So that others would also learn
not to steal and not to kill, (otherwise)
they will pay for it. Otherwise here in
Israel, everybody will steal and murder,
and nothing will be done . . . I would like
J. R. to go to prison. Sue Ellen is also not
so innocent with her adultery, and Pam I
would want to be pregnant and to have a
baby of her own, and everything will . . .

ITZCHAK: You talk as an Israeli. I want to
tell you one thing . . .

MACHLUF: I've never been to America.

that viewers can enjoy their own libidinal
drives, while rejecting them at the same
time. In both her early and recent work
on soap opera, Herzog (1941, 1986) develops this approach.

85. ITZCHAK: The word adultery in Israel is still
a little important, but not in Europe.
There it's something completely normal.
That means one cannot judge a woman
because she was unfaithful; the court
would not take it seriously. She did not
commit a crime against the law. You talk
as a Jew. In a religion like the Jewish
faith, a wife is not allowed to commit
adultery because she is not a wife then.
But in Europe . . .

ADI: Why do you look at *Dallas?* Why do
you watch *Dallas?*

CECILE: It's not better or worse than another series. There is no choice (in programs) here. Also all the beautiful things
which one sees—the ranch and the
richness. That's why one views; one en-
joys watching, but no more. One doesn't
expect anything of the story.

MACHLUF: The film is made out of scene
after scene, and each is a sequence in itself. In every episode, you see the beginning and the end. Within this they show
you the life of Americans.

CECILE: So you're answering the first question—that this is how you imagine America.

Interpretation: Itzchak's reaction to Zehava's criticism of Sue Ellen reflects his difficulty in finding himself in a process of
historical and social change where people
do not behave according to the norms he
has internalized and which he uses to assess the world. He seems to be disturbed
by people in his own society who do not
act according to norms—and yet are not
punished. Since he cannot deal with this,
he takes the violation out of his world
and describes it as if it were in the context
of another—namely, Europe, where it
can be reframed.

86. MACHLUF: . . . the richness in America, the
luxury. And it's foreign for me, and we
love to see it. The private pools, the elegant dress. I live in sixty-four square
meters, and there (they have) kilometers
and kilometers. And cows. And every-

Acculturation: The rhetoric is familiar, cf.
"And shall I not have mercy on Nineveh
the city which hath more than 120,000
people who cannot tell their right hand
and their left and many cattle?" (Jonah
4:11)

thing. I want to see it because I haven't got it.

7. CECILE: I, on one hand, don't like the children to watch . . .

Gratifications: Comparing Machluf's "I want to see it because I haven't got it" to Cecile's "I don't like the children to watch," sums up the conflict participants experience in viewing *Dallas*. Not to have it is frustrating, but to want or expect it threatens the group's precariously balanced normative system.

8. YOSSI: The Israelis love this series because it was the only one in color in the beginning. (general laughter) I don't like *Dallas*, but I prefer this over *Moked* or some *Mabat Sheni* or some concert.

Moked (Focus) and *Mabat Sheni (A Second Look)* are current affairs programs on Israel television which place heavy emphasis on politics and information (and, thus, on studio talk shows which are inexpensive to produce) and not much on entertainment (cf. Williams (1974) on the difference between public and commercial channels).

9. CECILE: I'll tell you. For me it brings a change. I don't know if that's true for everybody. I, for instance, here in Israel, am fed up with the war and with what there is in the news and what there is every day—this one was killed and that one was something else. This way one sees a more quiet life, in this sense. Then we also can think of different kinds of problems.

Gratifications: Cecile is expressing the classic, often-criticized function of television—that it is an escape from reality. Since this conversation was taped in February 1983 when the Israeli army was in Lebanon during what could be described as a war of attrition, the reality in this case is not humdrum and routine but anxiety-provoking and tense.

5
—— CULTURAL DIFFERENCES IN THE
—— RETELLING OF AN EPISODE

The focus discussions opened with a request to the group to retell the episode that had just aired. If understanding is a process of negotiation between the text and the viewer, each anchored in a different culture, then retellings ought to reveal the negotiation process at work. And if the model of negotiation is correct, attention should be paid to what viewers bring to the program, not only to how they use it or what they get from it. In this chapter, therefore, we will examine how viewers apply their own narrative forms and their own explanatory schemes to their retellings—that is, their editings—of the story.

Group discussions were based on four consecutive episodes of the second season of *Dallas*. Approximately one-quarter of the groups from each ethnic community saw each episode. The analysis of retellings reported here is based on the second of these episodes entitled "The Sweet Smell of Revenge," which followed "Little Boy Lost," the episode discussed by the Moroccan group in Chapter 4.

Of course, the discussion groups bring not only their values, their psychology, their traditions of story-telling, and their perceptions of what is legitimate to express in public, but also their different notions about the aims of the study (Tannen, 1982) and different attitudes toward the researchers. In the last analysis, the group's culture, its place in the society, and its presentation of self influence their retellings. We shall not even try to sort out these different influences; rather, we attribute them all—legitimately, we think—to culture. It will be more than enough if we can show that the ten (more or less) focus groups assembled from each ethnic community share commonalities among themselves and that they differ from the others. It is obvious from our method and from the case study of the previous chapter that within each group it is possible to identify a range of different attempts at retelling, since the request, "Please retell the story that you have just seen, making believe that you're

68

telling it to a friend or somebody at work" was addressed to the group as a whole, and any or all members might attempt to respond. Our analysis, therefore, is based on a judgment about the form and content of the retelling that predominates in each of the groups. This is not an arbitrary judgment, however, since our coding decision is based on the reactions of the group members themselves to the various starts at retelling. Typically, only one of these starts "takes." Of course, we could have avoided this problem by working with individuals. We did not do so by design, however, because the very idea of "interpretive community" seems well simulated in these discussion groups, where interpretation, indeed, arises out of the collective effort to make sense. In the case study of the Moroccan group, for example, Yossi's several starts at retelling and his more cynical view of the story are explicitly rejected in favor of Cecile's and Machluf's step-by-step, almost reverent, version of the events of the evening and the motives of the characters.

The Researchers' Retellings

One of us read through a subsample of discussions of the episode. Each of the ethnic groups was represented in the subsample. On the basis of this reading, and with Barthes's (1975b) classificatory scheme in mind, three types of retellings seemed to emerge, each with its own idiosyncratic form and content. We call them linear, segmented, and thematic, where the linear form focuses on a sequential story line, the segmented on the characters, and the thematic focuses on messages, virtually ignoring events and characters. These correspond, respectively, to Barthes's functional, indexical, and paradigmatic levels of the narrative.[1]

Using these three rough categories, a second reader then ranked the three narrative forms according to the degree of their applicability to each of the fifty-five discussions in our corpus.[2] This coding was done blind in that the reader did not know the ethnic identity of the group (though he could perhaps guess if he tried), and more important, he did not know the research hypotheses connecting these forms to retelling of ethnic differences.

At the same time, we went back to the script and videotape of the first episode in order to retell the story for ourselves using each of the three forms. We wanted to see how much the story lent itself to each form, or how much and what kind of editing needed to be done to transform the story-as-shown to the three types of story-as-retold.

The researchers' analysis revealed that there were two main plots which ran parallel to each other and were interwoven in the four acts and some thirty scenes of the episode. The two stories dealt with the two brothers, each of whom was trying to produce an heir before the other, one by means of regaining a child who may or may not be his own, the other by means of adoption. Both women were punished for their efforts to act independently—Sue Ellen for leaving with the child, and Pam for attempting suicide—and both ended up more dependent on their men than before (Swanson, 1982). In turn, both brothers moved from acting according to the rules to acting illegally—the one from the law court to kidnapping, the other from legal adoption to illegal purchase. Both brothers acted to save their wives from themselves—that is, to rescue them from individualism and emotion and to restore them to family and obligation—once more showing the similarities between the good and the bad brothers. This fits Gerbner's description (Gerbner et al., 1979) of the diminishing difference between heroes and villains in TV fiction. The good and the bad are not different in their aims nor in the methods they use. The criterion, rather, is the degree of efficiency in achieving their aims. Thus, the evil J. R. can qualify as a hero more than the chaste Bobby.

In addition, some five subsidiary plots were sprinkled over the thirty-odd scenes of one- or two-minute duration. These plots included crises in the marriages of other Ewing couples—that of Mitch and Lucy and that of Ray and Donna—and mounting tension in the competing dynasties—between Cliff and his mother and between Mitch and his sister Afton.

Each scene typically consisted of two people, usually a man and a woman, exchanging intimacies—scenes which are in themselves often more compelling than the plot line they serve, inasmuch as the plot is alternately predictable or reversible but always unending (Thorburn, 1982).

This analysis made clear that there was no simple linear story. A faithful linear retelling would entail the perception that there are two stories that proceed in parallel, one belonging to each brother. Moreover, this linearity does not proceed along classical Proppian lines, which require movement from a situation of lack to a happy resolution (Propp, 1968). Rather, the two parallel stories are at once Proppian and anti-Proppian, depending on who is defined as having the lack. Thus, if fulfillment of women is defined as the lack, this episode moves away from fulfillment—in the sense of independence and emotion—toward deprivation, passivity, and dependence. If, however, familism is defined as the lack, this episode moves classically from the threat of break-up to reunion. The former is an anti-Proppian story where the brother-villains undermine the women as separate beings with emotional needs and overcome would-be heroes like Dusty and his father Farlow, who could fulfill their lack (though Dusty might be more promising if he were not impotent). A dilemma of modernity is involved here; there is women's emotional fulfillment on the one hand, and fulfillment of her role as wife and mother on the other. Heroes of the one are villains of the other, and vice versa. Thus, just as there are two linear stories at work, there are also two potential narratives within each linear story. Sue Ellen is emotionally more fulfilled the more her status as wife and mother is threatened; that is, the process of overcoming one kind of lack makes the other more salient and demanding of attention. Hence, a single linear retelling along Proppian lines is by no means representative of what is going on, unless the retelling brings out the dialectical tension between the two linear stories.

Continuing the researchers' analysis, we move from the consideration of a linear model to a segmented model. Following Barthes, a segmented—or indexical—analysis focuses on the characters, their motivations, and their interrelations. Thus, a segmented retelling might identify a character and recount his or her interactions with different situations or with other characters in no particular sequence. The emphasis is not on recounting a narrative but on sampling from the narrative those segments which highlight the personal attributes and motives of one or more of the characters. In other words, rather than the character playing out a function in the story, the story serves to illuminate key aspects of the character or the dynamics of her or his personality. Retelling the story in this way, for example, one might focus on the causes and consequences of the personality of J. R., explaining what made him so ruthlessly competitive and how this central attribute of character expresses itself in various situations.

Even if this form of telling sounds as though it fits the disjunctive form of the soap-opera script a priori, one should take note of two complications involved in a segmental retelling of an episode of *Dallas*. One is, obviously, that the personalities of the characters must be appraised over more than a single episode. The other—almost a contradiction of the first—is that the storywriters themselves transform the personalities over time in order to stretch out the story in all its possible variations. J. R., of course, can easily switch from bad to good, but one may say that this is part of his essential personality. Not so for the others who are more fixed. Bobby, for example, is good until somebody decides that the story would be better served if Bobby, finally, became less good. Thus, a simple retelling along characterological lines is also not completely faithful to the story.

The third form of retelling is thematic or paradigmatic in the sense that one cuts through the story and the characters in search of a theme or message to sum up the moral. Thus, one can propose, paradigmatically—as certain critics and academics have done—that the story is about the failure of women's liberation (Swanson, 1982) or that it is about the superceding of the Horatio Alger myth of American mobility by the Godfather myth (Mander, 1983) of corrupt, self-contained networks that hold the key to success. Newcomb (1982), taking the Texas setting seriously, reads the story as a modern Western in which shoot-outs do not take place in the bar on Main Street but over the telephone and in the boardrooms of the *Dallas* skyscrapers.

Our own paradigmatic reading is that there is a conservative and primordial message, going beyond what Swanson has suggested. While Swanson emphasized the basic unity of the family as a criterion in terms of which actions are rewarded or punished by the storytellers, our reading does not see the primal unit as family but as generational continuity in the male line. It is true that there is family loyalty in *Dallas*, but while the father-son relationship is sacrosanct, the collateral, horizontal relationship among the brothers and between wives and husbands is open to backstabbing and competition. While this analysis is elaborated elsewhere (Liebes and Katz, 1988), the paradigm we are proposing is of a father-son relationship which imposes competition among the sons for the father's favor. This competition is expressed both in business and in the demand for male children which the sons transfer to their wives. The loyalty of the women is placed in further doubt in that they maintain their ties with rival dynasties. These connections are the only sources of power for *Dallas* women, as they can activate them as Trojan Horses inside the Ewing compound or in the rival families. Marriage, therefore, is more of a political transaction than a romantic affair, and its success depends on the adequacy of the exchange of security and status in return for the provision of children.

The Viewers' Retellings

We can now contemplate (1) whether there is a correlation between real viewers' cultural backgrounds and their choice of forms for retelling, (2) how closely real viewers' forms of retelling correspond to our own textual analysis, and (3) what one can infer from the choice of form about the chooser's perception of the relationship of the program to real life. We make the assumption that the other three episodes of *Dallas* seen by our discussion groups are constructed along the same principles as the episode that we analyzed in detail. This must be true almost by definition, i.e., the linear story must have at least the J. R. and Bobby strands; a segmented version must be distorted by the writers' intentional inconsistencies of character portrayal; and the thematic or paradigmatic must be constant across episodes. We, therefore, move directly to an analysis of the total retellings of the four episodes rather than treating each retelling separately.

The coding of the fifty-four discussions in terms of the three forms of retelling reveals a correlation between ethnicity and narrative form. Linear retellings ranked first among the Arab and Moroccan groups. On the other hand, the kibbutz and American groups more often offered segmented retellings. For their part, the Russians put aside the story—in both linear and segmented forms—in favor of a thematic retelling. Table 5.1 is a key to the types of retelling characteristic of each of the groupings.

Thus, there is confirmation that readings of *Dallas* fit the three forms of retelling and that each form characterizes one or another of the ethnic groups. This does not mean, however, that the three forms, as told, correspond to the

Table 5.1. The Three Forms of Retelling by Ethnic Groups

Level of Narrative*	Forms of Retelling	Predominant Focus	Typically Employed by
Functional	Linear	Action	Arabs, Moroccan Jews
Indexical	Segmented	Character	Americans, kibbutzniks
Paradigmatic	Thematic	Message	Russians

*Barthes (1975b)

researchers'—that is, our own—attempt to provide an optimal fit between the story and each of the forms. Instead of the complex fittings which seemed correct to us, the discussions tended toward much simpler retellings in which selective perception plays an important part. Whereas we perceived two linear strands moving in parallel throughout the story, the linear retellings of Arabs and Moroccans focused on only one of the two. They choose not Pam's suicide attempt but J. R.'s kidnapping operation, perhaps because the latter is a more obvious story of action. The story is retold in great detail, often invoking direct quotations for the highly melodramatic moments:

INTERVIEWER: First of all I would like to ask you to retell the story of the episode you have just seen as if you were telling it to a friend who has missed it today.

WILLIAM: J. R. is trying to get Sue Ellen and the child back home. So he goes off to try to get a monopoly of 25,000 barrels of oil—or maybe it is 50,000; I don't remember the exact number.

HYAM: Yes, it was 25,000.

GEORGE: To get his son back. He's trying to get a monopoly on the oil wells.

MARINETT: Yes, he told him . . .

GEORGE: So he takes (control of) all the oil in order to empty all of the refineries.

WILLIAM: It's in order to provoke (them) and organize an exchange. And he (Farlow?) said to him, "Others, bigger than you, weren't able to break me." After J. R.'s father was in South America on business. He (J. R.) talked to him and told him, "Come back."

HYAM: Jock phoned J. R. and said, "Your wife and the child will be . . ."

WILLIAM: J. R. called his father and said to him, "When you come home next week, Sue Ellen and the child will be back home." (Arab group 46)[3]

Just as the Arabs and Moroccans select among the possible linear retellings, so the American and kibbutz groups select among the characters for their segmented retellings. It is no wonder that the most popular choice for this kind of characterological reporting is Pam, whose story is presented as possessing deep psychological roots. Indeed, these segmented retellers are often aware that their focus on a character abstracted from the larger context of the story is the result of his or her psychological interest or emotional effect.

SANDY: The main thing I would tell them would be about . . . (laughter) I'm trying to think of a character in the picture, Victoria Principal.

GREG: Pam.

OTHERS: Pam.

SANDY: That she was, you know, upset about a lot of things inside herself and that she wanted to kill herself and that her husband was trying to talk her into committing herself to the hospital to help her. That is the main thing that got to me in this episode because emotionally that's what got to me, that she would want to kill herself. And that is the strongest point in this episode. (American group 3)

Within the segmented readings, another retelling does not speak of a particular character but of the interaction between two characters who are often
connected in some primordial way. It may be the relationship between J. R.
and Sue Ellen, Bobby and Pam, Miss Ellie and J. R., and so on. For example, in
retelling the story, a kibbutz group proceeded as follows:

> HILLEL: There was Lucy and her husband with their problems, and there
> was Bobby and Pam and their crisis, and J. R. and his son.
> ORLY: There was a crisis in the marriage of Bobby and Pam. Until now they
> were the ideal couple, and suddenly, they have these problems.
> IGAL: Sue Ellen is beginning to get discouraged by her what's-his-name, and
> with Pam and Bobby it simply exploded. They were always the ideal
> couple. They knew between them that it wasn't so. But at least exter-
> nally . . . But that's it. It just exploded. You can't bluff the whole way.
> (kibbutz group 85)

But neither of these forms coincides fully with the sorts of problems that
may be said to constitute a fully segmented reading. In particular, the viewers'
segmented retelling ignores nuances and changes that writers ascribe to the
characters, apparently in order to make identification easier. This is not a very
serious misreading, of course. More serious, perhaps, is the extreme selectivity
in focusing on one or two evocative characters at the expense of all the others
who make up the story. The fuller versions of the segmented retellings—those
which account for most of the characters—probably represent the best fit between the story as presented and the story as retold. Following is an example
of a relatively full retelling in the segmented form.

> DON: You have Pam trying to commit suicide because of her mother. You
> had J. R. being his typical self scheming . . .
> BEVERLY: Cliff Barnes, his sister, his stepsister, whatever, I think was a little
> upset that the mother gave him the business or gave him the running of
> the business.
> DON: Then you have the little gal and her husband split. What's her name!
> Oh, Charlene Tilten and her husband split up—Lucy, yeah, and him
> being offered a job that he really doesn't want.
> LINDA: Then Bobby got a picture of what's-her-name's baby, and he's got
> hope again.
> DON: Kristen's baby. Kristen.
> BEVERLY: Which is really his brother's.
> DON: The gentleman called on the phone and said he wanted money for
> more information regarding the baby. (American group 7)

There appears to be a correlation not only between ethnicity and forms of
retelling, but also between gender and retelling; indeed, it is possible that the
ethnic differences themselves may be explained in terms of the differential
participation of men and women in the linear retellings on the one hand, and

in the segmented retellings on the other. The Arab women are very reticent to enter the conversation; they appear to enter it when they have something "expert" to add. It is certainly true that the opening of the discussion is dominated by men. By contrast, the American and the kibbutz groups—who specialize in segmented retellings—are egalitarian; it may be that kibbutz women speak even more than the men, although this has not been studied formally. Recall in this connection the possibility —suggested by Modleski (1984) and Allen (1985)—that the soap opera genre is "feminine" in the sense that it deals less in action or in one-time solutions than in words, feelings, and ad hoc management of the continuing flow of crises. If this is so, it follows that the greater number of segmented retellings, which emphasize the psychology of characters and their embroilments, in these two groupings may be attributed to the greater participation of women, whereas more linear retellings—aiming at final solutions—may reflect the greater "manliness" of the two more traditional cultures examined.

Unlike the ad hoc character of segmented retellings, the linear and, even more, the paradigmatic impose an organizing principle on the story as a whole putting the pieces together in a kind of cognitive map. In the paradigmatic retellings, a general principle is applied deductively to construct a story. Here, for example, is the beginning of a discussion in a Russian group:

MISHA: The program reflects the reality in America.
INTERVIEWER: Let's get back to the last episode. What is it about?
SIMA: The financial problem plays an important role; J. R. wants to revenge himself using his economic background. Through the oil wells. In this particular episode, the financial problem plays an important role.
INTERVIEWER: That's what?
ROSA: That the oil is the main theme.
INTERVIEWER: Can you go back to the story?
ROSA: The oil is the main problem in the program. (Russian group 63)

It can be seen in this exchange how the three attempts of the interviewer to get beyond the thematic level and into the details of the story were to no avail. This refusal to get into details reflects not only a reluctance on the part of the Russians to show involvement in a television program which is defined as trivial, but also a statement of concern over the threat of a program like *Dallas* being capitalist propaganda. Repeatedly in the Russian groups, the program is retold paradigmatically in terms of a message. Moreover, the message is not considered innocent, but one which serves the hegemonic interests of the producers or of American society. The Russians are the only ones who responded in this way to the interviewer's request to retell the episode. The Russians' inclination to get to the message of the program will also be seen in an analysis of statements which deal explicitly with the message or moral of the program, i.e., "What the program/the producers/the writers want to tell us is . . ." Consider the following examples from three different Russian groups:

ALONA: I started to ask myself what is the secret of the popularity of the series. Why does it attract the middle class to such an extent? It is comforting for them to know that the millionaires are more miserable than themselves. Well, a poor millionaire is beautiful. Deep down, everyone would very much want a millionaire to be miserable, and on the other hand, they themselves would like to be millionaires. In the program they see millionaires as if they really were that way. (Russian group 62)

HANNA: The program praises the American way of life. It shows the America of the rich, and at the same time, it shows the American middle-class viewer that our country is beautiful and rich. We have everything, and those rich people, of course, have their problems. (Russian group 67)

MISHA: The program is propaganda for the American way of life. They show American characters. The program deals with the dilemma of life in America. It is actually advertising—or, more accurately, propaganda— for the American way of life. They show the average person in an interesting way the ideal he should be striving towards. (Russian group 63)

Thus, it may be said that the Russians are not interested in the paradigm per se but in the relationship between the message, the motives of the encoders, and themselves as audience. The message far overshadows the details of the narrative in importance because the program is perceived as a social and political strategy with an ulterior and destructive aim. Like the critical theorists, the Russians who read the story paradigmatically focus on the macro level, and their analysis, therefore, is on a different level than the analysis of any one episode. It is at a political level; their perceived message, in fact, corresponds to one of the two conflicting messages that Thomas and Callahan (1982) attribute to television's high-class family drama: the message of solace for those who are not invited to move to the top.

Characteristics of the Forms of Retelling

Each of the three patterns of retelling implies an orientation to time and different degrees of openness and inevitability. Whereas linear and thematic retellings are deterministic and closed, the segmented retellings are more open. Linear retellings are closed because they relate to a story that has mostly happened in the past, even if it is not altogether concluded, and thematic retellings are closed because they treat the continuing story as timeless repetitions of the same narrative principle. Thus, the Arabs and Moroccans, in their linear retellings, tended to tell an almost completed sequence which is presented as inevitable: J. R. has lost his baby, but he is getting him back, and the family is going to be reunited in the ancestral estate; or (recounting an earlier episode), Sue Ellen used to be unhappy, but now she has finally found a normal home for her baby and a romantic lover for herself (Moroccan group 20).

By perceiving these episodes as stories with happy endings, linear tellers, ironically, blind themselves to the essence of the serial, which is, it must go on!

Table 5.2. Characteristics of the Three Forms of Retelling

ms of elling	Frame	Openness of Text	Time Orientation	Reader Reception	Epistemological Perspective	Reference to Program	Subjective Criteria Guiding Retelling
ear	Referential	Closed/predictable	Retrospective	Hegemonic	Sociology	Family role	No explicit mention of criteria
mented	Ludic	Open/unpredictable	Prospective	Negotiated	Psychology	Names of characters/actors	Emotional arousal
matic	Critical	Closed/predictable	Constant	Oppositional	Ideology	Names of producers/titles of episodes	Cognitive/persuasive effect on self and others

Instead, they constantly seek to impose a Proppian scheme, which cannot work. Their characters are forced, thereby, into a more stereotypical mold than the producers require to keep the program going—which they do by introducing variations of personalities. For example, Sue Ellen was neither the hopeless victim that the tellers report nor will she be the happy mother and lover they foresee for her future. The paradigmatic retellings treat the series on the whole as a constant and monolithic message, regarding any individual episode as a manifestation of the ruling principle. Any variation has to be dictated by this principle.

Put differently, the linear and paradigmatic forms employ inductive and deductive reasoning to attribute inevitability—or closedness—to the story. Thus, the linear stories proceed inductively not from a principle but from the presumed reality of the characters, and thus, the closedness of linear retelling results from it being unthinkable that the story can turn in a different direction—just because the producers have got to continue. The paradigmatic story is closed because it is thought to derive from an ideological formula which is applied by the producers to the various subplots and episodes. The linear retellings may be said to be anchored in a referential mode, while the paradigmatic retellings are rooted in a more critical mode.

It is an obvious step to the conclusion that the linear retelling—anchored, as it is, in the referential—correlates with a hegemonic reading in which the reality of the story is unquestioned and its message presumably unchallenged. The association of the linear and the referential—invoking the reality principle—brings normative criteria in its train, and the imposition of such criteria contributes, for example, to the perception of Sue Ellen as engaged in a desperate effort of self-redemption, providing justification for what would otherwise be an unacceptable violation of the marital norm. Traditional Arab society has put women to death for less. In other words, normative acceptability influences retellings (and, indeed, legitimates viewing itself). The paradigmatic retelling, on the other hand, is more likely to accompany an oppositional reading (Morley, 1980), whereby critical awareness of an overall message surely sounds an alarm that the message may be manipulative.

Narrative closedness of both types—the linear and the paradigmatic—lead to stereotyping. The linear stereotyping is of the characters: they are made to seem more consistent. The paradigmatic stereotyping is of the producers, as we have said: they are reified into single-minded propagandists.

Unlike the linear and paradigmatic forms, the segmented retellings are more open or future-oriented. Armed with the knowledge of the characters and their motivations, the segmented retellings treat the story prospectively, using what has already happened to speculate on possible continuations. Thus, rather than looking for deterministic principles in the plot, in either the lives of the characters or the ideology of the producers, the Americans and kibbutzniks (who specialize in segmented retellings) search creatively for new complications which might emerge from the temporary narrative solution. Here are two such speculations from an American group:

> DEANNA: Cliff met his sister for the first time.
> JILL: This sounds like it's gonna be another lead-in for another one of J. R.'s romances. (laughter)
> DONNA: Pam's sister?
> DEANNA: Oh, well, one he hasn't tried yet . . .
> JILL: Just from the program and watching J. R. all the time—if it's got a skirt on—he'll get it or try.
>
> * * *
>
> DEANNA: Now it seems she (Katherine) has kind of got her eye on Bobby—and in this one episode—it had just a little bit of a hint that she might have her way.
> JILL: That'll snap Pam out of her depression fast enough.
> DEANNA: Or put her into a worse one. (American group 7)

It is easy to see how this kind of ludic inventiveness can spill over from discussion of the imminent machinations of the characters to taking the producer's perspective in having to decide what to do next. This explains why the segmented retellings also give attention to the real-life personalities of the actors, their traffic accidents and heart attacks, and the state of their negotiations with the producers.

One can also think of the three forms of retelling in terms of the epistemological perspectives with which they are associated. The linear retellings explain the story in sociological terms; the segmented retellings tend to psychological or psychoanalytic explanation; and the paradigmatic patterns are mostly ideological. These epistemological perspectives help to explain why the different forms of retelling focus on different subplots or characters and contain particular forms of labeling the characters. The linear stories are told from the perspective of kinship where the characters are motivated by social and normative considerations having to do with the hierarchical order within the family and the continuity of the dynasty. This explains the preference for the subplot dealing with J. R. and his efforts to reunite his family rather than for the subplot in the same episode dealing with Pam's troubled psyche. It also makes clear why J. R.'s plot to retrieve his child and wife is explained in terms of his commitment to his father and, in particular, why the relatively short and functionally unimportant telephone conversation with his (already dead) father is told in such great detail (see retelling on p. 73); this conversation is retold in direct quotations and is accorded high dramatic value by the Arabic group.

The invocation of the sociological perspective also appears to explain the relatively frequent use of family roles for labeling characters in linear retellings. Referring to J. R. as "the older son" and to Bobby as "the younger" may be the result of lesser familiarity with the characters or their foreign names, but it is equally likely that it is due to attaching more importance to family roles than to names. In the labeling of characters in the following example, the story would be as applicable to Esau and Jacob or other sibling rivalries as to J. R. and Bobby:

> AYAD: It's a rich family, with a large inheritance. They have wealth and oil and they have two sons. The older son is a cheat. He wanted to control by force all of the money of his father and mother. The younger wanted to share the wealth, but the older one plotted and schemed to get the money, and the two brothers fought with each other. (Arab group 49)

The segmented, character-oriented retellings focus on emotional problems in order to explain what happens on the screen. The psychological motivations and conflicts can belong either to the characters in the program or to the actors behind the scenes. Thus, the actions and frustrations of the various Ewings are often described as generated by unsolved internal conflicts, sometimes originating in childhood traumas, sometimes the result of present interpersonal crises. Pam's problems are explained as a result of being abandoned by her mother as a baby or, alternatively, as a result of the collapse of her marriage; J. R. has to prove his worth to his parents, who are thought to have favored his two brothers during their childhood, etc. These same developments are also explained by reference to show business. Pam's suicide attempt is the result of her wanting out of the show. Goffman's (1974) term "keyings" is helpful here: Segmented retellings may be keyed either to the narrative of the program or the narrative of show business.

Since psychological retellings relate to personalities, the characters are alluded to by their on- or off-screen names. Naturally, Americans, who are exposed to extensive gossip about the show's stars, tend to be more familiar with the actual names than Israeli viewers. Consider Don who begins:

> DON: Then you have the little gal and her husband split. What's her name? Oh, Charlene Tilten and her husband split up—Lucy, yeah, and him being offered a job that he doesn't really want. (American group 7)

Like the Americans, the Russians seem to obtain a sense of control by looking behind the scenes.[4] But while the Americans are concerned with an understanding of the manipulation of the characters by the producers, the Russians see the producers being manipulated by big business. In the Russian way of retelling, or rather of not telling, the episode has an ideological corre-late. The Russians sense an overall conspiracy intended to pacify and comfort the viewer. This concern directs their attention not to kinship roles, not to characters' names, not even to names of actors, but to the names of producers and writers as manipulators of the characters and to the titles of episodes as clues to the manipulative process. That the Russians memorize lists of credits was one of the real surprises of the study.

Conclusions

In order to analyze how popular American family drama is perceived in other cultures, we asked viewers, organized in intimate focus groups, to retell an episode of *Dallas*. The viewer retellings are fit to the three levels of narrative structure derived from Barthes's functions, actions (and indexes), and para-digms, which take forms that we call linear, segmented, and thematic, respec-tively. These types of retelling invoke sociological, psychological, and ideologi-cal perspectives.

The two more traditional groups—Arabs and Moroccan Jews—prefer lin-earity. They retell the story in a modified Proppian form. They select the action-oriented subplot for attention, defining the hero's goals and his adven-tures in trying to achieve them. They tell the story in closed form as if it were an inevitable progression, and the characters they describe are rigidly stereo-typed; indeed, they are often referred to by role—family role, of course—rather than by name. Their perspective is sociological, that is, the story is of the recognized reality of extended family, in an ancestral house (Lévi-Strauss, 1983), holding itself together in the face of contests of power both within and without. The cultural proximity of these groups to the *Dallas* story may seem surprising in view of the ostensible modernity of *Dallas*. But there is consider-able support for the argument that *Dallas* is, in fact, an old-fashioned family saga (Herzog-Massing, 1986; Swanson, 1982), less like the stripped-down, mobile nuclear family of the West and more like the premodern clan in which economic, political, and religious functions still inhere and the division of labor by age and sex is still prescribed.

A study of the reception of *Dallas* in Algeria (Stolz, 1983) gives strong support to this argument. The concern of Arabs and Moroccan Jews with power and relative position in family and society may be related to their social position in Israel, Arabs as a politically suspect minority, Moroccan Jews as an ethnic minority with experience of status deprivation.

The Russians speak of the episode in terms of themes or messages. They ignore the story in favor of exposing the overall principles which they perceive as repeated relentlessly, and which, in their opinion, have a manipulative intent. Like the Arabs and Moroccans, their retellings are closed and deterministic, but the determining force is ideological rather than referential. Unlike the Arabs and Moroccans, they perceive the story as being a false picture of reality. They are also aware that their illustrations from the story are chosen, self-consciously, to highlight the potential persuasive power of the program. Their interest is in the story as a product of hegemonic control.

This suspiciousness on the part of the Russians seems over-determined; it is almost too easy to explain. Dmitri Segal suggests that the Russians, especially Russian Jews, learn early to scan their environment for signs of where true power is hidden; they learn to read between the lines (Inkeles, 1950). Their literary training is another determining factor; unlike the Arabs or the Moroccans, Russians are steeped in a tradition of literary criticism which they apply relentlessly and with flaunted superiority to the texts and images they encounter in their new environment. What is more, these are refugees who are well trained in applying ideological criticism to other people's ideologies as well as to their own. They are also continually alert to sources of potential manipulation.

While the Russians invoke ideological theory, Americans and kibbutzniks tell the story psychoanalytically. They are not concerned with the linearity of the narrative but with analyzing the problems of characters intrapersonally and interpersonally. Their retellings are open, future-oriented, and take into account the never-ending quality of the soap-opera genre. One version of these psychological retellings relates to the business constraints and interpersonal problems on the level of actors and producers. In these keyings, the drama behind the scenes becomes the real story of *Dallas*. Segmented retellings label the characters in terms of their on-screen or off-screen personae. Their illustrations from the story are chosen in terms of emotional effect rather than the cognitive effects of the thematic retellings. These comparatively secure, second-generation Israeli and American viewers are fascinated by psychology and group dynamics, and can afford the luxury of interest in the individual, i.e., in themselves. They have no illusions about the reality of the story; they allow themselves to dive into the psyches of the characters, oblivious to those aspects of the ideology, the morality, and the aesthetics of the program that occupy others. Their definition of both the viewing and the retelling as liminal (Turner, 1985) permits a playful subjunctivity in their negotiations with the program, with fellow viewers, and with the discussion leaders.

6
MUTUAL AID IN
THE DECODING OF *DALLAS*

We believe that the decoding of popular culture is more than a Bakhtian dialogue between multiple voices within a lone reader addressing a text; it is a forum that goes on within communities from which meaning is forged and legitimated. In Chapter 4, therefore, we examined the conversation of one focus group and noted in minute detail the variety of types of decoding and group dynamics that took place both during the viewing and after. In Chapter 5, we climbed to the macro level to make comparisons among the discussion style of the several ethnic groups.

Both Chapters 4 and 5 illustrate the processes of collective meaning-making which is the basic concern of our study. Focus groups serve well precisely because they permit tentative interpretations to be floated by someone and shot down by someone else, because they permit bullies to try to impose themselves on the others, because expert opinion is sought out for guidance, because interpretations are moulded and twisted to fit the underground loves and hates that permeate interpersonal relations. This is what happens in life. That is why we favor the ostensibly "unscientific" and certainly awkward method of focus-group discussions over the neat individual interview or questionnaire, where only one's own multiple selves are available to keep one company and to help decide which category to tick off. Collective reading (and, we might add, collective writing) is a more authentic method, if only because one can observe the processes of negotiation through which individual readings are selectively accepted and rejected and refashioned as candidates for incorporation into the culture.

This chapter deals with the steps through which television programs achieve legitimacy within the culture of the group. The first step is the operation of mutual aid in legitimating understandings, interpretations, and evaluations (moral and aesthetic) of what the program means, indeed in giving approval to the very fact of viewing and discussing the program. A second step draws on these agreed meanings to further other conversations. We will bring together examples of these two types of interaction between group and text and subclassify them. We are still operating at the qualitative level of Chapter 4 in which we attempted to illustrate and code different types of exchange among group members. We referred there to a first type of collective meaning-making as mutual aid. Here we add conversational resource as a second type. Each of these types has the possibility of serving as a launching pad for testing proposals for para-social and social change.

Mutual Aid

Mutual Aid in Legitimation

The most elementary form of mutual aid gives social legitimation to overcome the variety of hesitations that viewers have in attending to the program and treating it seriously. Without mutual support of this kind, many groups would have trouble in acknowledging their own interest in the program, in allowing themselves to assume that others watch it, in accepting its priority over alternative forms of spending time, and in considering it a fit subject for respectable conversation.

For example, the kibbutzim rescheduled the traditional Sunday-evening meeting time in deference to the kibbutzniks' avid interest in the serial. The Russians perceive *Dallas* as required reading for participation in the polity. Family and friends invite each other to view together and help each other to view the program oppositionally (Hall, 1985), whether as moral, aesthetic, or ideological critics,[1] thus, like researchers in mass communications, to have the cake and eat it too.

Some groups find positive value in the program, even when they know that it is morally rotten. The Moroccan group 20, for example, finds the program morally outrageous but consoles itself in the escapist function (helps us forget Lebanon, poor housing, etc.), the safely distant glamour of the program, as well as the moral opposition which it mobilizes.

Mutual Aid in Orientation

Social interaction helps define what happens on the screen by filling in gaps in the plot or by identifying characters in the thick foliage of the Ewing family tree. Such mutual aid in orientation is expressed in dialogue while viewing a program and may be especially salient in serials which require knowledge and understanding of what has come before, of the parallel plots, and of the complex array of characters who wander in and out of the story. Since most of the action is in the words, help is often needed. The group thus becomes a recourse for viewers who happen to be out of the story for one reason or another or who have trouble following the story, often because of the speed or difficulty of the subtitles. The husband of Massudi in the Moroccan group (see

Chapter 4, note 3) helps her over the language hurdles by interpolation during the viewing and by cram courses later at night. The group also assists in translating alien concepts into language familiar to members of the group. In the Moroccan group, for example, Machluf converts the dollar value of the alimony that the judge awarded to Sue Ellen into shekels.

Another orienting function of the group is to prepare its members for up-coming surprises and shocks, such as Cecile's expression of shock and outrage in anticipation of the shame that will befall Dusty—and to themselves as reluctant witnesses—when the secret of his accident-related impotence is revealed in court. "He is not a man anymore," says Cecile, attempting to forewarn the others.

In another Moroccan group, meeting in their cooperative settlement at the outskirts of Jerusalem, Ziviah, middle-aged and illiterate in Hebrew (certainly in English), is puzzled over the disappearance of Jock Ewing, whose absence is unexplained. Other group members included her husband Joseph, her sister Miriam, her sister's husband Salah, and her friend, Zari.

> ZIVIAH: Where's their father? Why don't we ever see him?
> MIRIAM: I think the father's dead.
> ZIVIAH: That's what they say.
> ZARI: He died a few weeks ago, and it hardly matters.
> ZIVIAH: (indicating the screen) That's Bobby's wife; she's dying to have a child.
> MIRIAM: No, she's in a mental hospital now.
> ZIVIAH: Oh, yes, yes; that's right.
> YOSEF: Really.
> ZIVIAH: Yes, yes.
> SALAH: She's in a hospital now?
> MIRIAM: A mental hospital. (Moroccan group 32)

Note that Ziviah does not ask her questions interrogatively but tries a guess or hypothesis about what she thinks is going on and awaits affirmations or corrections.

Even the offer of orientation, however, cannot be free of the implicit censorship of group norms. In the following exchange, an Arab group finds it culturally compatible to *assume* that Sue Ellen (having run away with the baby from her husband, J. R.) has returned to her father's home rather than to the home of her former lover, Dusty, and *his* father. Thus, mutual aid in orientation edits or "koshers" information to a form that is acceptable to fellow group members.

> GEORGE: He is trying to monopolize all the oil in order to destroy Sue Ellen's father . . . He wants to use it to pressure . . .
> WILLIAM: Sue Ellen's father.
> INTERVIEWER: Sue Ellen's father; is that right?
> WILLIAM: Wasn't that Sue Ellen's father that was with him?

HYAM: Yes, Sue Ellen's father; that's him.
INTERVIEWER: Where was Sue Ellen at the time?
HYAM: She is staying at her father's. (Arab group 46)

The idea that Sue Ellen might be at her lover's ranch is too much for this group; traditional Arab society metes out severe punishment for lesser crimes. A sympathetic character like Sue Ellen is better off returning to her father's home. Mutual aid among viewers comes to the rescue; clearly, we are not only dealing with the technical assistance of orientation but also with a well-clothed Emperor.

Mutual Aid in Interpretation

An even more frequent form of mutual aid is exigetical; it offers help to fellow group members who need an explanation or who find interest in why something has happened or why a character has behaved in a certain way. Typically, this type of aid involves the application of members' understandings of life to the goings-on in the story. Even when the explanation is drawn from within the story itself, it is filtered through the viewers' understandings and experiences of life.

In a Russian group, for example, a discussion of the reasons why Sue Ellen won custody of the baby—is it "justice" or "the document?"—reflects two competing conceptions of the legal system. According to one, social institutions are arbitrary, formalist, and legalistic, and according to the other, they are founded on a concept of inherent justice.

LIUBA: Justice has a lot to do with it.
MISHA: What justice? It was the medical certificate (attesting to the impotence of the man with whom Sue Ellen is living) that helped, not justice.
MILE: No, it's justice, not the medical certificate, that helped her to win.
SOFIA: It was proven that Sue Ellen left him not to go to another man but to a sick man whom she was going to help at a difficult moment, and that was the decisive factor in the court's decision.
MISHA: Nothing would have helped without the certificate.
MILE: Misha, he's not potent, this new husband of hers.
LIUBA: She didn't go to a lover, but to . . .
MILE: Remember, she can't have any more children. So it's justice.
MISHA: What justice? It's the medical certificate.
MILE: You're wrong.
ALL: You're wrong. It's about justice. (Russian group 65)

Often, such debates on matters of interpretation spill over into discussion of the principles underlying the debate, that is, into discussion of the personal and communal experience from which the interpretation is drawn. This process is what we call referential. When such referential matters trigger interaction—usually about matters of common concern, such as norms governing marital relations, corruption, tradition, the legal process, etc.—we use the term "forum," or "referential forum" (see Chapter 4).

Russian group 65 provides another example that is of interest. In the course of retelling the episode, Misha proposes that the high point, both moral and dramatic, is Pam's suicide attempt. Mile joins in by agreeing that Pam's illness is the central theme of the episode. This triggers an argument between Mile and Sophia about the reasons for Pam's lengthy illness:

> SOPHIA: The illness is a result of the couple's having no children; this is the main reason for the illness.
> MILE: I don't think the reason is not having children. She's simply a sick woman.
> SOPHIA: To me it seems that she's sick because of these reasons. Maybe Bobby thinks that if they have a child—even an adopted child—it will help Pam out of her problem.
> MILE: In spite of this, I stand on my opinion. She's simply a sick woman, but the problem about children made her illness even worse.
> YITSCHAK: There's a professional speaking.
> SOPHIA: I remember a conversation with a professor (the psychiatrist). When he (Bobby) asked the professor whether the child will help to cure her, the professor said she wasn't sure that a child would help. That means that not having children is not the real reason. (Russian group 65)

A further example of competing interpretations comes from a kibbutz group, two of whose members differ over the reasons for Sue Ellen's victory in the trial:

> AMALIA: If she weren't a rich woman, she would not have managed to keep the child.
> SARAH A.: This time it's not money that counts.
> AMALIA: Yes (it is). It's because she had the resources to hire a good lawyer . . .
> SARAH A.: Well, it is not true. One borrows money for such . . .
> AMALIA: She would not have succeeded.
> SARAH A.: It's not true. One borrows money for getting a good lawyer when one wants to. On the whole, every person, when he really wants something, gives his soul for it. First of all, this is everything that he wants; and, second, this is his pride. Look at how couples who are about to be divorced behave . . .
> AHARONCHIK: I never tried it; I wouldn't know. (kibbutz group 82)

A Russian group cooperates in interpreting J. R.'s efforts to please his father. There is little disagreement but a cumulative enrichment of the various members' perceptions:

> SIMA: I'm surprised by his (J. R.'s) attitude to his father. He must be feeling that his father is superior to him financially, as a businessman. What we

see in the course of the program is that he is constantly telling his father, "Father, don't worry, the boy will come home, don't worry, everything will be all right," as if he were giving a report to his father, as if he were bowing down to him.

MARIK: In my opinion, he has inferiority feelings toward his father . . .

MISHA: He's a very complex person . . . He has many contrasts. One can't say that such a person is very positive, although he does have certain positive qualities. I can't say that business for such a person, and his ambitions for achieving his goals, are negative. Without such qualities he couldn't work and make money, and making money is his profession.

MARIK: Agree.

SIMA: For him, everything is divided according to priorities, according to their importance. In business, let's say everything has to be organized. In a family, there has to be an heir. Everything as it should be.

INTERVIEWER: Do you mean without emotion?

SIMA: I wouldn't say without emotion. Maybe yes. It seems to me that he wants his son not because he loves him; he's not so devoted to him. He simply knows that's the way it should be. He knows that he's his father's heir. I believe that he's living according to his father's code. (Russian group 63)

These examples make clear that mutual aid in interpretation is not always based on need and does not always involve hierarchical relations between a knower and a non-knower. Rather more typical is an egalitarian argument between exponents of competing explanations, each bolstering his or her case with come combination of data from the program and data from life.

Sometimes, the very same data can be marshalled to support competing positions. In Moroccan group 20 (see Chapter 4) Machluf explains that the baby cannot be J. R.'s by citing Sue Ellen's own admission that he is not. Cecile, however, refuses this proof, arguing that Sue Ellen herself has no way of knowing.

Mutual Aid in Evaluation (Moral, Aesthetic, Ideological)

Some groups, or certain members in a group, may think well of the outcome of an issue raised in the program, while others disagree. Thus, groups sit in judgment of the values of the characters through the marshaling of their own values to evaluate or censure. For example, Moroccan group 20 debated whether it was right that Sue Ellen was given custody of her baby. Recall that the women defined parents' rights in terms of the amount of effort and suffering that goes into bearing and caring for the child, while the men upheld J. R.'s rights as "author of the seed" and heir of the dynasty.

Such arguments are not limited to taking sides over issues within the program. A theme in the program as a whole is sometimes interpreted or evaluated against an opposite position which is embedded in the culture of the viewer group. A kibbutz group provides such an example of overall opposition:

SARAH A.: When I see them, I only pity them.
AMALIA: I live better than they do.
SARAH A.: And I tell myself how terrible it would be if I were one of them.
AMALIA: With all that they have money, my life-style is higher than theirs.
   (kibbutz group 82)

The Arab groups are equally harsh but more specific in their condemnation of the American materialism reflected in *Dallas:*

HYAM: This is America of the aim justifying the means.
ISA: It's bourgeois, and the result is disintegration, social crumbling. When materialism dominates, society falls apart, and the material begins to be everything. (Arab group 46)

HALIL: One can deduce from the serial that there is a disintegration of family ties in American society, in capitalist society, and in all Western society. There's no respect, no patience, none of the things which are considered good and which, to our mind, are the basic principles.
SHARIFA: (*Dallas*) portrays the family falling apart. (Arab group 47)

Not all moral criticism is directed at the pros and cons of wealth. Some of it is closer to a cultural superiority. In Russian eyes, particularly, Americans are boorish, without books or decent media:

LARA: The program shows that Americans have no culture. One never shows them reading a book or going through a newspaper.
ZVI: And they don't listen to the radio.
SIMEON: They (the Americans) astonish us with their superficiality. Whenever I look at this serial and see their primitive life, I conclude, each time, "that's what it's like in America." (Russian group 64)

But rejection is by no means the universal reaction. Many of the groups are not so quick to reject the material values in *Dallas*. Indeed, even the groups that do reject them at one point in the discussion may reconsider at some other point. More typical, perhaps, is the following exchange from a group of North African immigrants in a semirural cooperative settlement:

MIRIAM: Money will get you anything. That's why people view it. People sit at home and want to see how it looks.
SALAH: These are special people. Somehow they get it all, and we don't.
ZIVIAH: Right.
YOSEF: Everybody wants to be rich. Whatever he has, he wants more.
ZARI: Who doesn't want to be rich? The whole world does.
MIRIAM: Wealth also makes an easy life.
ZIVIAH: It's the best thing. (Moroccan group 32)

Note how easily a consensus is built around these truisms. One member of the group makes an assertion about the desirability or undesirability of some elementary value, and if it strikes a responsive chord, the other members join in, one by one, to reinforce the commitment. These are classic examples of finding reinforcement for prior values in the mass media.

There are at least two other kinds of evaluation, and these, also, are typically embedded in mutual aid. One is further elaboration of moral evaluation which, however, does not confront the morals of the characters but the morals of the producers as businessmen and as representatives of the ruling elite. The focus is on deception or manipulation. What we call moral evaluation implies acceptance of the Ewings as representatives of the dynastic rich, rejection of the desirability of their life, and an awareness that their unhappiness is the result. This is different from those who perceive an unreality in the program— an intentional distortion of reality that misrepresents in order to sway the viewers ideologically. The Russians are specialists in this. They assert, repeatedly, that the program represents the rich as unhappy because that is what the producers want us to believe! This variant of moral evaluation might be called ideological evaluation. It is a rejection of the values of the program by means of what Gouldner (1976) calls a socialist reading, which refers to the decoding practices of readers who learn to read between the lines in order to discern the true message.[2]

A third form of evaluation is aesthetic evaluation. It appraises the program not for the values of its characters or for the ideological manipulation of its viewers but for its artistic quality. Yossi's complaint (Moroccan group 20) that the program "is the same every week" is an example of this kind of evaluation in which the Russians and the Japanese are also particularly active. The Japanese complain that the characters are too black-white; that there is too little of the subtlety that they seek in their home dramas. They complain that they talk too much, too quickly, and that the serial drags on endlessly without any sort of resolution:

YOSHIE: The program's tempo is too fast.
AISUKO: There are too many elements, and still it must go on.
YOSHIE: When she (Pamela) offered (Miss Ellie) to set the table it reminded me of Japanese manners a generation ago. Does it convey the way of an American life?
ASUKO: Compared to Japanese, they might be stiff, but such things can happen. (group 5)

The Russians compare the program unfavorably with classic family sagas in their literature, such as Tolstoy's works. By comparison, the Ewing family lives in a contextless space, disconnected from any relevant reality. Year after year, they say, the characters remain the same age, never growing old (Russian group 68). Adding to this complaint, an American group member says that an atom bomb could be exploded somewhere, "and the people in *Dallas* would not even take notice."

Through interaction, a sharpening of aesthetic evaluations takes place in the same way that moral and ideological consensus arises. For example, consider the way in which a Russian group develops and refines its thinking about the dramatic function of a single episode within the flow of the serial:

> RINA: A special episode. Nobody killed or raped anybody.
> LARISSA: There have been episodes in which people were killed. They looked for the killer. Here there's nothing.
> HILLEL: You mean former episodes.
> LARISSA: Yes, this episode lacks something. It's static.
> LIUBA: This episode is the key to many of the coming episodes.
> LARA: Every episode is the beginning of the next episode.
> LIUBA: In this episode there are at least three themes for new beginnings in the episodes ahead. (Russian group 66)

Americans have more technical resources to invest in aesthetic analysis, and members of the American groups help each other to deploy these resources. Note how one American group (1) defines the characters in comic-strip terms—that is, in terms of another genre—in order to point out their simplemindedness; (2) defines the genre to which *Dallas* belongs, marking the difference between it and ordinary soaps; (3) characterizes the genre as a plot which, by nature, is unresolved; (4) modifies this generalization by indicating that certain of these issues are resolved while others are not; and (5) points to a structural analogy between the informative genre of the news show and the genre of soaps, an idea that has become fashionable among television researchers in the past years.

> NORM: These people act like comic-strip characters. They are predictable. Boring. Not credible.
> JANET: No, basically *Dallas* is a soap opera that goes on at night.
> LIL: Sure—it keeps you waiting from one episode . . .
> JUS: Don't they call it a nighttime soap?
> NORM: Nothing gets resolved.
> WILLIE: Just continuing episodes.
> JANET: No, lots of things get resolved like it should in a normal family. The only difference is where the fantasy comes in—they keep you hanging so you'll tune in tomorrow—the day after tomorrow—just like you're a news buff. (American group 4)

Having reviewed these four types of mutual aid, we can examine the statistical distribution of these interactional forms within different types of discussion and among the several ethnic communities. We coded each of the three types of mutual aid—orientation, interpretation, evaluation—according to whether it transpired in the context of what we called discussion or debate. (We omit mutual aid in the matter of legitimation, because it is expressed in the preliminaries of the group gathering or, more typically, long before the research began.) By discussion, we mean that there is interaction, even cumulative layers, shaping the consensus around some matter of orientation,

Table 6.1. The Rhetorical Context of Mutual Aid (in percent)

Type of Mutual Aid	Discussion	Debate
Orientation	34	17
Interpretation	47	74
Evaluation	17	10
Total units of interaction	(517)	(433)

interpretation, or evaluation, but that there is no disagreement. Debate, on the other hand, is a discussion that includes disagreement.

Table 6.1 shows clearly that interpretation is set in a more combative context than either orientation or evaluation. In other words, the latter two forms of mutual aid tend to be more hierarchical and authoritative, with "experts" handing down a judgment to their fellows. Interpretation, however, is more egalitarian.

The frequency of the three forms of mutual aid also varies by ethnic community (see Table 6.2). The Americans concentrate on interpretation. They do not need much orientation (for obvious reasons), nor do they take the program seriously enough to evaluate it. They are interested in the motivations of the characters and in the soap opera as genre. The highest frequency of mutual aid by orientation is among the Moroccan groups; almost four in ten of all types of mutual aid are of this type. The Arabs and Russians have the highest rates for evaluation. The Arabs are particularly exercised over moral matters, while the Russians concentrate on aesthetic evaluation.

Dallas as a Conversational Resource

Each consensus that arises from the process of mutual aid—whether of legitimation, orientation, interpretation, or the several forms of evaluation—takes on a new life as a conversational resource. The group makes use of these shared concepts and values. The group adopts into its culture the array of words, characters, metaphors, ideas, and attitudes which were verbalized as mutual aid and uses them as a symbolic vocabulary to enter even deeper into

Table 6.2. The Ethnic Context of Mutual Aid (in percent)

Type of Mutual Aid	American	Moroccan	Arab	Russian	Kibbutz
Orientation	21	38	25	13	22
Interpretation	72	47	52	62	65
Evaluation	7	15	23	25	13
Total units of interaction	(257)	(350)	(70)	(189)	(92)

relevant issues and problems. Thus, we are thinking in terms of two steps. The first involves the generation of consensus about such things as the meaning of the characters; the agenda of social issues, like the status of women; or the proposition that the rich are unhappy. The second step involves the application of these shared formulations to facilitate further interaction within the group. Following Jakobson (1972) in spirit, we call these conversational resources phatic.

The Phatic Function

The phatic function serves to keep open the channels of communication among group members. It is empty and content-free. In this sense, *Dallas* is like the weather. It brings people indoors, seats them together, offers them a shared experience and a subject for safe, ceremonial conversation. The shared image of a J. R. or Miss Ellie is available to facilitate interaction.

Not all groups require this kind of external catalyst to conversation. Obviously, intimate groups that are continuously bubbling will find little use for this kind of facilitation. People who told us—like the new immigrant from Russia—that viewing *Dallas* is like doing homework for other conversations are experiencing the kind of marginality which the phatic function helps to overcome. Being able to relate to what happened on *Dallas* the night before helps to bridge the gap between newcomers and oldtimers, both in the workplace and in the larger society.

Referential Functions

Unlike the phatic function which provides people with a neutral mechanism for establishing a comfortable public space, various referential functions serve groups that possess relevant topics for conversation by providing alternative loci for their discussions. Several different functions may be grouped together as referential, in that they all employ group consensus about the program to lubricate discussions of real life.[3] It is often easier to discuss real-life problems by distancing them onto another planet or somebody else's ranch.

The Metaphoric Function. The most elementary of these referential functions is the metaphoric, in which J. R. and the other characters serve as a vocabulary for labeling people and problems within family and community. Every neighborhood has a J. R. Thus, Reggie and Sandi make use of J. R. in order to discuss themselves and another couple, Inez and Don, who are not participants in the focus-group discussion.

> REGGIE: Well, J. R. certainly doesn't stand up for the family; he doesn't stand up for the company; he stands up for himself and, you know, if I was the head of the family and I owned the company, I would do more things that kept the family together than I would that kept everybody apart and fighting, and he doesn't seem to be family-oriented.
>
> SANDI: Well, no, it is kind of like Don and Inez . . .
>
> REGGIE: He is self-oriented.

SANDI: Yeah, he is self-oriented, but I think the family is a direct . . .

REGGIE: I think he would keep them in the house and pay the rent on it, but I don't think he would pay the goddam electric bill; you know, he would keep everybody on the farm, but he is just too, you know, for himself, he is no family . . . (American group 10)

Responding to Reggie's characterization of J. R.'s egoism and neglect of the family, Sandi suggests that their friend Don is a kind of J. R. Reggie agrees and develops the idea. In this way, the Ewings are proposed as metaphors, and part of what fuels the discussion is the question of how appropriate these metaphors are.

Beverly and Don, another American couple, use J. R. metaphorically as part of a fantasy game where the wife plays the superego and the husband plays the id.[4] Beverly hopes she will never have a son like J. R., but Don says he would be delighted to have such a child:

BEVERLY: J. R. and Bobby, their mother is just heartbroken with the things that J. R. does, and she is sick for Bobby because he doesn't get the things that he wants, and this kind of thing, well, that is every mother's reaction, but in our case, I hope to God that I never have a son like J. R. I would have to be, you know, that sick about it. (ha, ha)

DON: I would love having a son like J. R.

BEVERLY: Ah, phoo.

INTERVIEWER: You would love to have a son like J. R.?

DON: You betcha. You betcha.

INTERVIEWER: Why is that?

DON: I would like to have one that is as smart as J. R. (his wife laughs hard) A conniver, a doer.

BEVERLY: And you would sit back just like Jock.

DON: I made a mistake once, just after we watched *Dallas* for about a year or a year and a half or something, I told my oldest daughter that I thought J. R. was my idol, the kind of guy that you admire and respect; even though he is a fink and a crook, you admire and respect him. She went out and bought me a picture of J. R., and hung it on the wall in my den. (ha, ha)

INTERVIEWER: Do you still feel that way about him, that you have some admiration for him and some respect for him?

DON: Well, you have to have admiration for the guy; he accomplishes most things he sets out, no matter how, no matter who he has to step on to do it, and if you are a successful businessman and handling that much money, I think you have to do that in the world today. I don't think you can be Mr. Nice Guy and make twenty million dollars. I think you've got to step on somebody. (American group 7)

In several discussions, Israeli Arabs labeled Saudi Arabian sheiks as J. R.s, while General Sharon (Israel's defense minister at the time of the study and just implicated in the Sabra-Shatila massacre by a judicial committee of inquiry) was called J. R. in several of the kibbutz discussion groups:

SHAUL: He (J. R.) is Sharon.
AHARONCHIK: Sharon is a miniature version.
SARA A.: He steps over the bodies of his best friends. There are a lot of
   people like that. Take people in politics. It's almost the same thing; the
   only difference is that they are not shown on television as *Dallas*.
SHAUL: Don't smear. Why are you smearing?
SARA A.: It's exactly that. It's so; it's so. Politicians are dirty people.
AHARONCHIK: Sharon is not politics. (kibbutz group 82)

The morgue of Israeli characters who are labeled J. R. includes a busi-
nessman-politician convicted of bribery, a bank manager convicted of larceny,
and a member of the Knesset convicted of marital cruelty. Television characters
enter the folklore of the global village and give added depth and breadth to the
gallery of local characters. Thus, the local becomes global, and the global becomes local. Stolz (1983) believes that the globalization process is the predominant one, and that local heroes are relegated to the realm of dying folklore.[5]

Roles Within the Discussion Group. Discussion of the program creates another
rather different kind of conversational resource in that it contributes to the
emergence of differentiation based on roles and statuses within the group.
While we encounter these roles in the artificial circumstances we have constructed, we believe that they simulate real-life circumstances.

Many groups have an identifiable archivist, somebody who is expert in the
genealogy of the Ewings, in the history of what has transpired, and, sometimes, in the behind-the-scenes connections between the story and the real
lives of its actors. We have seen Cecile (see Chapter 4) playing this part,
although she is no less formidable as an interpreter. This archival expertise,
however, is not uniformly rewarded high status. In the groups that are more
skeptical about the value of the program (or of the research on it), being an
expert on its gothic intricacies is considered lowly or no better than "women's
work." Indeed, the Russian groups look to their women for orientation, not
only because the men do not know (they often do, it turns out) but also because
it is unbecoming to know. Other groups that treat the program and the research less equivocally give due respect to those who play orienting roles.

There are two oppositional roles that constantly emerge. One is that of the
cynic—like Yossi in Moroccan group 20—who dismisses the program as trivial
on aesthetic grounds. The Japanese groups are full of such role players (see
Chapter 9). The other role is that of moral oppositionist, such as Machluf (also
group 20). The Russians have the additional role of ideological opponent, who
points out how the program attempts to manipulate the viewers.

Some Russians refuse to participate altogether, insisting that they will take
a seat, drink tea, and wait for the others to finish. Very few actually walk out. A
more participatory role is that of traffic director, or a chairperson, who im-
plicitly nominates appropriate speakers for the several topics. Zehava played
this role in Moroccan group 20, and also served, in part, as agenda-setter,

pointing out which real-life topics are implicated in various aspects of the discussion of the program.

There is also often a specialist—an intellectual or critic—in the nonreferential aspects of the program, that is, in the aesthetic elements that go into its construction: structural aspects of the narrative (villains and heroes), aspects of the genre in comparison with other genres, and aspects of audience attractions and gratifications.

Rehearsals for Real-Life Roles. There is another kind of role-playing—different from the roles played in the discussion—whereby scenes and characters from the program, as commonly interpreted, are used for temporary redefinitions of identity, as in situations of play (Stephenson, 1967). Thus, the conversational resources generated through mutual aid and consensus, permit groups to act out alternatives to their usual perceptions, attitudes, and behaviors. It is an opportunity to enter what Turner (1985) calls a liminal moment during which viewers try on other roles subjunctively. This aspect of social interaction with a text is found useful by psychotherapists and other agencies of social change (Kilgus, 1974). The psychodynamics of these as-if experiences are not necessarily explicit, of course, but the observer sometimes gets a glimpse which enables him to reinterpret an entire sequence of group interaction. This is well illustrated in the Moroccan discussion of Chapter 4 where Yossi and Zehava invoke the episode to work through some of the tension between them: Zehava's wifely role, for example, and Yossi's drinking problem.

There are a number of groups in which women use *Dallas* to preach a feminist message to each other. Amalia, for instance, calls her friend, Sarah, a feminist because of the way she retells the episode:

> AMALIA: I would say "Have you seen that! She succeeded. She won (over J. R.)."
> SARAH: You're telling it so proudly because you're a woman. (kibbutz group 82)

Sophia and Tamara, similarly, debate whether women can identify only with other women:

> SOPHIA: It's as if the characters of Miss Ellie and Sue Ellen were taken from real life.
> TAMARA: Maybe because we're women we experience female characters more keenly.
> SOPHIA: Why? Even as women you can experience the characters of the men just as strongly. (Russian group 67)

Many times, participants use the programs in order to clarify their positions vis-à-vis their spouses who are also present in the group, as do Yossi and Zehava. They clarify relevant and concrete issues of their lives within the group discussion of the Ewings' family relations. Part of these interactions are playful and arouse laughter in the group, canalizing the tension away from its true locus. George, for instance, is worried about his wife, Karen, who identifies with Pam in her longing for a baby, and Greg thinks that Sandi is defending *herself* when she accepts Sue Ellen's excuses for her alcoholism:

> CAROL: She wants a baby.
> JACQUE: Well, she thought she lost a couple of babies.
> KAREN: She couldn't have one.
> GEORGE: (laughter)
> INTERVIEWER: Why is that, George?
> GEORGE: Because she wants more children, and we can't afford any more.
> KAREN: Because I want another baby. (American group 4)

> SANDI: But look at Sue Ellen. She is an alcoholic, and that was all bad, and she lost her son because of it, but she overcame and developed into a better character, I mean . . .
> JOHN: OK, well, she was all mixed-up. (chuckle)
> SANDI: Well, I know, but she did, I know, but she overcame it.
> GREG: Alcoholism isn't evil, it's . . .
> RENEE: It's a disease.
> GREG: It's an emotional problem. (laugh)
> SANDI: But what I'm saying is . . . (laugh)
> GREG: "I have an emotional problem." (American group 3)

The punchlines which end these two sequences of dialogue express the essence of the exchange and lay it to rest. They are typical of this kind of revelation during the course of the group discussions.

Some of these intimate exchanges take the form of subjunctive fantasy games that permit tension release and invite good-spirited response and supportive laughter. Thus, Don (American group 7) jokes about his wife's poor management of the household budget in response to her dreamings about what she would do with J. R.'s money if only she had it.

Unmasking Pluralistic Ignorance and Rehearsal for Change. Once the program is firmly understood, viewers can use it reflexively to clarify where they themselves stand on the issues. This is a different way of establishing identity: not by trying on fictional roles subjunctively, but by soberly confronting alien values with one's own. It is a next step, following the evaluation of the Ewings, to take this consensus as a basis for self-examination, as done by Machluf in his call for a rallying around Jewish identity (Moroccan group 20, Chapter 4).

In this kind of interaction, group members sometimes discover one of their number expressing something they did not expect, or that the momentarily deviant group member did not expect of himself—certainly not in the presence of the others. The response of the group to such anti-normative outbursts is a measure, for the group, of the strength of its commitment to its norm and, for the deviant, of the extent to which the group will tolerate deviation. At the extreme, such moments may unmask pluralistic ignorance—everybody thinks that everybody else unequivocally favors the norm—and may hinder any radical change in the norm.

Somewhat less extreme than rebellion against the perceived consensus is an ambivalent expression, whereby a member "floats a trial-balloon" to indicate that he is not altogether certain of his adherence to the norm. Consider Greg, who first insists that he wants to be like Bobby and fifteen minutes later—in reaction to the conversation about J. R.—expresses deep admiration for J. R.:

GREG: You admire anyone that clever.
JOHN: Anyone who can do a job well, even if he's a rat, you have to admire him for it . . . Anybody who can do a good job like that, you got to . . .
SANDI: And get away with it; you've got to give them credit, right?
JOHN: Yeah, and get away with it.
GREG: I kind of fantasize myself as Bobby, acting like a Bobby, but I admire J. R. more than I admire Bobby, too. Bobby is a dummy. (laugh)
(multi-conversation with Sandi saying something about Bobby being a sensitive, loving person)
GREG: Just his ruthlessness. (lots of laughter) No, it's his ability to survive, to come back from the bottom and bounce back up and come out on top again, you know; and no matter how many times you get him down, he'll bounce back up and keep trying and somehow come out a winner, you know. He'll have to step on a lot of people to do that; survival is something to be admired, the ability to survive.
SANDI: No, uh, huh, I don't admire that. (American group 3)

The change in Greg's position is characteristic of other situations, but typically, viewers are less likely than Greg to be aware of their own internal conflicts and of the influence of the group to change their positions. For instance, Janet is a woman who repeatedly denounced J. R. in the course of the discussion, characterizing him as vindictive, rotten, braggart, egotist, sadist, as someone she would like to see "get it up the kazoo." Ten minutes later, she loves him because of his strength, explaining little more than that "underneath all our weakness lies something in us that would like to come out strong." She suggests that her subconscious identifies with J. R.'s strength:

JANET: Because he's always so vindictive. He's rotten to his brother; he's worse to his wife. He's . . . he's . . .
GUS: He flaunts his money.
JANET: He's a braggart, he's an egotist, he's a sadist.
GUS: Yep . . . oh yeah . . .
JANET: He's just a mean individual. I just don't like him. I'd like to see him get it right up the kazoo.
LIL: But he's a good actor.

Later, in the course of the same conversation, Janet speaks differently:

GUS: And I like his little grin—like he swallowed the canary.

NORM: He doesn't go roughshod—things happen.

WILLI: I liked him in that swimming pool tonight. (laughter)

JANET: Yeah. I like him even though he is a stinker. Everybody I think basically likes a strong domineering—even though we may consider ourselves meek—but I think underneath all our meekness lies something in us that would like to come out strong . . .

GUS: You'd probably like to be that strong.

JANET: Yeah, I would.

LIL: Does that mean you respect him a little?

JANET: Yes, yes, I do, definitely. I respect his being that strong and nasty . . . I like him.

WILLIE: We don't know why his wife left him you see. I mean maybe he was . . . (American group 4)

Janet reveals what she really feels—admiration for J. R. whom she would like to resemble but does not—only after she detects that the group is much softer on J. R. than she implied in her original declaration of war on him. This suggests that ambivalent statements of the sort that are less likely on a personal questionnaire are all the more likely in the context of a group which is weaving its way toward consensus.

We believe that this process of expressing ambivalence in the group context may be a rehearsal for possible normative change in the group. In any event, if we view these expressions of ambivalence as parallel to the earlier conversational function of the ludic trying-on of roles, these two types of role-playing may be schematically summarized using a quasi-psychoanalytic scheme. Thus, the informal—mostly subjunctive—statements are playful. They relate, in various ways, to identification with characters (Freud, 1961). Identification takes several forms. In its most elementary sense, it involves the perception of like/unlike. But, in addition, it may involve the desire to be like/unlike him. Independent of these two is the affective like/dislike. The combination of elements is revealing about the dilemma posed by *Dallas* to viewers, and hence, its potential for playfulness and fantasy (see Table 6.3). Many viewers dislike J. R. but admit to wishing to be like him. They like Bobby, J. R.'s more humane younger brother. Some feel they *are* like him but are wary of saying (or thinking) that they *want* to be like him. Hence the folk summary of J. R.'s popu-

Table 6.3. Types of Identification

	I am like him		I am not like him	
	I want to be like him	I don't want to be like him	I want to be like him	I don't want to be like him
I like him	1	2	3	4
I dislike him	5	6	7	8

larity—love to hate him—seems quite understandable, and from here, it is an easy step to hating oneself for being attracted to him at all, or perhaps for feeling ambivalent.

The discussions clearly reveal these varieties of identification. The first variety, of course, is the straightforward: I am like him, I want to be like him, I like him; or, conversely, I am not like him, I do not want to be like him, I do not like him. Some of this fantasy is in the indicative "I am," but much more of it is in the subjunctive "I would like to." In any case, these are imaginary games in which one fancies oneself as one of the characters or associated with one of the characters in an opposite (counter) role. "I would lose 20 kilos," said a Jerusalem woman, if "Bobby would go out with me even for one evening."

A second, more frequent type of identification presents the self as juggling different, often competing, attitudes or identities. Being playful, these are less constrained by the rules of cognitive consistency, but the strain is evident in at least some of our participants. One kind of dissonance, then, arises from contradictions. Another kind of dissonance involves shuttling back and forth between liking and disliking one of the characters, or between wanting and not wanting to resemble two different characters, typically J. R. and Bobby. Still another kind of ambivalence involves identifying with one particular attribute of a character—if I were rich like him—and speculating on how one would play out other aspects of his life. Some invent situations—if my son were a bank robber—that are products of association with the television narrative. Participants try on different roles, consciously or unconsciously, and sometimes look to the reactions of others.

When these forms of fantasy enter into the discussion, the other group members often—not always—react. Reactions may take the form of serious discussion, even debate, but quite frequently interaction of this kind has a comic aspect, inviting jokes, barbed statements, and laughter. For example, group members may discern and remark on the betrayal of attraction or identification with a character by another of their number. Spouses sometimes remark, jokingly, about the deeper meaning of being attracted to or identified with one of the characters. Or, one group member may make a statement about his or her identification with a character or about ambivalent feelings about two characters and evoke responses from others which take the form of ludic interactions or even more extensive discussions or debates.

These examples of the way in which the group draws its own readings of the program—in effect, mobilizing resources for conversation from orientation, interpretation, and evaluation—are then fed back into the group's self-definition. Most of the conversational resources discussed in this chapter (except the phatic function) are a part of the corpus of referential uses of the program, whereby the members of the group move from consensus about the program to discussion about life in general and about their lives in particular. The referential is the subject of the next chapter.

7

REFERENTIAL READING

The referential (Jakobson, 1972) connects the program and real life. Viewers relate to characters as real people and in turn relate these real people to their own real worlds. The critical (Jakobson's metalinguistic) frames discussions of the program as a fictional construction with aesthetic rules. Referential readings are probably more emotionally involving; critical readings are more cognitive, dealing as they do with genres, dynamics of plot, thematics of the story, and so on. They may be just as involving as referential readings, nonetheless, and just as pleasurable.

To say that the referential is more involving would be to ignore the fact—which we repeatedly observed—that the *investment* in the critical is no less than in the referential. If involvement is defined in terms of investment of resources such as thought, time, energy, or emotion, there is no basis for saying that the one is more involving than the other. Even if one were to define involvement solely as emotional involvement, the critical is not without emotion; certain types of critical statements are full of passion. In addition, certain uses of the critical may betray an effort at self-protection, a refusal to admit emotional involvement. Moreover, the referential includes cognitive as well as emotional statements, even if the referential inclines to the "hot" and the critical to the "cool."

It is more useful, then, to speak of these distinctions as patterns or types of involvement rather than of degrees or extent of involvement.[1] We prefer to think of involvement as investment, and emotional and cognitive involvement as forms of investment. We, therefore, add to the distinction between referential and critical involvement a further distinction between emotional or hot and critical or cool.[2]

This chapter and the one following deal, respectively, with the two basic types of framing, the referential and the critical. The present chapter begins by clarifying this distinction and goes on to distinguish, within the referential, three further variables which, taken together, constitute the second dimension "hot" and "cool." The following chapter makes the same distinctions within the critical frame. In other words, these chapters address the mechanisms through which the viewer interacts with the program, becoming involved with it, and perhaps affected by it.

We extracted from the fifty-four group discussions (excepting the eleven Japanese groups) every statement that connects an observation about the program with an observation about real life or about the program as text or artistic construction.[3] The overall ratio of the two types of statements is better than three to one in favor of the referential. A question of interest is whether or not the naturalism of television, in both content and viewing context, invites referential associations and makes difficult the distance required for critical thought. Here are two examples. The first is critical; the second, referential:

REUVEN: It's impossible to achieve one's goal in this series; I'll tell you why. It's what they call a soap opera in the States. Are you familiar with this term? It's a series that goes on for years on end, and in order to get the audience to stay with it, it ends in the middle. The audience hopes the missing end will be told next week, but it never is. They always manage to get to another scene that won't be completed either. That's the way they hold the audience for years, endlessly. If they get to some ending, if everybody gets what he wants the following week, nobody will view . . .
AVI: The series will end. (kibbutz group 81)

LARA: It's not clear to me why he wants so much to get his son back.
NATASHA: As somebody explained to me, in the United States family status—whatever is going on behind the curtains—is very important for one's career. Every big manager has a family picture on his desk, his wife and children. That's why all the flirting is unconnected with the career. That's why his family status is so important, from the point of view of his career. (Russian group 66)

Comparing ethnic communities, we find that the groups differ significantly in the ratio of referential to critical utterances. The most critical utterances (relative to the referential) were made by the Russians, followed by Americans and kibbutzniks, followed by Moroccan Jews and Arabs (see Table 7.1). Higher education also increases the proportion of critical statements,[4] but even when education is held constant, the rank-order of ethnic differences remains unchanged.[5]

Had the American groups far exceeded the others in making critical statements, it would have occasioned little surprise. The Americans do not take the program as real or serious, because they are obviously well acquainted both with the real Dallas and with real Hollywood. That the Russians and kibbutzniks should match and even exceed the American proportion of critical statements invites a different kind of explanation. (The Japanese were the most critical of all.) For the moment, let us say that we are led by these findings to

Table 7.1. Statements in Referential and Critical Frames, by Ethnicity (in percent)

	Americans	Moroccans	Arabs	Russians	Kibbutz
Critical (metalinguistic) frame	27	10	11	37	28
Referential frame	72	90	88	62	72
Number of statements	(293)	(264)	(167)	(251)	(187)

suggest that these cultures all provide training in critical framing of texts and dramatic forms, and that this kind of socialization transfers from one medium to another and from familiar to unfamiliar genres.

A high ratio of critical to referential statements does not necessarily mean that the absolute number of statements about life is low. The kibbutz groups, for example, were high in both types of statements. On the other hand, the very high number of statements about life of the Arab groups is inverse to the number of their critical statements.

About What? The Subjects of the Referential Statements

While the thrust of this chapter is on the how of referential framing, we look first at what they are about.[6] All referential statements that figure in the interaction within the discussion groups were coded by topic, and the twenty-three resulting topics were then reduced to four. These are: (1) motivations for action; (2) kinship relations and norms; (3) moral dilemmas, having to do (mainly) with the price of success; and (4) business relations. There is substantial similarity among the ethnic groups in the rank-order of attention given to each of these topics. With the exception of the Arabs, motivation was the most discussed topic in all groups; reference to the motivation of the characters in the story led to talk of motivation in real life, and vice versa.

The Arabs focused their referential statements, first of all, on the subject of kinship roles and norms; for the other groups, this was the second most frequent referential category. Thus, relations among story spouses, generations, siblings, and so on were frequently used to discuss kinship relations in real life, and vice versa. Moral dilemmas occupied the kibbutz groups and the Arabs disproportionately; only the Americans made frequent reference to business relations in the story and life.

The large measure of agreement over the rank-order of the topics discussed referentially suggests that programs such as Dallas may be able to impose an agenda on diverse communities of viewers. It seems a better bet, however, that the social agenda proposed by the program coincides with pervasive and pre-existing concerns over primordial human motivations and interpersonal relations, particularly within the family. This is a clue to the ease with which a program like Dallas crosses cultural frontiers and engages participation.

Within these broadly defined topics, however, the different groups display different tendencies in their interpretations. In explaining motivation, for example, the Americans and the kibbutz members invoke a sort of Freudian theory, perceiving individuals as governed by irrational drives and connecting these with childhood events. Thus, J. R.'s personality is thought to derive from his having been second to Bobby in his mother's favor. Interpretations of this kind, of course, relieve individuals of much moral responsibility. In contrast, a large proportion of the Russian statements invoke determinism of another form, as if people behaved in a particular way because their roles impelled them to; as if businessmen, for example, or women, were programmed by society. The Moroccans also blame society, but invoke a Hobbesian model in which individuals must fend for themselves in the jungle of the world. Only the Arabs—who focus not on motivation but on family interrelations and moral dilemmas—find the individual free and responsible enough to struggle against temptation and constraint.

While there is little variation among the ethnic communities in the subjects of the referential statements, there is substantial difference in their formulations. We shall analyze these differences in terms of a series of further variables: two kinds of *keyings* (real and play), three kinds of *referents* ("I," "we," "they"), and two kinds of *value orientations* (interpretive or value-free, and evaluational or normative).

The Keying of Referential Statements: Real and Play

Most statements have a straightforward, serious character; they are indicative in form. When they relate the story to life, they do so realistically. In contrast with these, stands another set of statements that take a more playful form; they are more poetic, in Jakobson's sense, relating the story to imagined situations in life in a subjunctive mood.[7] They involved the trying on of characters, i.e., group members imagining how wonderful or awful it would be to be like them. Following Goffman (1974), we call both of these forms keyings, the one real and the other play. (It is noteworthy that most of the play utterances come in the first, more open, portion of the group discussion and decline sharply as the questions become more closed, as Daniel Dayan had suggested.)

Consider the following examples. The first is a realistic keying from a Russian group:

SIMA: Pam feels that Bobby neglects her; he's never home.
MISHA: It's true, but what can he do? What's a man busy with? To be occupied only with family is not practical; it's not realistic. Either he has to stop worrying about money and tend to his family all day long, or he has to be busy with something else—that is, with work. In fact, if a man works twelve hours a day, he can't be occupied with his family the way a woman can. (Russian group 65)

Next is an example of a ludic keying, illustrating how viewers take an idea from the program and play with it subjunctively in their minds or in interaction with others:

> BEVERLY: I think we have to be a scuzzy person to be able to act like that to begin with. I mean, if I had a million dollars (he's talking about fifty million dollars for just a place to store his damn oil), if I had fifty million dollars I would give it to all my friends, all my kids; I wouldn't connive and cheat just to get more.
> DON: Give her a hundred bucks and she splits five ways. (ha, ha) Twenty to each kid. (American group 7)

The American and kibbutz groups specialize in this kind of ludic keying (though, as we shall see, even they make many more serious than playful statements). Thus, in discussing the almost-collusion between Miss Ellie and her son J. R. in his diabolical plot to kidnap his son away from his estranged wife, an American woman (group 9) said, "If my son robbed a bank, would I drive the getaway car?" The subjunctive and ludic character of this kind of trying on of roles fictionalizes life, almost making the speaker a character in a story.

> NOAH: He (Bobby) seems to me the most balanced, the most considerate of the lot.
> YIGAL: It reminds me of our kibbutz admissions committee. Truly, I swear. (laughs)
> NOAH: I'm the admissions committee. It's OK.
> DINA: In short—you'd accept him.
> NOAH: He might not achieve what he wants but . . . in stages, what's called slowly but surely, he gets there somehow.
> GILA: Zehava, what do you think of Bobby?
> YEHUDIT: When her husband is in the army—then she thinks about him . . . (laughter)
> ZEHAVA: I'll compromise on him too. (to Yehudit) You're disgusting. (kibbutz group 84)

The statistical summary of the proportion of the two kinds of keying is presented in Table 7.2, which makes clear that the Americans and the kibbutzniks engage in ludic keyings more than the others. The Russians, who make critical statements more often than the Americans and the kibbutzniks (see Table 7.1), do not distance themselves when it comes to keyings. Their statements about the relationship of the story to life are as serious as those of Moroccans and Arabs. Indeed, the Russians are equally serious, even passionate, about the manipulative intent that they discern in the ideological message of the program. Hence, we shall see that the Russians are hot not only with respect to referential keyings but even within the context of the ostensibly detached critical frame. The Americans, for the most part, are cool both in the referential and the critical.

Table 7.2. Real and Play Keyings in Referential Statements, by Ethnicity (in percent)

	Americans	Moroccans	Arabs	Russians	Kibbutz
Real keyings	79	87	87	92	75
Play keyings	21	13	13	8	25
Number of referential statements	(213)	(236)	(147)	(145)	(135)

About Whom? The Referents

More light can be shed on ethnic differences by examining the sociolinguistic patterns in which the subjects of these utterances reside. We classified each statement, first of all, by referent, employing the pronoun—the object to whom the referential statement refers—in order to determine which part of reality is triggered by the program. Secondly, we classified each statement by whether it is simply an interpretive utterance or whether a moral evaluation is involved, that is, whether the statement is normative or value-free. Thirdly, we classified the referential statements in terms of the extent to which they are essentially playful or serious. The pronouns employed by speakers in transferring a story reference to real persons divide into primary references to self and family; references to ethnic group and the nation; and universal references—distant from self—to abstract social categories such as businessmen or women. We call these "I," "we," and "they." The universal "they" is the dominant referent for all groups, but the Russians far exceeded the others in reference to universals: three-fourths of their referential statements are of this more abstract kind:

> MARIK: Woman was created for the family, and I think that for her, "child, kitchen, and church" as the Germans say, is the most important thing . . . A woman who has a lot of leisure and doesn't use it as is necessary, that is, it's important to find her some specific occupation. I don't mean she has to have a job, but something specific for her.
> MISHA: Something to fill the free time, otherwise she has a real problem. Why do they write about Princess Diana who also has a tough problem. Her husband is occupied with sport, government affairs, and is very little at home.
> MARIK: Let's compare her (Sue Ellen) with Princess Diana.
> MISHA: Same thing.
> MARIK: I think that, when a woman marries somebody like J. R., she ought to know how a man like that occupies himself, what he can give the family and what he can't give the family. That is, can he give time to the family as Sue Ellen imagines? (Russian group 65)

By contrast the American and kibbutz groups are lower in "they" references and high in references to self and family:

SARAH A.: The funniest was when they tried to kill him. Her (Sue Ellen's) behavior was simply . . . How could she suddenly . . . ? True, you feel guilty; then you worry about a person, but to suddenly love him . . .

DAUGHTER: It was because she was feeling guilty she was afraid.

SARAH A.: What, then, because I think I'm guilty, I should suddenly sell myself, my personality? . . . In the beginning when what's his name, the father, got a heart attack. She looked at the house as if it would be hers, and then her mother-in-law said, "Don't worry, you will not be here."

SARAH B: But that's how people are.

SARAH A: It's not true. You hated her for this behavior . . . The way she used to despise her sister-in-law . . . Now you feel sorry for her.

AMALIA: Because she was jealous.

SARAH A: What did she have to be jealous about?

SHAUL: If they would have shown the good things about her in the beginning . . .

SARAH A: Then I have to be nasty? I can be jealous inside myself.

AMALIA: Situations in life can cause you to be nasty, frustrated.

AHARON: No, no, I don't accept that.

SARAH A: I don't accept it.

AHARON: I believe that if you would be in her situation and were living with someone like J. R., you might have behaved in the same way. You forget she's living with someone I would not be prepared to live with for one minute, and she lives with him. And she was watching him all the time being unfaithful. It isn't *she* who started being unfaithful. It's *he* who did.

SARAH A: No, I don't have to descend to the other person's level. I have to rise above it. Why didn't she run off?

AHARON: Where would she run off to? Did she have anywhere to go? . . .

SARAH A: To live in all this luxury. I would throw everything behind me and become a servant in someone's house in order not to have to live that kind of life.

AHARON: You have not been in such a house yet. Don't say you would throw it all away.

SARAH A: I think so. (kibbutz group 81)

Far more than the other groups, the Arabs use Arab society ("we") as a frequent reference.

RAVIA: Sue Ellen as well—I agree she's rebellious and stubborn. Tries to get revenge against her husband. In all the ways he was unfaithful to her, she's unfaithful to him. In our Arab society it's different. In our society the man will do anything and the woman wouldn't. (laughter) Because that's the way we were brought up. It's difficult to change.

MOGED: (to Ravia) You think all men in our society are J. R.s?

RAVIA: Almost, yes. (laughter)

MOGED: A small J. R.

RAVIA: J. R.'s sons. (Arab group 42)

Table 7.3 shows that the Americans and kibbutzniks are highest in the use of personal and primary references ("I"); while the Arabs are the only group to

Table 7.3. Referents of Referential Statements, by Ethnicity (in percent)*

	Americans	Moroccans	Arabs	Russians	Kibbutz
Primary ("I") referents	44	24	18	14	38
"We" referents (ethnicity, nation)	2	13	18	10	11
Number of referential statements	(213)	(236)	(147)	(145)	(135)

*As explained in the text, "they" is by far the most frequent referent for all groups. This table compares only the "I" and "we" referents because these distinguish best among the groups. The columns do not total 100%.

make substantial use of "we" categories, referring to ethnic or national identification.

Comparing these different uses of the referent form suggests that the abstract referents of the Russians ostensibly reiterate the kind of distance from direct personal involvement in the story which we observed in their predilection for the critical over the referential. Here we see that, within the referential, the Russians again choose cool involvement by alluding to general social categories rather than to themselves. On the other hand, such abstract generalization betrays an almost believing attitude in the truth value of the program, of the sort we have seen in the Russian use of real keyings. They are less likely to say "I have an uncle who is like J. R." than "capitalists have to act that way." Indeed, it might be argued that the abstract generalizations of the Russians— "women belong in the kitchen"—leave no room for distance between story and behavior, while the personal references of the Americans and kibbutzniks may create distance, at least in the sense of leaving room for myriad other possibilities. Thus, it is possible that by bringing story and themselves closer together in this way the Americans and kibbutzniks may be distancing the truth value of the story, while the Russians with their universal truisms may be bringing it closer.

Even if this counterargument is correct, however, it should be made clear that it is *our* argument, not the Russians'. From the speakers' point of view, surely "they" is more distant than "I" or "we." It is only from the observers' point of view that the question can be raised as to whether this is not simply rigid. Since this chapter deals with referential statements from the viewers' vantage point, we shall rank "they" as more distant than "I" or "we." We will also maintain that "we" is more committed than "I" because the "we" invokes a role, a public persona, taking an official stance on behalf of a group, whereas "I" is lighter, less committed, less consistent.

The Arab groups are most engaged. They do not simply analyze the program, as do the Russians using "they," or simply personalize, as do the Americans and the kibbutzniks; they actively argue. They read the program as a challenge to their own values and experience the need to dissociate themselves. They reassert their own opposing values.[8]

Value Orientations

Continuing this exploration of the rhetoric of the referential, we distinguish between statements that are interpretive without being judgmental (which we call value-free) and statements that are both (which we call normative). The latter include interpretation but go beyond this to include a stand in favor of or against the behavior being interpreted. We apply this distinction to all statements that are keyed as real.[9]

Consider an example of an interpretive, value-free statement:

GUS: I would imagine that some of those wealthy families are kinda like that; I bet the Kennedys were.
NORM: No, they went East.
JANET: I don't think you have to be wealthy to be like that; you can have a stinker in any family.
GUS: Yeh, but look at the old man; he chased Gloria Swanson and all those girls.
JANET: Who are you talking about? The Kennedys or *Dallas?*
GUS: Kennedys.
WILLIE: Fitzgerald, the old man Kennedy.
NORM: Joseph Kennedy.
GUS: She just asked do you think they are real people.
JANET: Yes, of course, but I said you don't have to be a powerful, wealthy family to give birth and raise a stinker, a lot like J. R. or Kennedy.
GUS: That's true.
NORM: You may not be like that, if you didn't have that money.
JANET: C'mon. (American group 4)

All groups have far more value-free interpretations than normative utterances. The Arabs, however, differ from the others in their relatively high use of the normative:

ANISE: Sue Ellen is J. R.'s wife, but Arabs believe that she is a bad woman, she's too free and gone astray.
SHERIFA: A bad woman. Considering the behavior of her husband, there may be some justification for what she does, but I wouldn't behave that way.
ANISE: I think so, too. According to our norms, she is forbidden both to drink and to smoke. In this final analysis, I pity her. (Arab group 43)

An examination of Table 7.4 makes clear that the Arabs are the only group making substantial use of the evaluational orientation. They are more likely than the others to add a normative verdict—approving or condemning, often with some degree of passion—to their interpretations. The Moroccans, too, may be said to be slightly more normative than the three Western groups.

Table 7.4. Value Orientations in Referential Statements, by Ethnicity (in percent)

	Americans	Moroccans	Arabs	Russians	Kibbutz
Value-free: interpretation	90	85	60	92	90
Normative: interpretation and evaluation	10	15	40	8	10
Number of referential statements, real keyings only	(169)	(204)	(127)	(131)	(102)

Patterns of Involvement in Television Fiction

To this point, we have analyzed four rhetorical forms in which viewers of differing ethnicity couch their statements about *Dallas*. Taken together, they combine to form a typology of patterns of involvement. First of all, of course, there is the basic dichotomy that we call referential and critical. Each of these is a frame for involvement. (Parenthetically, it should be borne in mind that we are talking about referential and critical *statements*, which although they vary in extent among communities, do not necessarily represent either individuals or communities; that is, a statement is necessarily one or the other, but an individual or a community may be high or low on both.)

We have also presented three rhetorical forms in which the referential statements are couched: real versus play keyings, "I"-"we"-"they" referents, and value-free versus normative orientations. On further consideration, each of these forms may be considered an expression of an underlying dimension which we label hot or cool. Thus, we define as hot those statements that are more emotionally loaded, while the cool are more cognitive. Hot statements treat the program confrontationally. Within the referential, confrontational statements are those in which the viewer feels called upon to defend group norms, to treat the program as real, to relate to it seriously, and to evaluate it in terms of the norms. In Chapter 4, for example, *Dallas* is challenged by the culture of the Moroccan group as representative of American anomie.

Hot confrontations may be identified in the critical frame as well, but at the ideological level of the message rather than at the referential level of reality. The Russians specialize in these hot, critical statements. Cool statements, by contrast, are oppositional but not confrontational. They may be defined in terms of their snubbing of the reality or the seriousness of the program and, hence, of its invitation to moral outrage.

Having recoded the three referential forms in terms of hot and cool, let us do the same for referential and critical, defining the referential as more hot and the critical as more cool. This is not very elegant methodologically because for most purposes we wish to treat the two dimensions as orthogonal. Nevertheless, we allow ourselves this departure because the array of the four variables (framings, keyings, referents, and value-orientations) in terms of hot and cool scale in an interesting way, as Table 7.5 shows.

Table 7.5 positions each ethnic group on each of the four dimensions which express the hot and cool patterns of involvement.[10] It will be recalled, for example, that Americans and kibbutz members tended towards play keyings, while the other three groups tended towards the real. Accordingly, in the *Keyings* column, Americans and kibbutzniks are labeled 2 (play), while the others are labeled 1 (real) because they take the reality of *Dallas* for granted. Similar tabulations have been made for the other three dimensions of rhetoric.[11] The table makes clear that the Arabs and the Americans stand at opposite extremes of the scale. The Arabs speak most referentially, hardly using the critical frame at all (see also Table 7.1). They talk real rather than play (see also Table 7.2). They speak for their group and their culture in the language of "we" (see also Table 7.3). Their interpretations are also more engaged; they are the only group that speaks normative evaluations (see also Table 7.4). The Americans and kibbutzniks are most cool; their involvement is of a more cognitive nature. They use the critical or metalinguistic frame to a high degree (see Table 7.5); their keyings are playful; their referents are to the less committed "I"; their value orientations are neutral rather than normative.

There is a variety of in-between patterns. In some ways, the Russians are even cooler than the Americans in that they use the "they" referent most, and the proportion of their critical statements is highest of any group (see Table 7.1). On the other hand, they take the program seriously; they use real keyings rather than play keyings (see Table 7.5).

The Moroccans are also in between, but they are more difficult to position. They are as hot as the Arabs in frame and keyings, but they are not as normative.

In sum, the Americans and the kibbutzniks—native-born, and most "modern" of the Israelis—are coolest. They address *Dallas* more critically, personally, and playfully. Although the Russians are even more critical, invoking

Table 7.5. Hot and Cool Patterns of Involvement, by Ethnicity

	Referent[a]	Keyings[b]	Frame[c]	Value-Orientation[d]
Arabs	1	1	1	1
Moroccans	1	1	1	2
Russians	1	1	2	2
Kibbutz	1	2	2	2
Americans	2	2	2	2

[a]1, more hot: high proportion of "we"; 2, more cool: high proportion of "I"

[b]1, more hot: low proportion of play keyings; 2, more cool: high proportion of play keyings

[c]1, more hot: low proportion of critical statements; 2, more cool: high proportion of critical statements

[d]1, hot: high proportion normative; 2, cool: low proportion normative

most meta-textual references, they are not so lighthearted about the program; they seem to take it very seriously at both the referential and the critical level.

That the program should be hottest for the more traditional groups suggests that they recognize the familiar in *Dallas* as well as the exotic. In spite of the ostensible distance between Lorimar's Texas and the Middle East, there may be real similarity—as Stolz (1983) argues in her study of *Dallas* in Algeria—between the patrilocal and patriarchal Ewing clan, the locus of political and economic power, and traditional family structures. This would explain why the Arabs and Moroccans are challenged by the program to defend themselves, to respond confrontationally by flexing their own values in light of what they perceive to be the real but threatening option of changing values without a corresponding change in social structure.

Conclusions

Most statements in all groups are based on perception of the program as real. That is, there are far more referential than critical (metalinguistic) statements, and within the referential, far more keyings to the real (serious, indicative, familiar) than to play (fantasy, subjunctive, hypothetical). Moreover, most statements in all groups refer to people in general or general categories of people ("they"), and few statements are in the "I" or "we" form. These statements are usually interpretive in character—observations and explanations of behavior—without value judgments; evaluational (normative) statements are far fewer. "Pragmatic" may be a good way to describe this overall tendency to the real and the value-free.

Overall, one may say that spontaneous discussion of *Dallas*—presuming that we have successfully simulated such discussion—accepts the program as real and as morally unproblematic in spite of the back-stabbing and corruption which underlie the human relations that are the subject of the referential statements.

Patterned deviations from the dominant pragmatic pattern (real and value-free) are of particular interest. On the one hand, we are interested in use of the critical (metalinguistic) at the expense of the referential and in use of play keyings at the expense of real keyings. That is, we are interested in identifying those groups and those situations in which the viewer distances himself from the reality by using metalinguistic frames and ludic keyings. On the other hand, we are equally interested in the move from the abstract "they" and the value-free in the direction of more intimate referents ("I" and "we") and more evaluative—therefore more emotionally loaded—orientations.

Arraying the cultures on the multidimensional scale of involvement, the ostensible conclusion must be that the more "modern" groups are cooler, that is, more cognitively involved in the program, while the more traditional groups are more emotionally involved. The hot framing of the more traditional groups appears to be influenced by several sources. The referential, for one thing, is closely allied with storytelling forms favored by traditional cultures (Ong, 1983; Goody, 1977; Olson, 1977), and these, in turn, are reinforced by their compatibility with the storytelling forms of television (Fiske and Hartley, 1978). Secondly, the program may be framed as real because it is about a culture whose reality is a function of what is shown on the screen of a medium that is itself officially associated with reality. Thirdly, certain familiar elements of kinship structure are recognizable in the narrative, and therefore, its message of moral deterioration within this context is perceived as provocative or hot. In the absence of alternate forms of framing and keying, the admission of the hegemonic agenda of the program to the most intimate circles—even women are gradually infiltrating the traditionally male audience, sometimes even sitting together—poses a competing paradigm which cannot but shake the system.

We should reiterate here our postulate that hot and cool statements may be equally involving, the one expressing more emotional investment, the other more cognitive investment. If Marshall McLuhan had deigned to deal with messages he would have agreed that cool is more involving, because his cool is cognitive, i.e., it is a response to the openness of ambiguous media technologies, such as television. Others might argue that the cool is *less* involving because of their unspoken definition of involvement as emotional. By now, we hope to have made clear that both of these forms are involving if involvement is defined as investment of self, whether emotional or cognitive.

It is worth clarifying how our usage compares with McLuhan's. The hot and cool of *Understanding Media* are syntactic attributes of technologies and have to do with ambiguity, i.e., hot media deliver messages in high-definition and unambiguously and do not, therefore, require the user to invest himself, cognitively, in their decoding. It is in this sense that cool media are involving. We, however, label as hot and cool not the media but the response of the audience. Such response, moreover, is not to the medium but to the message (in McLuhan's sense). It may be either to the semantics of the message, which are mostly referential and hot, or to the syntactics of the message, which are typically critical and cool. In other words, hot and cool are not determined by the medium or even by a particular genre or program but by the viewer.[12]

There is a certain sense in which we "understand" McLuhan and even find ourselves in sympathy. When McLuhan postulates that it was the combination of hot radio and a hot Hitler that evoked the primordial passions of the Germans, he surely did not mean to say that they were uninvolved. Rather, he seems to be saying that the combination of medium and message were so imposing that they left no room for critical response, i.e., for the kind of cool, cognitive processing which he defines as participatory. Cognitively, there is nothing to "work with," and hot emotional involvement is not participation for McLuhan. Our sympathy for this position is based on the observation that the message of *Dallas* is typically accepted as more hot than cool, that is, as more referential than critical, as more serious than ludic, as more emotional than cognitive. One might say that hot is hegemonic or that the modal response to

Dallas—looking at statements, not people—is hegemonic in the sense of un-critical acceptance of the self-definition of the text. Such readings, McLuhan might say, are helplessly dominated by the text.

Here is where we disagree. Not only critical readers engage the text opposi-tionally. Our findings suggest that even referential, hot readers have a defense in their ability to invoke moral opposition. Emotional involvement, that is, need not be passive and unthinking; one may accept the reality of a text and actively confront it, nevertheless. In the case of *Dallas*, this means that hegemonic readers—referential and hot—can also enter into negotiation with the text, even if they are more likely to experience unease in their confrontation with the program, inasmuch as they have given it a standing which other types of readings would deny it. It may be, therefore, that the referential, hot read-ings of the more traditional groups do, indeed, allow the message of the pro-gram to seep in.

8
CRITICAL READING

The status of the viewer has been upgraded regularly during the course of communications research. In the early days, both major schools of research—the so-called dominant and the critical—saw the viewer as powerless and vulnerable to the agencies of commerce and ideology. Gradually, the viewer—and indeed, the reader and the listener—were accorded more power. With the rise of gratifications research, the viewer began to be seen as more selective and more active than was originally supposed, at least in the sense of exercising choice in the search for satisfaction (Katz, 1986), and as less isolated. The neo-Marxists have recently acknowledged that the media can be consumed oppositionally or in a mediated sense and not only hegemonically (Parkin, 1971; Hall, 1985; Morley, 1980), thereby adding the notion of conscious decoding to counter the instrumental and even intuitive matching implicit in gratificationism. It appears that recent literary theory has followed a similar course, abandoning the idea of readers uniformly fashioned by the text in favor of readers as members of interpretive communities that are in active negotiation with the text, both aesthetically and ideologically (Fish, 1980; Radway, 1985). Although it may seem that the reader posited by gratificationists is most powerful of all because he is free to bend the text in any way he sees fit—indeed, virtually to abolish the text—the fact is that his seeking is determined by his needs, and his needs—so the critics say—may well be determined by the media (Swanson, 1977; Elliott, 1974).

In short, the reader/listener/viewer of communications theory has been granted critical ability. The legendary mental age of twelve, which American broadcasters are said to have attributed to their viewers, may, in fact, be wrong. Dumb genres may not necessarily imply dumb viewers. There are creative options within formulaic popular culture which may challenge both producers and readers (Eco, 1985).

Empirical evidence for critical ability is still very sparse: Neuman (1982) and Himmelweit (1983) have made a start towards classifying viewers' reactions to programs and their critical vocabularies. So far, one can say only that there is a growing consensus among these and other scholars that the operational definition of "critical" coincides with an ability to discuss programs as constructions, that is, to recognize or define their genres, formulae, conventions, narrative schemes, etc. We would give equal credit for critical ability to viewers who are able to perceive a theme or message or even an issue in a fictional narrative, such as the message "there's room at the top," for example (Thomas and Callahan, 1982). We would code such a generalization as critical, all the more so if it takes a more complex form such as "the program says that mobility is possible because this is what the producers have been paid to tell us." We would also credit as critical viewers who are aware that they are using analytic criteria—such as schemas, scripts, frames, roles, and other notions of viewer processing and involvement in their responses to the program.

Two of these categories, either the semantic—themes, messages, etc.—or the syntactic—genre, formulae, etc., relate to the viewer's awareness of the text as a construction. The third category relates to the viewer's awareness of the processing of the program by the cognitive, affective, and social self. This third form of criticism, we shall call pragmatic.

If most referential statements are hot, by our definition, most critical statements may be considered cool. But just as we find cool involvements in the referential frame—in playful responses to the reality of the program, for example—so we find hot involvements in the critical frame. These hot responses concentrate in the semantic realm.

Each of the ethnic groups uses the program more referentially—as a connection to real life, including their own lives—than they use it critically. The ethnic communities, however, vary considerably in this regard. About 30 percent of the framing statements made by Western groups—Russians, Americans, and kibbutz members—are critical, compared with only 10 percent of the framing statements made by Arabs and Moroccans. This difference holds even after educational differences are taken into account; indeed, among the lower educated, the *only* metalinguistic statements are made by the more Western groups. Japanese viewers made the most critical statements, proportionately, of all.

Using an altogether different coding method, we attempted to validate this pattern by analyzing replies to the more specific question, "why all the fuss about babies?"[1] In reply, some participants told us that the program dotes on babies "because they are needed by dynasties as heirs"—a statement we coded as referential. Others told us that babies are good for soap operas because they permit parents to fight over them—a statement we coded as metalinguistic. Consider the following quotes, illustrative of referential or metalinguistic "babies," respectively:

RINA: The emphasis on the issue of babies in the family shows the importance of babies in a monarchy. They cannot risk (the possibility) that the empire they have built would vanish with their death; continuity is important. (Russian group 62)

REUVEN: There are a lot of problems around babies in such a family—the real identity of the baby, sicknesses, kidnappings—which provide a lot of possibilities for the writer of the series in constructing the plotline. (kibbutz group 81)

Table 8.1 reports on these differences in relating to babies. The referential divides in two: statements which speak of the function of babies for life and statements which speak of the function of babies for the characters in the story, as if they were real. Critical or metalinguistic "babies" speak of the function of babies for the producers and writers.

In the analysis of these data, the three Western groups again exceeded the others by far in their use of critical explanations, but this time the Americans showed a marked preference for this kind of framing. They make almost twice as many critical statements as the Russians and the kibbutzniks and six times as many as the Moroccans. The Arabs gave almost no metalinguistic explanations for the fuss about babies. Further examination of these data by educational level (of the group) shows that the higher educated make most of the critical statements but that the ethnic differences persist.

We have already speculated that the Western groups' higher rate of making critical statements about television programs may reflect their greater experience with the medium or their greater training in criticism or, perhaps, their greater familiarity with the society being portrayed. That the Americans are strikingly more critical in response to the more specific question about babies suggests that they do, after all, have more experience with television genres and their production than even the other Western groups. The Americans seem especially able to respond to specific questions of this kind, although we do not know why. Thus, in the discussion of babies, they seem to be aware of the difference between the function of a baby for the story and his appearance on the screen—both critical framings.[2] They are also the only one of the ethnic groups seeing a demographic message in the appearance of babies, apparently because Americans are having to struggle between the ethic of self-fulfillment versus the ethic of altruism.

Table 8.1. Function of Babies (in percent)

	Americans	Moroccans	Arabs	Russians	Kibbutz
Story babies: for the characters	14	19	24	16	16
Real babies: for people (life)	58	75	74	67	66
Drama babies: for the producers	28	5	1	15	19
Total statements	(120)	(175)	(68)	(82)	(61)

With this basic distinction in mind, we now can analyze the critical realm. The critical involves awareness either of the semantic or syntactic elements of the text or of the roles of the reader as processor of the text. Obviously, an analysis must focus disproportionately on the three Western groups who participated most in the metalinguistic realm, but it is important to keep in mind that most of the statements of these viewers, too, fall into the referential realm, and thus, that the sophisticated viewer should be seen as a commuter between the referential and the critical, and not just as one or the other.[3] The critical categories employed by the Japanese groups are included here as well. (It should be noted that the Japanese have hardly any referential statements at all since they had no opportunity to get into the program.[4]) We wish to show how ordinary viewers frame everyday television critically, or metalinguistically, and to map the several ways in which they subdivide the frame.

Table 8.2 suggests that the several communities differ in the target of their critical statements.[5] The Arabs and the Russians give greater emphasis to the semantic—to the thematics of the program, its ideology and its message— while the Americans concentrate on statements about form.[6] The Americans (and the Arabs, although the absolute number is small) give more emphasis to statements about the functions of characters in the dramatic construction, showing awareness of the dimensions in terms of which the characters are polarized (good-bad, strong-weak, etc.)[7]

Semantic Criticism

Theme

The form of criticism closest to the acritical, referential realm is the ability to discern and generalize the theme of the narrative. Viewers who say that the program reflects the egoism of the modern world are taking a first step away from the referential, where they would say, "J. R. tricks people. This is interesting because it is the only way to succeed. I, for instance, am going to do the same thing myself. I am going to accumulate money, acquire land, and use my cunning" (Arabic group 46). As hegemonic theorists would expect, the

Table 8.2. Critical Statements, Semantic and Syntactic (in percent)

	Americans	Moroccans	Arabs	Russians	Kibbutz
Syntactic statements:					
genre, formula	48	43	20	49	48
dramatic function	40	25	35	12	21
Semantic statements:					
themes, ideology, message	12	31	44	38	31
Total critical statements	(80)	(28)	(20)	(86)	(52)

referential viewer takes for granted that J. R. is real and speaks as if *Dallas* were some sort of documentary. The critical viewer—even at this elementary level—shows awareness of the program as separate from reality and is concerned with the accuracy of the relationship. In this realm, there are notable similarities between Arabs and Russians who see the program as representation of moral degeneracy or rotten capitalism, although the Russians somewhat more than the Arabs question the accuracy of the representation.

The Arabs are more likely to blame moral degeneracy for the ills of modern society, whereas the Russians see more political causes. But it is often very difficult to separate the two; indeed, four of the Arab focus groups employ Marxist rhetoric to assert that the program reveals that capitalism is to blame for the moral and political degeneration of the West—for example:

> ANISE: (*Dallas*) embodies Western capitalism and shows that the more freedom there is for people, it becomes too much because it has already led to anarchy. (Arab group 43)

A possible explanation of the high sensitivity of Arabs in Israel to the dangers of Western culture is offered by Smooha (1984) who claims that (1) Israeli Arabs are at a different stage in the modernization process (with respect to the status of women); (2) Western culture is associated with the colonial administration under which they suffered, and which, in their opinion, favored the Jews over the Arabs; (3) even after the withdrawal of colonialism, Western culture continued to be associated with it, and Israel itself is considered a present-day colonial power; and (4) capitalism is perceived as a threat to the traditional social system. Arabs, therefore, have more reason than others to dissociate themselves from the culture of *Dallas*.

Some of the Japanese viewers claim that *Dallas* is compatible with a sense of a creeping recession. In America, which has come to realize that it is past its prime, bitter, unhappy, unharmonious dramas express the zeitgeist (group 4). Put differently, one Japanese participant saw the adventures of the Ewings as demonstrative of the end of the era of the American rich (group 5). Indeed, some of the Russian groups go so far as to wonder whether the text is not itself critical of Western society and its economic and moral order, reminding us of Fiedler's (1982) contention that the best of popular culture is subversive. Hanna, a member of one of the Russian groups (group 68), claimed that *Dallas* is a "socialist text."

Messages

These discussions of theme may appear either as inferences of the viewers or as intentions—messages—ascribed by the viewer to the producers. Thus, the most frequent theme perceived in *Dallas*—that the rich are unhappy—may be mentioned as the viewers' own conclusion or may be thought to be what the producers are trying to teach. Yet a further step—one particularly characteristic of the Russians—is not only to ascribe intent to the producers but to ascribe manipulative intent, in the sense that the producers are telling something they want believed but do not necessarily believe themselves:

ALONA: I started to wonder why the series is so popular. What happens there? Why does it attract the middle-class person that much? It's nice for him to know that the millionaires are more miserable than himself. Sure, a miserable millionaire is a nice thing because everyone within himself wants a millionaire to be poor, and nevertheless, he himself wants to be a millionaire. Here he sees the millionaires portrayed as if they were real. (Russian group 63)

Thus, we are dealing here in three levels of thematics—the elementary, the one closest to the referential, on which the viewer makes an inference about the theme of the program; a second level on which the viewer makes an assumption about the producer's didactic aims in introducing the theme (message); and a third level, on which the viewer suspects the producer of trickery, even if the speaker himself sees through the trick. Some of these statements are as hot as many referential statements are. In other words, critical statements are not simply cool and contemplative but can also express intense feelings.

Our coding of messages does not permit us to distinguish easily between "the program teaches us" and "the producers are trying to tell us," although we did code manipulative intent separately.[8] Messages, like themes, are sprinkled throughout the discussions, although many are concentrated in reply to our explicit question, "What is the program or the producer trying to say?" Nevertheless, it is interesting to note that the Russians and the kibbutzniks (to a lesser extent) are most active in spotting messages, anticipating our explicit question long before it was asked. As Table 8.2 shows, the Arabs and Moroccans—not the Americans—follow the Russians and kibbutzniks in the frequency of themes and messages, although most of their replies are in answer to the explicit question. From the nature of these replies—Arabs give particular emphasis to the theme "the Americans are immoral" more than to the theme "the rich are unhappy"—it seems that the Arabs are responding in the realm of themes rather than intentional messages. Table 8.3 summarizes the relative

Table 8.3. Types of "Messages," According to Ethnic Groups (in percent)

	Americans	Moroccans	Arabs	Russians	Kibbutz
"The rich are immoral"	18	26	13	22	16
"The Americans are immoral"	—	13	34	2	12
"The rich are unhappy"	33	28	16	18	43
"The Americans are unhappy"	—	—	—	—	9
"The Americans are uncultured"	—	2	3	9	—
Other	49	31	34	49	20
Total number of "Messages"	(27)	(58)	(39)	(55)	(32)

frequency of messages per group as well as the content of several of the predominant messages.

But what happened to the Americans this time? In the domain of messages, the Americans tend to be resistant. Not only do they offer fewer messages than any of the other ethnic groups, but they also protest that *Dallas* can have no message for them since it is just entertainment, only escape. Paralleling their playful statements in the referential, the Americans refuse to acknowledge that there can be anything serious about *Dallas*. When the Americans do acknowledge a theme or a message, they tend to say that the message will be so perceived by foreign viewers who do not know that the program is just escape and not about anything real. When the Americans perceive messages for themselves—and this is relatively rare—they ascribe didactic and meliorist intent to the producers, e.g., the producers think that it is important to have a strong father figure in society or that babies are a good thing after all and that one can have babies and go on being egoistic.[9] In this realm, at least, the Americans are surely less critical than the others, and thus, perhaps more vulnerable to manipulation. They believe that the producers do good homework, and that they have a sense of responsibility on which the viewer can depend.

Archetypes

A higher level of thematic criticism might be labeled archetypical in that generalization about the narrative is based on the perception of an underlying theme that unites a class of texts or performances. The image of the good sheriff entering the enemy camp unarmed and staring the villain into surrender to justice and civilization is equally applicable to the classic Western movie, President Sadat's heroic visit to Jerusalem (Katz, 1980; Liebes-Plesner, 1984), and an American detective shaming a mafioso off his private island (BBC, 1972). The essence of this form of criticism is intertextual, revealing an awareness of similar dynamics among different texts; at its most classic, it is archetypical in the sense of Oedipus, Joseph, or Cain and Abel. This form is not very frequent in our data, although the occasional archetypical allusions are dramatic indeed. Thus, we heard J. R. compared to Arab sheikhs in the Persian Gulf and—from both Arabs and kibbutzniks—to General Sharon. Of course, the reference to classic sibling rivalries in a dynastic context is much more frequent, although most of these do not make explicit mention of the various pairs of biblical brothers.[10] A Japanese viewer notes that the image of an ancestral father bestowing his blessing on that son who will deliver a first heir also figures in Japanese stories of dynastic intrigue.

At the extreme of archetypical themes, the viewer is saying in effect that the theme must have influenced the narrative, consciously or not. Semioticians sometimes speak as if the writer or producer is merely an instrument through which these classic stories retell themselves. This structural aspect of storytelling, therefore, stands on the borderline between semantic and syntactic criticism: Insofar as it deals with themes, it belongs in the domain of the semantic; insofar as it alludes to a classic sequence of actions or to themes that are elements of an identifiable narrative genre, it belongs in the domain of the syntactic—to which we now turn.

Syntactic Criticism

Critical ability in the syntactic domain reveals an understanding of the component elements of a genre or formula and the nature of the connections among these elements. Almost two-thirds of the critical statements of each of the four Israeli groups are of this character—relating either to *Dallas* as a soap opera or to a comparison of *Dallas* and other genres or to the rules of storytelling which dictate the behavior of characters and the sequence of events in the corpus of *Dallas* episodes. An even larger proportion of the critical statements made by Americans are of this type, but rather than be impressed by this syntactic ability of the Americans, one should be impressed by the high level of similar ability shown by the non-Americans who are far less experienced with the regularities of American television drama. It should be noted that Israel has never televised a proper soap opera; *Dallas* is the closest they have.

Genre

Nevertheless, Israeli viewers often volunteer quite precise definitions of what we would recognize as soap opera, even when they cannot name the genre. Consider the following examples from two members of kibbutz groups:

> MIRI: Every week the program focuses on the story of one of the stars. Every now and then they move from one to another and succeed in showing a few minutes of each star, to show that the story progresses a little bit . . . and they've introduced a new character, that is the daughter of the mother, and they leave us with some line of thought about each one—what will happen between her and what's his name. (kibbutz group 80)

> AVI: It's impossible to achieve one's goal in this series; I'll tell you why. It's what they call a soap opera in the States. Are you familiar with this term? It's a series that goes on for years on end, and in order to get the audience to stay with it, it ends in the middle. The audience hopes the missing end will be told next week, but it never is. They always manage to get to another scene that won't be completed either. That's the way they hold the audience for years, endlessly. If they get to some ending, if everybody gets what he wants the following week, nobody will view . . . (kibbutz group 81)

In Japan, on the other hand, viewers say that they will stay with a series only if all the characters are reasonably satisfied at the end of the episode. In comparing the formula of American soaps to the brand they themselves produce, viewers claim that, unlike *Dallas*—where an episode races at a fast tempo to end at the height of conflict after fifty minutes—the Japanese home drama goes on for two hours, at a much slower pace, ending on a note of harmony. According to the discussants, the Japanese cannot bear family conflict to drag on from one week to the next, as this would spoil "the mood of relaxing" at home. This incompatibility between the formula and viewers' expectations gives a clue to why American family dramas have failed in Japan.

It is interesting to compare these statements with Thorburn's (1982) analysis of the television melodrama, which argues that since the story's end is never in sight, the dramatic tension inheres in the short conversational segments with their heavy emotional loading. The steady barrage of these crises is what makes for the melodrama. Members of a kibbutz group and a Russian group put it rather similarly:

ORLY: I don't remember one scene which did not consist of a conversation between a man and a woman, not necessarily married. He talks to that one, then they change the scene, and she talks to that other one. There is a lot of tension in these conversations, actually in every scene. There is no sex in the program, but the relationships between the sexes are very prominent. (kibbutz group 81)

TAMARA: Normally, the series of events would be sufficient for a hundred families; suddenly everything fell on the family. . . We forgive Katzman (the series's producer). It's true he has to hold the audience, to drag the time. (Russian group 63)

Attention is also given to the repetitiveness of the story. The point that the story is always the same was proposed in one of our Moroccan groups but was rejected by the others. Thus, Yossi (group 20) counters the interviewer's request that the group relate the story by saying "the same as last week; believe me, (they are) the same faces." But the group ignores him in favor of a detailed discussion of what the story is about. The Americans, on the other hand, are much more insistent about the formulaic aspect of the story; they point out that J. R. plays a weekly trick with somebody as his intended victim.

MICH: Well, it's very well written though they'll always let you hang, you know, at the end of the program, and you, well, like we say, we got to tune in and see what happened—to so-and-so and so-and-so from the episode.

DEANA: And two years ago they ended the season when J. R. got shot and we had to wait a couple of months to find out who shot him, and this year they had the big fire, and now you're going to have to wait for couple of months to find out what happened. (American group 16)

Apart from identifying *Dallas* as a soap opera, there is occasional awareness of the way in which *Dallas* is *not* a soap opera. The Americans specialize in these nuances, emphasizing that *Dallas* is in prime time, and that the leading character, in this devil-like surrealism, is somehow different. "Without J. R.," someone says, "the rest of it is soap garbage" (group 14). Comparisons are made between *Dallas* and its successors, like *Dynasty*, in character delineation, geographic location, dramatic inventions, and rhythm.[11]

Sometimes *Dallas* is perceived as belonging to less obvious genres. A number of comments compare *Dallas* to Godfather stories, noting the similarity to the adventures of a Mafia family, just as Mary Mander (1983) does in her academic analysis of the program. Japanese viewers prove more familiar with American culture than Israelis, and several of them join Michael Arlen (1980) in associating the Ewings with the legendary oil dynasty of Edna Ferber's *Giant*. Made famous in its Hollywood film version, this saga depicts intrigue and sibling rivalry of a wealthy family living in an isolated, large, gloomy ancestral mansion. One Japanese discussant recalls *Gone With the Wind*, describing the attachment of Southern gentry to Tara and the land.

Many comments compare *Dallas* to the genres of their own cultures, emphasizing differences. The Russians, in particular, make pejorative comparisons to the family sagas of Pushkin and Tolstoy, for example, while the Japanese also make analogies to the family dramas of Chekhov, defining *Dallas* as a "family collapse story," moulded on the pattern of *The Cherry Orchard*. Americans mention *The Forsythe Saga* and *The Brothers*, pointing out that the stories of these families, unlike that of the Ewings, are interwoven with political and historical process. *Dallas*'s characters are afloat in space and time. They do not even age. Comparing *Dallas* with *Forsythe*, an American group member remarks:

> CAROL: If you watched it for six to eight weeks, and you started when they were twenty and you ended when they were sixty, the whole life went through what was happening in the country at the same time—the strikes in 1926 and so forth. Here, nothing. I mean the atom bomb could be blown up somewhere, and the people in *Dallas* wouldn't care. (American group 4)

The syntactic critics see the program as a story of endless turn-taking between the good guy and the bad guy rather than as a developing narrative. Indeed, one American went so far as to say that it is not so much a moral struggle as an amoral entertainment, like wrestling, he says.

> GREG: When I watch it, sometimes I feel like I'm just about watching wrestling team matches or something like that. The bad guys keep squashing the good guys, using all dirty tricks, and then every once in a while, some good guy will resort to the bad guys' tricks and, you know, stomp on the bad guy for a while, and all the crowd will go, yeah, yeah, yeah, and then the next week, the bad guys are on top again, squashing the good guys. (American group 3)

Dramatic Function

Analysis of the dramatic functions of the characters is part and parcel of the same kind of critical ability. By their response to our question, "Why all the fuss about babies?" the three Western groups—but especially the Americans—revealed an awareness of how babies propel the story along, in generating conflict, for example. The Americans are aware, further, that the babies need not even be seen on the screen but only to be present in the minds of the characters. In this connection it is interesting to note that some Japanese viewers—they are not acquainted with the serial—retell the first episode in terms of the potential dramatic function of the two persons perceived as the central characters.[12] Thus, the two keys to how the narrative will continue are identified as an internal and an external force. From within the family, they predict, J. R. will move the story along by virtue of being a trickster, while as an outsider, Pamela, the newcomer wife, will advance the story through her love for Bobby, thus breaking the vicious pattern of the rival families' feuds, transforming Bobby and making the newlywed couple into the spiritual, if not material, winners. One of the Japanese viewers speculated on the delicate balance between the central characters needed to make the story interesting: "If Pamela is going to control J. R., the program won't be interesting because what is interesting is J. R.'s tricks."

The obvious references to the personification of good and evil or to the function of the minor strands of the story in providing tension-release are further examples of sophistication about how stories are constructed and punctuated.

> MICH: They kind of use (Ray) as a fill in . . . I seem to focus on the hard-core stuff, and every time they show Ray in there, it is just like a side-track when you go and get a cup of coffee.(American group 16)

Business

The Americans, again, are the most sophisticated about that other set of building blocks of television narrative, namely, the business behind the box. Their critical statements show keen awareness that characters come and go, not only as a function of the needs of the story but also as a function of the deals they strike with producers and of the accident rate on the Santa Monica Freeway. Two of the American groups contemplated the possibility that Pamela's attempted suicide may be related to her contractual state. The similarity in the narrative of *Dallas* and *Dynasty* are also remarked upon and attributed to the "invisible college" of writers and producers. Consistent with such economic or gossipy framing, Americans—when asked how the serial can ever end—tend to say "by catastrophe," as if to say that only some deus ex machina can do it. This is in contrast to other groups who—when asked the same question about how to end the story—say either that there will be a happy end for everybody or that the good and bad will be appropriately rewarded. These latter endings are consistent either with a more referential view of the characters as real or with a metalinguistic view of a traditional story. By their catastrophic ending, the Americans seem to be saying that the story cannot be stopped by inherent or conventional means and that only radical external intervention will do. The Americans also note that the great climaxes at the end of the season create a tension strong enough to hold the viewer through the summer months and that the best programs are broadcast during the semi-annual special ratings ("sweeps").[13]

While far less knowledgeable than the Americans about what goes on behind the scenes, the Russians know, nevertheless, that something is going on. They are not interested, however, in actors' contractual relations but in the business of buying and selling audiences and are suspicious of the ideological control of the program by elites. Indeed, the Russians, curiously, are the only ones who take the credits seriously. They know the names of the producers, speculate on what motivates them, and sometimes believe that they are being manipulated from on high, that the producers are propaganda mongers.[14]

There is no question that the Americans are far ahead of the others in the making of metalinguistic statements of all kinds. They are the only ones who show awareness or interest in the business aspect; they are the most sensitive of all groups about the nuances of genres and why *Dallas* is and is not a soap opera and how and why it compares with its several spin-offs. The Russians also show a high level of syntactic awareness but their emphasis is more on the formulaic aspects of the story and its valuelessness as literature; they are also more likely to suspect that some sort of propaganda is at work. Kibbutzniks tend to pay more attention to the segmental structure of the program as a sequence of two- and three-person conversations interwoven through the episode and its never-endingness.

Pragmatic Criticism

Self-awareness of the nature and causes of involvement in the semantics and syntactics is what we call pragmatic criticism. Some groups express this awareness with respect to the nature of their involvement in characters and themes; others are aware of the ways in which the structure of the program captures and occupies their imagination.

The naturalness of the characters is remarked by a number of discussants, particularly Americans. It is the awareness that the characters are acting "themselves"—that it is very difficult to separate between character and actor in the ubiquitous genre of soap opera—that puts people in this particular kind of critical mood, for example,

> DEANA: This guy is such a jerk I really get mad. You know I always thought that these women that saw actors and actresses in airports and called them by their stage names or whatever was the last part they played . . . but I honestly feel that if I saw this guy in the airport—I would be tempted to tell him off—even knowing actually that this is a part, I would really like to ram him hard. (American group 9)

Viewers are also self-aware of the way in which involvement may result from the similarities between family problems in the story and family problems of their own:

EITAN: I would say that somehow we enjoy it because the problems the Ewings have evoke some of the dark secrets which exist in every family. I used to say that my family was a zoo until I discovered that every family has different animals, but everybody has a zoo at home.

HELEN: If you will take your own family and create a series for us every week . . . I would not like to hurt you . . .

EITAN: No, you don't hurt me. I agree with you, this is my own family zoo, but I think every family has such zoos. (kibbutz group 80)

The genre, too, is recognized as a source of involvement. A number of discussants mention the built-in compulsion to find out what will happen next week, or better, to spend the week inventing possible solutions to the last show's problems or contriving next week's continuation. This participatory function is well known from the earliest research on radio soap opera (Herzog, 1941) and, indeed, from literary research on novels published in installments in popular magazines, such as Dickens (Iser, 1978).

Altogether, the point of this pragmatic criticism is that it connects reflexively between the text and the reader's self-definition of his experience or of his role. Thus, the ludic viewer fancies himself in the role of putative writer as well as reader or of a sports spectator placing bets on likely outcomes. Indeed, one viewer called *Dallas* a game of risk, and another called it a wrestling match.

More traditional viewers refuse to play games and insist that they are viewing—licentiously perhaps—as people with moral convictions that predetermine their response to the program. The Arab groups, for example, regularly speak of the program in terms of "we" and "them," and although this polarity is by no means metalinguistic, it does imply a self-consciousness about the role of the reader. The following is a familiar illustration:

MACHLUF: You see, I'm a Jew wearing a skullcap, and I learned from this film to say (quoting from Psalms) "Happy is our lot" that we're Jewish. Everything about J. R. and his baby, who has maybe four or five fathers, I don't know . . . I see that they're all bastards. (Moroccan group 20)

The Japanese, as well, explain their noninvolvement in the program in terms of the difference between the two cultures[15] and in terms of their attitude toward American society. As one nonviewer claims, the Japanese *could* have been affected by the series "some years ago (when) Japanese had admired American life and society." Now that they are more critical of the Americans, they see beyond the glamour into the violence within the family, and it only makes them wary.

By contrast, the Russian and American viewers show their self-awareness by explicitly excluding themselves from the kinds of effects that they attribute to others. In pointing out the ideological manipulation they perceive in the story, the Russians are saying that others, not themselves, will be affected. Similarly, the Americans who insist that the program has no message or moral for them are equally insistent that the rest of the world will misread *Dallas* as an image of America full of neurotic people walking on streets paved with gold.

Further Development of the Critical Code

When the Japanese focus discussions reached us—some three years after we had coded and analyzed all the other groups—we noted the high concentration of critical statements among the Japanese. The Japanese make very few referential statements—fewer, proportionately, than any other group—probably because they had not seen the program previously. In order to compare the critical statements made by the Japanese with those of the other groups, we decided to expand on the categories of Table 8.2. In doing so, we added the pragmatic realm to the list and further subdivided the semantic and the syntactic, adding construction (awareness of the program as having been put together) and mimetic (reflection on the reality of the program and on how reality is presented). The units of analysis are far more refined than in the previous coding, and as a result, there is a much larger number of critical categories.[16]

Table 8.4 compares the distribution of critical statements made by the Japanese groups with the combined distribution of the Russians and Americans, the two most metalinguistic groups. The table shows the Japanese to exceed the Americans and Russians in their attention to genre and formulae. They also make many statements about themes, perhaps because of their effort to grapple for a summary of the first sampling of the serial. They are slightly higher than the other two groups in their attention to the pragmatic, giving most of

Table 8.4. The Critical Statements, by Category, of the Japanese Groups and the Russians/Americans (in percent)

	Japanese	Russians/Americans
Syntactic statements	45	60
genre	15	6
dramatic function	3	7
business	1	6
construction	26	41
Semantic statements	34	22
themes	12	1
messages	5	6
mimetic	17	15
Pragmatic statements	22	17
Total number of statements (N = 100%)	(453)	(1114)

their attention to the incompatibility between the program and Japanese expectations of home drama.

The two Western groups specialize in statements about the constructedness of the story, a new category which was added to give expression to the large number of statements betraying the viewers' awareness that the story is designed, blueprinted, and assembled by writers and producers.

Conclusions: Types of Opposition

Having examined differences among types of critical statements, we are in a position to conclude the discussion of viewer involvement. We now argue that certain forms of critical decodings may also be hot. In other words, critical reactions do not necessarily imply distance; indeed, some of them are as intense as referential statements and entail equal emotional investment.

We propose, therefore, to summarize our argument by cross-tabulating the dimensions referential/critical and hot/cool. Table 8.5 shows the four resultant forms of involvement: moral, ideological, ludic and aesthetic. As should already be clear, each one of the ethnic communities specializes in one of these forms. The more traditional groups involve themselves morally, that is, they relate to the program as real and argue with it. The Russians, as we have seen specialize in the thematics of the program, becoming hot and bothered over the manipulative message they discern. The Americans and kibbutzniks are more cognitively and playfully involved in the reality of the program and thus fall in the referential/cool category, while the Japanese—and sometimes the Russians and the Americans—focus on the syntactics of the critical realm.

Each of these four forms of involvement may be associated with a type of defense against the influence of the program. Thus, the combination referential/hot may produce moral opposition to the content of the program, while critical/hot, through awareness of the manipulative construction of the message, may produce what we have called ideological opposition. Within the cool mode, referential/cool is associated with the ludic, and critical/cool may produce aesthetic opposition. It is evident that each pattern of involvement includes a mechanism of defense. The Arabs, accepting the program's reality, reject the values of the characters. The Russians are anxious about producers; they take them seriously and treat them as threatening. These are both confrontational stances—hot. The Americans and kibbutzniks reject the idea that the credibility or the value of the characters deserve to be taken seriously but express no doubt about the motives of the producers. The Japanese, like the

Table 8.5. Forms of Opposition

	Referential	Critical
Hot	moral	ideological
Cool	ludic	aesthetic

Russians, also worry about the producers, not over their morality, but over their competence. The questioning posture of the Americans, kibbutzniks, and Japanese include a reflexive or self-doubting component and suggests a more cool and cognitive type of involvement.

It should be reiterated that these types of critical statements about *Dallas* emerged in the course of focus-group conversations that did not require discussants to use the critical register.[17] Indeed, the two more traditional groups in our study volunteered only a small number of the sort of metalinguistic statements we have analyzed in this chapter, and all six ethnic groups, excepting the Japanese, talked more referentially than critically.

Critical reactions do not necessarily imply distance; indeed, some of them are genuinely hot in the intensity of their involvement and, sometimes, outrage. Indeed, the coolest kinds of critical framing—the syntactic statements—may lower the barrier to the penetration of unchallenged messages. In this sense, the Arabs and Russians are better protected than the Americans. When the Arab groups speak critically, they express awareness of the politics of the program and of a theme or message to which they are opposed; this parallels the normative opposition of Arabs and Moroccans in the referential realm. Some Russian groups go even further and perceive conspiracy; they think the producers may be willfully distorting reality in order to influence viewers.

The Russians also reject the program on aesthetic grounds, by comparison with the literary genres with which they are familiar. This aesthetic opposition takes its place alongside their ideological opposition.

Again, the forms of opposition are diverse. Moral opposition may be either referential—when it accepts the message as reality, gives it standing, and argues—or critical, when it betrays an awareness of the (manipulative) construction of an ideological message. Indeed, all critical statements—certainly including aesthetic opposition—may be deemed oppositional in the sense of rejecting the referential reading.[18] This may clarify a confusion in some of the literature on oppositional readings (Morley, 1980).[19]

The types of opposition may be presented schematically, by cross tabulating the hot/cool dimension with the referential/critical. Table 8.5 shows that the combination referential/hot may produce moral opposition to the content of the program; while critical/hot, through awareness of the manipulative construction of the message, may produce ideological opposition. Within the cool mode, referential/cool is associated with the ludic, and critical/cool may produce aesthetic opposition. Each of these forms of opposition constitutes a different kind of defense against the message of the program and, contrariwise, a different form of vulnerability.

We have said at various points that each type of opposition may both defend a viewer and cause him to be open to influence. Thus, moral defense is based on giving a program standing and, thus, deeming it worthy of argument. Ideological defense is vulnerable because it is based on automatic transformations, as if to say that the opposite of the message *is* the truth. Aesthetic defense risks letting the ideological message slip by, while the playful escape of ludic defense may fail to return one to the ground.

9

NEITHER HERE NOR THERE: WHY *DALLAS* FAILED IN JAPAN*

To this point, we have argued that critical statements may be no less involving than referential ones. The cognitive framing of the serial—what we call cool, what Eco calls smart—may be a source of considerable satisfaction and no less a ticket of admission than referential framing to the networks of discussion of such programs.

Examining the Japanese focus groups reminds us that the critical is not *necessarily* involving. When we described critical framing as involving, the statements we analyzed came from regular, even enthusiastic, viewers of *Dallas*. Their critical statements about genre, dramatic function, mimesis, and the like—and certainly their playful reactions in relating to the characters— permitted them to enjoy the program while seeing through it. Even the statements based on ideological opposition to the program came from those who were attracted to the program while condemning it. Moreover, the makers of these statements were the same people who made the referential statements! The critical need not be associated only with the sophisticated enjoyment of analytic viewing, but it can also lead to rejection and disengagement. Even if the analytic work is pleasurable, it may take one away from the program rather than deeper into it.

The Japanese exceeded all the other groups in the proportion of their critical statements; in fact, the Japanese make very few referential statements. This may be due to their lack of knowledge of the program and its characters (*Dallas* having failed in Japan after being broadcast for only some six months). It may be due to extraneous factors, such as the misleading name of the program, or perhaps, as some discussants suggested, the lateness of the time slot in which

*Professor Sumiko Iwao is co-author of this chapter.

130

the program was broadcast.[1] But it may also be due to the fact that the program was explicitly tried and rejected, for reasons we attempt to determine.

Why did the Japanese rejected the Ewings when so many other nations, although not all, welcomed them so enthusiastically? To answer this, we will examine both the reasons explicitly offered by focus-group members themselves and the implicit explanations embedded in their discussions. The heavy proportion of critical statements made by the Japanese should be seen as a combination of their original attitudes toward the program proposed to them by the Asahi Broadcasting Company and the role that we may presume them to have assumed when we sat them down to view and to talk about a program which they knew to have failed. The Japanese differ from the other ethnic communities not only in approaching the program cold but also in their definition of the research situation. If the Russians suspected us of not noticing that they were viewing in spite of their better judgment, the Japanese saw themselves as helping us to understand why they were being consistent with their better judgment in *not* viewing. If the Moroccans felt that they were being tested and the Russians felt they were testing us, the Japanese surely felt that they were serving as our consultants on the problem of defining the limits to the diffusion of American popular culture abroad.

One might add that the Japanese respondents, more than the Israelis and the Americans, might be considered captive audiences who would otherwise have walked out on the program, as some of them claimed they would have done. It should be borne in mind that the Japanese have a highly developed television menu, consisting of the prestigious public broadcasting of the NHK and a variety of commercial networks.[2] The genres of Japanese television are a mixture of traditional and Western forms, and particularly relevant for our purposes is the Japanese version of the soap opera, the so-called home drama. Unlike Israel, where the only practical choice on a winter Sunday night was viewing the Ewings, the Japanese had a number of homemade choices to which they clearly felt greater affinity.[3] It is a sobering thought that if Israel had its own soap opera, and if it were aired at the same time as *Dallas*, the local program would almost certainly win out. We know this, in fact, from other nations whose indigenous soap operas are more popular, or certainly no less popular, than the much more elaborate imported ones.

The Japanese focus-group members, upon seeing the first episode of the American serial, refused the multidimensional invitation to involvement in the program. The Japanese willfully deployed their critical ability to stay away, to resist both referential and ludic temptations. They refused to let themselves get hooked. But they themselves admitted that at another time—when America was their model—the program might have been given a chance. Even now, some say, had they overcome their initial impulse to judge the program incompatible, they might well have begun to enjoy it. In other words, we have before us a complicated exercise in the self-attribution of consistency.

Putting these complexities aside, we will attempt through the realm of cultural compatibility to answer the question, "Why did *Dallas* fail in Japan?" A straightforward reading of the protocols of the eleven Japanese discussions leads inexorably to the proposition that Japanese viewers regarded *Dallas* as incompatible with their values and tastes. The theme of inconsistency emerges from their discussions, and we propose that this helps to explain why *Dallas* failed in Japan. But more than this, we believe that this concept may be projective of central concerns in Japanese culture. If we are correct in this belief, our research method may be useful not only for an understanding of different readings and reactions to an alien cultural product but also for a poor-man's anthropology of cultural differences. That is, we find it useful to immerse ourselves not in an authentic text of another culture—as Ruth Benedict (1947) did—but in the decodings by members of that culture of a text not their own.[4]

During World War II, Ruth Benedict (1947) and Margaret Mead (1953) tried to understand inaccessible cultures, particularly the Japanese, through close readings of their films. They attempted to *infer* the values of the culture from its visual (and verbal) representations. We chose to study culture at a distance through observation of members of different ethnic groups interacting with a major example of American popular culture. From our observations emerge self-revealing comparisons from which we can infer something of the values of the receiving cultures and the nature of critical concepts, as well as the aesthetic, moral, social, and psychological expectations addressed by each culture to television entertainment. The attraction of making these inferences explicit in the case of the Japanese was irresistible.

A Methodological Reminder

Inasmuch as *Dallas* had failed quickly and some time before the extension of our study to Japan, the focus groups we assembled in Tokyo obviously could not see the program on the air. Nor did we arrange for Japanese husbands and wives to view the program together, as this does not simulate the normal viewing unit. Middle-class husbands in Japan return home late after long working hours, a long commute, and the customary tension-reducing drinking session, and women typically view television alone or with children. Moreover, there is reason to believe that women are more spontaneous when in the presence of other women. For all these reasons, we chose to assemble eleven focus groups of either men or women, inviting them to discuss the first episode of *Dallas* in which Pam is introduced to the Ewings after her elopement with Bobby.[5] The episode was dubbed in Japanese, and had been broadcast about a year earlier, but almost none of the sixty or so discussants had seen it.

The eleven focus groups were contacted informally and invited to view the *Dallas* episode and to join in a discussion. The meetings were held in various places—community center, university, and homes—and were conducted by discussion leaders along the lines of the same interview guide used by discussion leaders in the Israeli and American settings. Similar background questionnaires were filled in by all participants.

The eleven discussions were translated from the Japanese into Hebrew and English, and the coding was done as reported in Chapter 8. Our analysis here, however, is qualitative and impressionistic within the overall guidelines of the quantitative materials already presented.

Inconsistent and Incompatible: Why *Dallas* Failed in Japan

Over and over again, the Japanese focus groups point to inconsistencies and incompatibilities that trouble them. One set of inconsistencies has to do with semantics, that is, with contradictions in the story and in the actions of the characters. At the syntactic level, too, they note how poorly the program fits any of the genres to which the program might claim to belong, especially how much it violates their expectation of the genre of home drama in which they place *Dallas*. At the pragmatic level as well, the Japanese are troubled by incompatibilities between the American narrative and the perception of their own culture and sociohistorical situation. The Japanese conceive the story as being compatible with an earlier period of Japanese culture from which they have since departed and possibly compatible with the culture they perceive to be characteristic of an America which—in the words of one viewer—has recently been abandoned as a role model. Some question the American reality that the program claims to depict. These are various forms of aesthetic evaluation, in terms of which the Japanese groups both analyze the program and explain their unwillingness or inability to become involved.

Inconsistency Within the Story Semantics

Japanese viewers are very attentive to inconsistencies in the construction of the story. They insist that the narrative is "neither here nor there." If Bobby and Pam elope, presumably against the wishes of their parents, how can they return to the parental ranch immediately after the honeymoon fully expecting to rejoin the extended family? If they are so rich, how is it that they set the table by themselves and do not have private tutors for their children? Inconsistencies of this kind seem to bemuse the Japanese viewers and lead them to question the worth of the program: "Although it describes family, how is it there is no love or sympathy? 'Wet' elements are lacking here" (group 6). Sometimes, however, such inconsistencies are praised; some Japanese viewers liked the idea that they are so rich they have their own helicopter but the bride carries in her own suitcase (group 1).

Mimetic problems also trouble the Japanese viewers, namely, that the characters are not believable and that there is a credibility gap between the story and their image of America, especially the American rich. "It is a story of a remote world," someone said. "Yes," agrees a fellow group member, "it is remote. It is not a possible story" (group 6).

The characters are too stereotyped for the Japanese viewers; they are not subtle enough: "I would like to have some more complex characters with shading," said a group member (group 1). There is no real character development. "Even the bad guys should have some weak points" (group 9) "so we can have pity on them" (group 5). "In this case, *Dallas* is more like a Western," said a viewer (group 5) where the good are good and the bad are bad. In other words, the characters are too stereotypically good or bad, strong or weak, without being tempered by the contradictory elements that characterize human beings in Japanese eyes. Columbo, for example, is liked in Japan because he betrays weakness and approachability. The *Dallas* villain is all black. The women are too uniformly strong, untempered by the weaknesses which make women attractive. The Japanese discussion groups agreed that they did not want to see women crying continually—that is too old-fashioned. But neither did they want too much assertiveness; indeed, they sometimes confessed that they wished to see women mistreated, as in the popular and serialized *Oshin*.

The Dallas characters are blatant, showing no restraint in their passions for power, wealth, and sex. Scenes of sexual overtures among coworkers or compromising sexual adventures are hardly hidden in *Dallas*, and the Japanese find these hard to enjoy. Altogether, the program violates Japanese sensibilities about how people would interact publicly and privately in order to achieve and maintain aesthetically harmonious relationships.

The Japanese perceive the characters as flat and, moreover, think they all look alike. At least in this first viewing of the series, Japanese viewers felt Americans indistinguishable from each other! "The story is too simple and foolish" (group 5). "The plot may be complicated, but the characters are too simple." J. R. is an exception to this oversimplification, they agree, because he is good and bad, but he is not subtle enough. "In *Dallas* the bad ones show their evil openly, whereas in Japanese drama they are more cunning and set traps in secret" (group 5).

They sense an incongruence between what is considered rich in *Dallas* and what they believe to be truly rich in America. Unlike our viewing groups from other cultures, some Japanese consider *Dallas* shabby—clothes, houses, characters, and all—and are unconvinced that this story is about the American rich. Other Japanese viewers, who accept the Ewings as a dynastic family, complain that marriage based on romantic love is a middle-class phenomenon and does not fit the upper class:

> KAZUKO: In the high society, marriage is very much like in Meiji Taishoo period in our country. Very conservative. Personal and warm relations in marriage are middle class and lower than that. Then it is hard for me to believe that such a marriage between Bobby and the girl, which is typical to the middle class, happens in high society. (group 8)

Perhaps, they propose, this is a story more about premodern or, maybe, postmodern American society than about the America that conquered Japan. The America of *Dallas* is either about the rugged pioneer days, some viewers suggest, or an anticipation of American decline. Reference is made to images of the old Texas, where everything was high, daring, ruthless, exploitative, and dynastic. Other viewers suggest that perhaps *Dallas* is a collapse story—a genre in which they also place Chekhov's plays—in which the back-stabbing and intrigue within class and family are metaphors for the disintegration of American hegemony.

An occasional voice, nevertheless, found the program believable. "Except for ranch and money," she said, "I saw it with a sense of nearness. I was rather attracted" (group 1).

Syntactic Inconsistency

At a more abstract level, the question of consistency also arises with respect to the construction of the story. Assuming that this is a melodrama, they ask, how is it that it begins only after the marriage of Pam and Bobby rather than during the courtship? And if it is a romance, why is Pam so ready to offer her loyalty to the rival, rich family that destroyed her own? In the words of Kyooru (group 5), "If it were a melodrama, she would have said 'let's leave such a home.'" If this is an escapist tale—and we shall see that the Japanese like such stories—then why do they not let romance and goodness flow? What they are doing is more fit for a documentary, they say, except that it clearly is not a documentary. A documentary would rightly show us the true character of high society, namely, that marriages are instrumental and not romantic. So why do they not make up their minds? "It's not this, and it's not that"—it is not science fiction, and it is not a traditional story—says another viewer (group 3).

Japanese viewers also have much to say about the way in which the program is scripted and filmed, beyond what they have to say about the plot. They say it is flat, and lacking in accent. They do not mean, apparently, that it is without crises, but rather that it is only a series of recurrent crises which do not build into a crescendo. This deprives the viewers of an opportunity for catharsis. Viewers also criticize the tempo of the program; many say it is too fast, too cluttered.

Unlike the never-ending American soap opera—about which they are obviously complaining—home drama tends either to tell a complete story each time (that is, the same characters return each time to tell of a new problem, as in a dramatic series, not a serial), or the story is serialized, moving—not endless—towards a resolution or attainment of a goal that comes in the last episode. The American soap has no last episode if it is successful—the best have been going on for thirty years or more.

Another inconsistency noted by Japanese viewers has to do with the title and advertising of the program. Focus-group members who actually sat through an episode realized that they had an altogether misleading image of what *Dallas* is all about. Some associated the title with the Kennedy assassination; others imagined "the lonely hot desert . . ." devoid of "any impression of love and humanity." Still others wondered why a story about landed gentry should be labeled with the name of an industrial city. Focus-group members made clear that these associations are unattractive for them or misrepresentations of the neither-here-nor-there sort.

Several of the respondents went so far as to suggest that had they not been misled and put off by the wrong images, they might have chosen to view the program. Some were on the verge of admitting that they would be interested if the program were given another chance. The problem of titles is one which occupies, of course, and the problem is all the more acute in the diffusion of cultural products across linguistic boundaries. Indeed, one might venture that *Dynasty* is called *Denver Clan* in Germany precisely to capitalize on the affinity with its predecessor, *Dallas*. One group blamed the staff of Japanese editors for poorly labeling the name of the episode (group 3).

Incompatibility with Present-Day Japan: A Pragmatic Problem

We used to identify with America, say the Japanese discussants, but we do not any more. We are beyond the stage of material aggrandizement, and we are not at the stage of decline. America was the model for postwar Japan, they say, where materialism, ambition, mobility, class differentiation, and competition were major values. But in present-day Japan, they tell us, there is a decline in the interest in money and achievement and a return to values of family and harmony in human relations. "Money-hungry stories are not popular among Japanese dramas," concluded one viewer (group 6). Obviously, we will not here judge the correctness of this self-image but merely report on what we have learned about it.

What we infer from their analysis is a three-phase theory of Japanese development—an old Japan, a postwar Japan, and a Japan of the present day. The old Japan was based on extended family and dynasty, where birth-order privilege, the centrality of inheritance, and the powers of mother-in-law were characteristic of the upper class and the feudal social system. In the second phase America was the model for Japan, and individualism, ambition, and materialism were central values. Present-day Japan—the third phase—is characterized by the return from competition to harmony and from individualism to familism.

Dallas, they say, is like phase one—dynasty, birth order, feuds over inheritance, etc. Indeed, it is noteworthy that the Japanese viewers often name the Ewings by the order of their birth—first son, second wife (i.e., Pam, the second son's wife), and so on, much as the Arabs do (see Chapter 5). It also has something of the materialism of phase two, they note, thus pointing both to the inconsistency of historical periods when translated into Japanese terms and to the fact that both of these periods are now behind them and well-forgotten: "We want to forget things like mother-in-law power" (group 5). "All we want nowadays,"—in phase three—is good relations with relatives; we are ready to abandon money, as they are not in America. Good life in old age is more important than money, which is taxed away anyway. Honor is more important than riches (group 5). In other words, Japanese viewers are saying that *Dallas* is old fashioned [sic!] and, therefore, dull.

Some discussants, less concerned with social change, point to the incompatibility between the program and primordial Japanese values. Atsuko of group 5, for example explains the incompatibility of the predatory themes in *Dallas*, not least the family infighting, with the basically "grass-eating" personality of the Japanese. The Americans, he insists, are "meat-eaters," and the character of their fighting is unacceptable to the Japanese. He expresses some sympathy for first sons and landed families who have something important to fight about. But not that way! says the respondent. If they were Japanese, they would do it otherwise:

> KYOOKO: As the firstborn (J. R.) has a lot of things to protect. And in order to protect his own honor he has no choice but to fight.
> ATSUKO: Well, if he were a Japanese, even if he has a lot to protect, he would not do what J. R. did. It might be the difference between meat-eating by people and grass-eating people. Europeans and Americans are warlike. (group 5)

Inconsistency with Japanese Expectations of Television Home Drama

In addition to the frustration over the lack of consistency in the construction of the story and in its mimetics, Japanese viewers feel frustrated over the incompatibility between *Dallas* and the kind of home drama they want and have learned to expect from television. They are concerned here not only with the structure of the narrative but also with its pragmatics. In other words, they regret their inability to become emotionally involved.

When the Japanese complain about *Dallas*, they have home drama in mind. They say that *Dallas* is cluttered with too many stories and too many people, and that it is too demanding in the sense that it always leaves you hanging in the midst of conflict over one or another of the stories. There is resentment that the episode is not complete in itself and does not end on a harmonious note. The Japanese do not like unhappy endings; said Misato (group 8), "If each episode ended with a happy ending it might have been different." Another group member added that the Japanese want to go to bed happy.

But, as is evident from some of the earlier examples, Japanese people also like to go to bed with dreams. "*Dallas* doesn't give us a dream," complained a member of group 9. We want something romantic, said many others, meaning that they want their emotions to be engaged by the program. Either give us something we know, something recognizable to ordinary, salaried people with dull lives, or give us romance, said a respondent in group 8. We do not laugh at them, but we also cannot identify, said a member of group 5, echoing the neither-here-nor-there aspect of Japanese criticism of *Dallas* as falling between genres. "It lacks the elements which are common in Japanese drama: humanism" (group 6).

Viewers complained that the program is too violent (group 5) and does not provide the "congenial, warm feeling" they expect; there is no sense of a family eating dinner together, one of the hallmarks of Japanese home drama. Many viewers summed up this disappointment with the verdict that the program is tiring, that it makes them tense (group 7). *Dallas* "is very dark," they say (groups 1 and 6). We don't want to live with unhappiness until next week is the way this theme was summarized.

An American program that received high marks in Japan was *Little House on the Prairie.* This, they said, is good home drama consisting of good people, solved problems, openness to strangers, romantic themes, and separate episodes. The Japanese verdict appears to be that *Dallas* is failed home drama.

Danger! Conclusion

We have tried to make plain that a central theme, perhaps *the* central theme, in Japanese reactions to *Dallas* has to do with inconsistency. *Dallas* is inconsistent within itself, with its title, with the genre in which it presumes to belong, with the romantic expectations the Japanese have of this genre, with their aesthetic criteria for the construction of a television narrative, with their image of post-war American society, with their image of themselves, and with their image of men. Some of this is internal inconsistency and apparent contradiction; some of it is incompatibility between the cultural product and this audience. In Russian and Arab readings of *Dallas,* we also find a high degree of complaining about cultural incompatibility—moral incompatibility in the case of the Arabs and Moroccan Jews and aesthetic incompatibility in the case of the Russian Jews—but this prevented none of these groups from viewing and enjoying the program. The Russians, it is true, viewed with some embarrassment; they apologized to us for being such avid viewers. But viewers they were!

This suggests that inconsistency and incompatibility is more of a deterrent for the Japanese than for the other groups. It is interesting to recall Michael Arlen's (1980) point that one of the attractions of *Dallas* is precisely its moral unpredictability, as if inconsistency were a rule for a modern society that is experimenting—at least in the ludic experience of viewing—with the absence of clear, consistent, and structured expectations. For Arlen, *Dallas* thrives on its inconsistency and normative improvisations, in which it also invites viewers to join.

A related observation can be made from a structuralist point of view, namely, that the aesthetic form of the program—not only its content—arises from combinations of improbable and contradictory genres such as the nighttime soap opera, the Western, plus the romance (Newcomb, 1982), a Mafia variant of *Gone with the Wind,* a violent detective story grafted onto a family saga. Better than other groups, the Japanese *see* all these things but reject them. Television is not the place for liminal experiments; a home drama should be that and nothing more.

If it were not for the fact that the academic image of the Japanese asserts something quite opposite to these conclusions, we would now rest our case. Unfortunately for our argument, the anthropological study of the Japanese character seems to suggest that the Japanese *do* live comfortably with inconsistency. They are said to have situational morality, allowing free movement from the norms of one situation to another without experiencing the tensions of guilt or dissonance. We cannot do more than reiterate that we seem to have stumbled upon a quite different orientation in response to the screening, and since we cannot presume that our inductions are more authoritative than the major scholarship in the field, we can only attempt to propose several possible forms of reconciliation between the scientific literature on Japanese culture and our summary of eleven focus-group discussions of *Dallas*.

One possible basis for reconciliation would be to say that the Japanese are particular about the aesthetics or artistic forms: they want art—popular as well as traditional—to stay within its chosen form. Another possibility is to take careful note of the viewers' concern, not with moral inconsistency, but with cognitive inconsistency. They seem troubled by the unpersuasiveness of the situation; they may be saying, simply, not that it is *wrong* but that it makes no *sense* for Pam and Bobby to elope and then move in—that it is neither here nor there—without having to explain or negotiate or acknowledge how these two actions can coexist. Perhaps it is the abruptness of the transitions that disturb them, the action without talk. Subtlety is sorely missed: in the editing, in human relations, and in the characters. The crudeness is incompatible with their expectations both of life and of art. It may well be, therefore, that the Japanese are indeed practitioners of situational morality but not of situational incongruity.

Our interpretations find some support in Lebra (1976). While endorsing the centrality of what she calls interactional relativism—whereby morality is fine-tuned to the symbolic interactions that underlie all interpersonal relationships—she emphasizes how much the Japanese invest sensitivity, compulsiveness, circumspection, and refinement in the creation and maintenance of pleasant and smooth social relationships. Everything must be brought into harmony or fusion in smoothing social relationships. The aesthetic sensibilities of the Japanese are concerned with small detail and staying in tune with the surroundings. Thus, *within* given situations, a consistency of tone must be achieved and maintained so that participants—and, indeed, the situations themselves—may find their proper place. Thus, perhaps the problem is not moral at all, but aesthetic. Even if the Japanese are flexible enough to allow for variations in morality that may be called for in different situations, they seem altogether perfectionist in their demand for accuracy and consonance of detail within a situation.

10
DALLAS AND GENESIS: PRIMORDIALITY AND SERIALITY IN POPULAR CULTURE

We have tried to show how *Dallas* invites very different kinds of viewers—educationally and ethnically—to become involved in their several ways. But what is it about a program like *Dallas*—or perhaps what is it about the soap opera genre to which it is related—that makes this kind of multidimensional participation possible?

In attempting to answer this question, we were led by the viewers to two aspects of the *Dallas* genre, the semantic dimension, which draws so heavily on primordial themes of human relations, and the syntactic dimension of seriality, which regularly combines and recombines this set of basic narrative elements to tell endless variations of the same story. We suggest that these two dimensions of the genre constitute invitations to the viewer to invest his emotions, empathy, and expertise as a card-carrying member of a kinship group and to invest his imagination and puzzle-solving predilections as a seasoned viewer in the game of guessing how the program will develop next week.

In fact, the idea of the universal appeal of soap opera as a drama of kinship in which we are all connoisseurs has been noted by others, both in general (Newcomb, 1974; Fiske, 1988) and with respect to programs like *Dallas* (Swanson, 1982; Tracey, 1985).[1] The idea of seriality as a form of aesthetic pleasure has also been stated, most recently by Umberto Eco (1985). Our point of departure does not proceed from a content analysis of the text to some imagined reader supposedly constructed by the text, but inductively from real readers—and the variations in their readings—to those aspects of the text which invite different levels of decoding and different forms of involvement. Thus, we can show that Eco's two readers (the naive and the smart), ostensibly corresponding to semantic and syntactic decodings, may in reality be the same person. To be able to show that these two model readers can coexist in the same individual is one of the advantages of our method.

On How *Dallas* Invites Involvement

However devoted we have been to the primacy of viewers' decodings and to examining meanings from the readers' perspective, we do not, by any means, wish to propose that the readers are writing the text. We made our position clear in Chapter 2, in which we dissociated ourselves from those theories in literature and communication which treat the reader as altogether sovereign and the text as if it were an ink blot or an empty clothes hanger. This is the point, then, at which we wish to reintroduce the text. We will dwell on those attributes of *Dallas*—and of the soap-opera genre more generally—that facilitate the multifaceted patterns of involvement which the viewers assume.

Primordiality

Dallas is a primordial tale, echoing the most fundamental mythologies. Consider the parallels, mutatis mutandis, between *Dallas* and Genesis. Just as our forefathers were the giants of their time, dividing the world among themselves, so the characters in *Dallas* fill the whole of the frame, dwarfing governments and shutting out any aspect of the real world which they do not control. Gradually, readers of the story come to believe that the dynasty *is* the world, at least the world from which will emerge a nation and its rulers. This is obvious in the case of Genesis and in *Dallas*, too. Both professional critics and the American focus groups point to the relationship between the America of the Kennedy clan and the Ewings. The producers help, too, by choosing names like John and Bobby.

Dynasty is the major preoccupation of the first book of the Bible. The favored marriage between a son and his father's brother's daughter or granddaughter functions to keep property within the family and to enhance the family's power. The domestic arrangements in *Dallas* have a similar function: all of the family live together, and the constant threat to parcel out the inheritance is repeatedly avoided. In fact, there are more examples of dividing up family property in Genesis than in *Dallas*.

The biblical entanglement of business and family predates the modern separation of the two. But *Dallas* reverts, nevertheless, to the primordial model. The two institutions are inexorably intertwined in the text: each invades the other, and the same rules apply to both. Family is as instrumental as business, and business is as affective as family. Marriages are power alliances, and the elemental passions—rather than the rules of the game—govern business. Thus, J. R. buys up all the oil wells in Texas in order to bring home his estranged spouse, as Jacob worked for fourteen years in order to obtain his chosen wife.

Altogether, one might say that the Genesis story is about "the social construction of family" or, alternatively, about God's intervention in the planning of unusual births and deaths and "in reversals of the iron law of primogeniture" (Alter, 1981).[2] Consider how closely *Dallas* fits Alter's analysis of Genesis as the repeated election of a younger son to carry on the line "through some devious twist of destiny." The brothers in *Dallas*—J. R. and Bobby—are simple variations on Cain and Abel, Isaac and Ishmael, Jacob and Esau. The brothers compete for their parents' blessing; each brother seeks to be named the official heir; each brother tries to outdo the other in the instrumental (not moral) tests that will prove his qualifications; the parents conspire, each with his or her favorite, and manipulate each other on behalf of this favorite; brothers and parents divide in their inclinations toward nature and culture, excess and moderation, wildness and domesticity.

In Canaan as in *Dallas*, the key women have problems with fertility; they repeatedly fail in the mission of producing an heir; they are forced to acquiesce in the acquisition of other women's children; they have to endure the tension of the presence of these other women, who are, often enough, their own sisters or predecessors. Both in Canaan and in *Dallas*, there is concern for the continuity of the house (Lévi-Strauss, 1983). In Canaan, this means seeking out alliances with distant kin in order not to assimilate locally; in *Dallas* it involves making alliances with rival dynasties to subvert them from within. For a reminder of what all this looks like—and how complex it is—see Fig. 2.1.

A striking difference between the two texts is that the women in Canaan have a lot more influence on their husbands, both directly and indirectly, than the women in *Dallas*, who are basically victims. Another difference is that the Bible prefers the sedentary home lovers—the studious, the dream-decoders, and the dwellers in tents—to the hunters and the Dionysians of *Dallas*. We refrain from pronouncing *Dallas* more archaic than Genesis, but that would seem to be the case. *Dallas* is the id unbound (Gitlin, 1983). Unlike the rest of soap opera, the hero of *Dallas* is a villain or trickster whom Fiedler (1982), for one, would find compatible with his theory that the best of popular culture—including media culture—is subversive of the bourgeois order, even if the message is regressive rather than progressive.

Even without explicit mention of sources, the mythic reverberations figure in many of the group discussions. For example, Ayad (Arab group 40) tells the *Dallas* story as follows: "It's about a rich family who have a large inheritance. They have oil, and two sons. The older son is a cheat. He wanted to grab control of all the wealth of his father and mother. The younger one tried to share in the property but the older one schemed and plotted to get the money. And two brothers quarreled." Notice how this quote omits the name of the characters in favor of their primordial roles and how familiar it all sounds. A more sophisticated version of this same kind of telling is by Eitan, a member of one of the kibbutz groups (group 80). "He was the elder son, and it's as if he was constantly trying to prove his worth to his parents. There was another (a third) brother whom the mother loved, and baby Bobby was loved by the father." A Japanese viewer also recognizes the primordial quality of these relationships but makes clear that these are better forgotten: "It certainly reminds us of the Japanese before the war. Elements such as inheritance, relationship between bride and mother-in-law—and powerful eldest son—these are points we want to forget."

There are different levels of sophistication; different theories that are invoked in telling, attributing motivation, and interpreting; and a different selection of issues. But sophisticated or not, mythic or not, we are all connoisseurs of these human relations and the psychology, sociology, and politics that define them. In other words, all viewers—at their level of sophistication and embedded in their culture—will find the narrative of the embroilments of kinship familiar and can become involved in how these characters are organizing their lives by comparing all of the other kinship texts they know—their own, their neighbors', and their forefathers'. It is likely that these kinship stories become so engrossing that the rest of social and political reality are shut out and not missed. This clearly has a political consequence.

Seriality

Involvement in these characters and their stories does not only reflect their enactment of human texts which are familiar to us but also reflects our week-to-week familiarity with them. We are connoisseurs not just of the situation but also of these very people who visit us so regularly. The familiarity which results from these weekly visits leads to the types of serious and playful identification with characters which we have already noted and to what is known as para-social interaction (Horton and Wohl, 1956), whereby people talk back to the characters, approvingly or disapprovingly, wishing them well or ill, urging them on, warning them of danger, worrying about the shame they will bring upon themselves. Indeed, seriality at the referential level often puts the viewer in a position of knowing more about a character than the character knows about himself, thus increasing the viewer's sense of control over the proceedings.

The Bible is a serial story, too; it is written as such and read as such. If repetitiveness is read as seriality, one may say that *Dallas* reenacts the same story with the same characters (they marry, unmarry, remarry continually; they die and are resurrected), while Genesis repeats the same stories in successive generations (Alter, 1981). If installments in-the-telling are essential to seriality, the weekly portions of the Bible read throughout Jewish and Christian worlds easily qualify. Moreover, Jewish synagogues have been "re-running" the Old Testament for 2000 years.

The open-minded nature of the family serial, of course, distinguishes it from some of the formulaic constraints of the series in which each story is self-contained and has to be resolved within fifty minutes (Newcomb, 1974). The serial allows for greater character development, more ambiguity, and more complexity. In a word, soap opera *is* more like reality, and it is no wonder that the stories enter into the realm of gossip. Moreover, the incomplete nature of each episode which leaves us hanging is reminiscent of the Zeigarnik Effect, which posits that interrupted tasks are better remembered than completed ones. This is yet a further dimension to help explain the active nature of reader involvement in serial narratives, as literary theorists (Iser, 1978) have already noted.

Seriality as an invitation to viewer involvement operates not just at the referential level but also at the metalinguistic level. At this level, viewers can name the genre and compare it to others; they can define its attributes and dramatic conventions, such as its division into subplots woven around characters and the staccato succession of two- and three-person dialogues. While the Americans compared the dynamics of *Dallas* to those of other television dramas, the Russians used the classic novel, much to the detriment of *Dallas*. It is clear from our study that television viewers are much better critics than they are usually given credit for. They become quite involved in these analyses and comparisons, which are often emotionally loaded. Indeed, some viewers, using the metalinguistic frame, can do things they do not do in the referential frame, namely, put the pieces together—combine and recombine them—as the writers do, while managing, nevertheless, to switch back and forth from the referential to the metalinguistic.

The key to viewer involvement at this level is in the realization that the story is like a contest in which the outcomes can repeatedly change or like a game in which the pieces can be put together in different ways. For long periods of time, the pieces are the characters as given—in number, gender, personality, and kinship roles. These characters can be rotated through a series of changing problems and relationships which are necessary to keep the story going. Viewers who relate to the program at this level become interested in how the characters will next confront a problem or each other. Consider Deanna (American group 9) who says, "Now it seems that Katherine has got her eye on Bobby, and in this one episode there is just a little bit of hint she will have her way." Continuing her thought, Jill says, "This will snap Pam out of her depression fast enough." And Deanna adds, "Or put her into a worse one."

Another viewer, Greg (American group 3), perceives a seesaw of domination and subordination at work, claiming it is like a wrestling match (see quotation on p. 123). Greg's involvement is in his intellectual perception of the program as contest and not in the emotions of soap opera. In the longer run, the characters themselves are changed, and viewers get the idea that the true pieces of the puzzle may not be the characters as given once and for all but structural attributes which are redivided among the characters. Thus, the good and the bad guys may not only struggle for domination but may actually exchange roles. This kind of jigsaw puzzle or Lego set or computer game invites the metalinguistic viewer to anticipate the combinatorial possibilities and to stay with the program to prove himself right.[3]

Primordiality, Seriality, and Types of Involvement

In an attempt to unveil what in the story motivates conversation and involvement, we have identified two major clues: primordiality and seriality. Primordiality evokes in the viewer an echo of the human experience and makes him an instant connoisseur of the *Dallas* variations on the elementary forms of kinship and interpersonal relations. Seriality is an obvious invitation to involvement in the regular visits of familiar characters, in the gossip of anticipation, and in discovering the rules of the producer's game.

The viewer may frame both the primordial and the serial either referentially or metalinguistically (critically). Thus, a referential framing of the primordial would experience the contemporary reality of sibling rivalry, for example, from both *Dallas* and Genesis. The metalinguistic framing would perceive both the similar paradigm that underlies the two stories as well as the different negative devices employed by the two sets of writers. Seriality may also be framed in either way. The referential framing of seriality attributes reality to the characters whose company we keep weekly—even between episodes (Booth, 1982)—while the metalinguistic framing of seriality is concerned with the art of construction of syntagmatic combinations.[4]

While Eco's distinction between the mythic and the strategic seems to correspond to our primordial and serial, we disagree with his exclusive attribution of the mythic to the naive reader and of the syntactic to the smart reader. For better or worse, real readers insist on behaving more ambiguously than the roles that theory assigns them. This is the point at which to recall that we have two kinds of readers: those who remain almost exclusively in the referential frame and those who commute between the referential and the metalinguistic. What we are now saying is that the primordial content of *Dallas* makes the referential reader more involved in reality, but so does its serial structure. That is, referential readers treat the characters as real not only because of semantics but also because of syntactics. For those readers who commute to the metalinguistic, we are suggesting that the serial structure gives them ample material for syntactic games but also that the primordial content allows them to play Lévi-Straussian games. There are two points here: (1) real readers often play both of Eco's roles, the smart and the naive; and (2) both major types of involvement (referential/naive, and critical/smart) are well served by the primordial/mythic and the serial/strategic dimensions of the story.

We cannot here presume to be able to solve the aesthetic problem of how commuting is possible, that is, how viewers can be involved at once in the reality of the narrative and in the strategies of its construction. One suggestion, however, arising from the present study calls attention to the compatibility of the family saga and the serial form. The naturalness of this fit would explain why the referential readers are so little disturbed by the ostensible artificiality of the construction. It may also explain why the commuters find it possible to move from the referential to the metalinguistic and back. The kinship story, obviously, repeats itself in reality, and we become aware of the structure of sameness and variation in real-life repetitions. It is an easy step from this reflexive position to thoughts of combining and recombining. It is another easy step from these thoughts to the awareness that the serial form is doing exactly this.[5]

The Structural Study of Myth: Our Own Game

In conclusion, let us try our own hand at playing this game. We can show that (1) the biblical paradigm of relations within and between generations finds an intertextual echo in *Dallas* and (2) that the workings of this paradigm are evident both in the parallel and intersecting stories of the two brothers. In other words, we will try to shuffle the elements of the story à la Lévi-Strauss so as to reveal the paradigmatic theme emergent from the sequence of events through which each of the brothers proceeds and in the relationship between the two syntagmas.

Taking together the episodes of the second season of the serial (the season on which we have reported throughout), one discovers a dialectic interaction between actions that tend toward disintegration of family relations up to the brink of total collapse and between actions aimed at preserving and continuing family unity. These actions divide according to the opposing norms that govern family relations between and within generations (see Fig. 10.1). The vertical line that connects grandparents, fathers, and sons is governed by the principle of loyalty to the continuity of the dynasty and by the norm of mutual respect and love between the generations and symbolic veneration of the founding fathers. The horizontal line is governed by opposite principles and norms. Husband and wife, brother and brother, sister and sister, brother-in-law and sister-in-law are in direct and brutal competition with no holds barred. These within-generation relations continually threaten to bring down the family, no less than the inheritance fights of Isaac and Ishmael, Jacob and Esau, Joseph and the brothers.

Sometimes, the intragenerational fighting is so fierce that the rivals explicitly threaten the father's patrimony (business or biology) and their own continuity; that is, they go to the brink of violating intergenerational loyalty in their obsession to crush their intragenerational rivals (see item 2 in the Bobby-Pam plot and item 8 in the J. R.-Sue Ellen plot in Fig. 10.2). This paradigm is not universal, it should be noted. In immigrant societies, for example, the

Figure 10.1. Vertical Harmony and Horizontal Rivalry

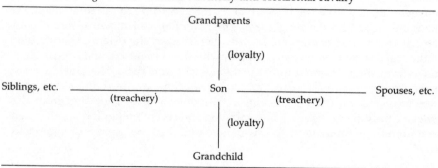

horizontal relations of peers are preferred to those of the vertical line between parents and children (Eisenstadt, 1956). Analyzing postwar British films, Gans (1979) finds a similar preference among former comrades-at-arms—who risked their lives together—at the expense of the vertical line. Relative to these revolutionary paradigms—as in Freud's primal murder of the father by the sons—the *Dallas* paradigm is a conservative one.

Fig. 10.2 presents the stories of the two brothers in parallel columns. (It may be useful to refer back to the Fig. 10.1 of kin relations while examining Fig. 10.2.) The rows represent the sequence of events over time, syntagmatically, and the columns highlight the elements of the paradigmatic structure. Each column is divided in half to show intergenerational loyalty (on the left) and intragenerational treachery (on the right).

The meaning of our retelling of the story becomes clear only by reading the four columns simultaneously. The stories of the two brothers parallel each other in time and content and can be understood only in relationship to each other. This is why it is so difficult to tell the story simply, whether linearly, segmentally, or thematically. Our respondents (see Chapter 5) were handicapped by being asked to retell an episode and to do so orally. Our retelling benefits from having a season of written scripts at our disposal and from being able to paste the pieces together systematically. The repetitiveness of primordiality emerges in serial sequence, and it helps to have a scripture at hand.

The program can be treated as an educational toy consisting of a limited number of pieces that can be fit together to reveal a whole, which, in retrospect, inheres in every part. Parenthetically, we might add a word in praise of the educational value of such games. Instead of ignoring popular culture or treating it as taboo—as is done in many classrooms, in spite of the inordinate amount of time spent on it by the students—there is a case to be made for its legitimation as a base for analytic exercises. Students can be asked to infer what images of American society—for example, what kinds of relations between the sexes—emerge from a favorite television program. They can be asked to classify the program in terms of an array of television genres and in comparison to the genres of other media, low and high. They can be asked to explain why a program is popular or, even better, to explain the relationship between the construction of a program and its appeal. The Lévi-Straussian method for the structural analysis of myth can be demonstrated with respect to a serial like *Dallas* as we have just done. All of us are connoisseurs of kinship relations. The satisfaction of interpreting a family saga can be rewarding both emotionally and intellectually, hot and cool, as it has been ever since Abraham and Oedipus. Mutatis mutandis, J. R. can serve this function, too. Let "the devil do God's work."

Figure 10.2. The Two Central Plots—Syntagmatic Sequence (Rows) and Paradigmatic Structure (Columns)

	THE J.R.–SUE ELLEN PLOT		THE BOBBY-PAM PLOT	
	Intergenerational Loyalty	Intragenerational Treachery	Intergenerational Loyalty	Intragenerational Treachery
1.		J.R. betrays Sue Ellen with her sister, who tries to kill him.	Bobby and Pam devote their lives to having a child, in spite of the danger to the baby and Pam.	
2.		Sue Ellen betrays J.R. with Cliff, leader of rival dynasty no.1.		Bobby asks his father to let him head the business instead of J.R., threatening that he will leave the family estate.
3.		J.R. suspects Sue Ellen of having tried to kill him, and she herself believes it.	Bobby invests all his energy in the family business	and neglects his wife.
4.	Because Jock intends to sell part of the estate which she inherited from her father	Miss Ellie threatens to divorce Jock.	Pam organizes a search for the mother (who abandoned her in childhood).	
5.	J.R. and Bobby make peace between their parents.		Pam brings her mother to Dallas	and warns her against her son Cliff (Pam's brother), who may try to extort her money.
6.	Sue Ellen gives birth	and announces to J.R. that Cliff is the father.		Pam sinks into a depression because Bobby is neglecting her.
7.	J.R. "proves" that he is the father of Sue Ellen's baby.		Bobby tries to adopt a baby legally to produce an heir while J.R.'s baby is gone.	

8. J.R. causes Bobby to fail, risking destruction of Ewing Oil in order to persuade his father that Bobby cannot run the family business.

9. Sue Ellen runs away with her baby to the estate of her lover, Dusty, the heir of rival dynasty no.2.

11. but without Sue Ellen.

13. J.R. destroys Dusty's father's oil business.

15. J.R. betrays his wife with Holly, the heiress of another rival dynasty.

8. Pam despairs over having a baby of her own and attempts suicide.

9. The psychiatrist explains Pam's illness on the basis of (as punishment for?) her mother's betrayal when she was a baby.

10. Bobby buys a baby illegally.

11. Katherine, half-sister of Pam and Cliff, enlists Bobby against her brother.

10. J.R. promises his father that he will bring the baby home and reunite the family.

11. J.R. tries to kidnap his son and to bring him home

12. J.R. defers to his mother and agrees to bring back the baby together with his wife.

13. In order to secure the return of his son,

14. Sue Ellen returns to Southfork for fear of losing her son.

11

DALLAS AS AN
EDUCATIONAL GAME

We wish to expand on the idea just proposed, i.e., that *Dallas* and programs like it may be put to use by professionals and policymakers in the fields of education and culture. First, however, it is appropriate to review the design of the study and the findings that seem most central. Thereafter, we shall turn to some proposals that bear on policy-making and to needed research that follows from the start we have made.

Reprise: Research and Principal Findings

We have been studying the ways in which members of different ethnic groups decode the worldwide hit program, *Dallas*. Our interest in this problem arose originally from the question of how such a quintessentially American cultural product crosses cultural and linguistic frontiers so easily. Despite the universal popularity of American films and television and the allegations of cultural imperialism which accompany their diffusion, almost no one has bothered to find out how they are decoded or, indeed, whether they are understood at all. Our subjects are people of some secondary schooling drawn from four ethnic communities in Israel—Arabs, newly arrived Russian Jews, Moroccan Jews, and kibbutz members—and nonethnic Americans in Los Angeles. Groups of six persons—three couples, all friends, meeting in the home of one of them— were asked to discuss an episode of *Dallas* immediately after seeing it on the air. We also conducted a parallel study in Japan—one of the few countries in which *Dallas* failed. We make no claim to represent the world, nor even to have a formally representative sample of the communities we have studied; we say only that the latter is quite likely. The focus-group method does not lend itself to large samples, but the internal consistencies within the several communities reassure us of the reliability of the differences we claim to have observed.

Obviously, this is not the research design that will lead to a conclusive answer to the secret of the popularity of American television overseas. We chose to study one such program, as a start, in order to observe the mechanisms through which people become involved—how they understand, interpret, and evaluate a program—and to compare these types of involvement across cultures. As a result, we now have some good ideas about how these programs manage to engage and enter the lives of widely different kinds of viewers.

Before we summarize these findings, we again dismiss the widely held view that the success of programs like *Dallas* can be explained in terms of their simple-mindedness or in terms of their rich visual appeal. The fact is that the program is not simple at all; one must learn the complex relationships among the large number of characters and how to make a coherent story out of the staccato series of scenes and subplots which are presented to the viewer without benefit of explicit connections. Moreover, the pretty pictures are by no means sufficient to give an understanding of the narrative; indeed, there is very little action. The story depends on words, and in Israel, for example, these words are subtitled in two languages, Hebrew and Arabic.

To view *Dallas* overseas—perhaps even in America—is to view a *program*, and not—as certain critics think—to view moving wallpaper. It is, in fact, more than viewing a program; it is becoming engaged with a narrative, socially, psychologically, and aesthetically, depending on the background of the viewer. Moreover, *Dallas* provokes conversation. People urge each other to see it and legitimize it as a social currency. In this process, people help each other to understand, interpret, and form opinions about the program, and, as a result, the shared images that emerge are invoked yet again for discussions of personal, social, and political issues. In Algeria, for example, Stolz (1983) argues that conversations about *Dallas* have replaced grandmother's storytelling around the fireside. The participants in our study endorsed this view, both in their reports on the frequency of viewing and discussing the program with others and in allusions to these conversations in the course of the focus discussions. Kibbutz members said that their commune suspended business on the evenings of the broadcast and was occupied with talk of *Dallas* on the day after. A new immigrant from Russia said that *Dallas* was compulsory viewing for anyone who wanted to become part of Israeli society.

The secret of the success of *Dallas*, we think, is in how it offers viewers at different levels and in different cultures something to do. We are not referring here to the superficial problem of understanding; in fact we found that all of the groups we studied had an elementary understanding of the story as a drama of human relationships. We distinguish, rather, among different types of understanding. These types of understanding are related to different types of involvement: referential and critical, emotional (hot) and cognitive (cool). Programs like *Dallas* invite these multiple levels of understanding and involvement, offering a wide variety of different projects and games to different types of viewers. Such programs may beam a homogeneous message to the global village, but our study argues that there is pluralism in the decoding.

On Viewer Understanding and Involvement

Programs like *Dallas* appear to be able to activate very different kinds of responses. Asked to retell an episode just seen, some groups chose to represent the story more sociologically, as if it were the story of a linear progress through a social obstacle course. Other groups retold the story more psychologically, emphasizing the motivations and personalities of the characters, while yet others retold the story in terms of themes and leitmotifs.

These and other responses of the viewers led us to distinguish between two broad categories of involvement in the program, the referential and the critical (or metalinguistic). For example, in answer to our question, "Why all the fuss about babies?" some viewers referred to real life and explained that families, especially rich ones, need heirs. Others said, using a metalinguistic frame, that babies are good material for conflict and that the narrative of soap opera needs conflict to keep going. Within the referential, we distinguished between real and ludic keyings. The one makes serious equations between the story and life; the other treats the program more playfully, subjunctively, and interactively— turning the group discussion into a kind of psychodrama. Making a further distinction within the referential, we observed that some viewers key the program normatively, judging messages and characters moralistically; others treat the program as observers and withhold value judgments. The moralizing statements tend to be couched in the language of "we": "Their women are immoral; our Arab women would not behave that way." Less moralizing statements come either in the language of "they" (businessmen, for example), for those who generalize from the program to the universals of life, and in the language of "I" and "you," for those who treat program and life more playfully. We made a further distinction in terms of emotionally hot and cognitively cool types of involvement, where hot refers to more confrontational ("us" or "them") involvement that is typically serious and moralizing, and cool is often more personal, more playful, and morally neutral. Referential and hot are correlated, but by no means exclusively.

Hot and cool also apply to the metalinguistic, where hot critical statements identify a message in the program and explicitly oppose it. Opposition in the informant and idealized opposition—of the sort we have seen to typify critical Russian reactions—are also classified as hot.

Patterns of involvement vary by ethnicity. The more traditional groups— Moroccan Jews and Arabs—do not stray far from the referential. Even the well-educated among them make comparatively few metalinguistic statements, although better-educated viewers in all groups use the metalinguistic frame much more. The Arabs, in particular, discuss the program moralistically in terms of "them" and "us." This pattern of relating to the program is at once involving and defensive: the program is discussed referentially and seriously, but, at the same time, it is rejected as a message for "us." Even if this rejection serves as a buffer against the influence of the program, it nevertheless reflects a high level of engagement. Their opposition to the program also takes a political or ideological bent (which we classify as critical) where American cultural imperialism, now including Israel, is identified with colonialism and domination.

The American and kibbutz groups show an altogether different pattern of involvement. The number of their metalinguistic statements is higher proportionately, and their use of the referential is often in the ludic mode. Their use of the critical frame is sometimes ludic, too, i.e., they take pleasure in the aspect of the genre in statements such as *Dallas* would be *Little House on the Prairie* if it were not for J. R.

The Russians are critical of the aesthetics of the story (comparing it unfavorably to Tolstoy's and to Pushkin's). Japanese viewers object to the inconsistencies in the construction of the story and to its incompatibility with their expectations of the familiar genre of home drama, to which they ascribe it. The Russians are even more critical of the message, which they regard as an ideological manipulation. Beware, say the Russians, of the false message of the program. They tell us that the rich are unhappy because that is what they want us to think!

Thus, we see two dominant patterns of involvement in these decodings, each with its own variations. The more traditional viewers remain in the realm of the referential and hot (the real, the serious, the normative) and mobilize values to defend themselves against the program. The more Western groups— the Americans and the kibbutzniks—are relatively more aware of and involved in the construction of the program, that is, in the critical realm. Within the referential, they deal with its reality more coolly and playfully. The Russians and Japanese are also metalinguistic but have idiosyncratic specializations. The Russians show more awareness of the message of the program than of its structure. This hot and critical concern seems to go together with the kind of seriousness with which the Russians enter the referential, just as the more constructionist concerns of the other Western groups go hand in hand with their more playful keyings of the referential. The Japanese specialize in the critical and cool, focusing on the pragmatic—that is, on the ways in which the text engages the viewers—in an effort to explain why they have resisted the program's appeal. Of course, that is what we asked them to do.

We cannot posit which of these forms of involvement and distancing are more likely to affect viewers. While it may appear at first glance that ludic keyings and metalinguistic framings are more resistant to influence, we are not certain that this is so. The ludic may be seductive in the sense that fantasy and subjectivity invite one to be carried away. Similarly, constructionist concerns distract attention from the ideological message. Even ideological decodings are vulnerable to influence in the sense that the decoders believe that their oppositional reading is the truth! Each community has its own defense. If we had to hypothesize which viewers are more vulnerable (in the sense of upsetting their balance), we would presume those viewers that accept the reality of the program—those that do not challenge its hegemonic agenda—even as they argue with it.

Implications for Policy

If we are correct in these findings, there are several implications for educational and cultural policy. All of these stem from the observation that viewers are much more alert and able than most critics give them credit for and that they put even highly standardized television programs to a variety of unanticipated uses.

1. Viewing escapist programs is not as escapist as it seems. In fact, viewers typically use television fiction as a forum for discussing their own lives. Concern over family, social issues, women's status, etc., are activated in response to these programs (at least in the context of the focus group), and there is good reason to believe that an agenda is set for discussion as a result of the negotiation between the culture of the viewers and of the producers. Techniques and ethics for the purposive use of such discussions as consciousness-raising devices should be further developed. Agents of social and psychological change have made beginnings in Mexico and elsewhere (psychotherapists such as Kilgus, 1974). Conservative programs may not be as conservative as they seem. *Dallas* may be ideologically conservative—in the opinion of some critics, including ourselves—but that does not mean that it is consistently used that way by viewers. Critical theorists themselves have observed how soap opera may be employed nowadays by female viewers to frame a "site for gender struggle" (Radway, 1985; Ang, 1985).

2. It follows that content analysis alone should not be a basis for international cultural policy. Audience decodings may surprise the content analyst and policymaker. We are not proposing to whitewash the export of industrial soap opera, but we do urge that the concern over cultural imperialism in the market of films and television be recontextualized. In the absence of the local soap opera—which is likely to be more popular than any import—a program such as *Dallas* may have some value. The value comes not from the program but from negotiation with it.

3. Given the decoding abilities of audiences, we propose that serious thought be given to the possibility of incorporating such popular texts into the curricula of classes for both children and adults. Our study gives ample evidence of what connoisseurship can result from viewing such programs, and how such a skill may be put to work as a basis for exercises in such things as the development of aesthetic judgment, the classification of artistic forms, the ideological underpinnings of a story, the attitude toward women and minorities, the values of another culture, and the like. School should bring in such external learning experiences and capitalize upon them. Both referential and

critical decodings of popular culture can serve as a basis for serious educational efforts.

4. Critical ability should be cultivated systematically. The best place to begin is at home with familiar television programs. Viewers can easily be shown—as our focus-group discussants were shown to their delight—that they are very able critics. An effort should then be made to see whether trained viewers are able to transfer their critical abilities to other media with which they feel *less* familiar. Perhaps the intuitive resistance to other visual and dramatic arts can be overcome by showing the potential audience member how his or her training in television criticism might apply.

Research Implications

We believe that a program like *Dallas* deserves serious attention, not just for the sake of understanding the secret of its attraction across cultures but also because it reveals something about the ways in which a program of this type is used, often quite creatively, by viewers in very different social circumstances. We do not wish to leave the impression that we are convinced that *Dallas* is a work of high art, even of high popular art; nor do we insist that the somewhat unorthodox concepts and methods developed in the course of the study have proven themselves conclusively. What additional data and what enhanced methods would help establish our conclusions? We propose a number of directions for further research.

1. We found a level of alertness on the part of television viewers that exceeds and appears qualitatively different than the findings of researchers who have followed routine TV viewing over the course of days or weeks. We must ask, therefore, whether our method created this high level of alertness? To answer that question, one must invent an alternative method which would be less obtrusive, both during the course of viewing as well as when people might be talking about or acting out what they have seen on screen. This is very difficult to accomplish. One method is anthropological, but this is very expensive and impressionistic (Bryce and Leichter, 1983; Lull, 1980). Another approach would be to develop a system of mass observation (Harrison and Madge, 1939), which the British attempted during World War II, wherein participant observers are trained to report on the behavior of people in the everyday social contexts to which they belong. Other possible methods are some adaptation of the beeper-diary method of Csikszentmihalyi and Kubey (1981) or the diary methods of Graber (1984), which distinguish, however, among different types of programs. Observations in public places such as bars, cafes, hospitals, etc. (Lemish, 1982), are another possibility. We do not yet know of any ideal solution, and this is certainly a generic problem of assessing the processing and effects of mass communications. Methodological development in this area deserves a high priority.

2. Some of the shortcomings of the focus-group method are also its

strengths. Constraining people to talk may be artificial, but it also may be a faithful stimulation of real talk. (In any case, artificial or not, the focus-group method has certainly established that people are *capable* of the types of understanding, interpretation, and evaluation that we have observed.) The further objection—that our method observes groups in action and cannot, therefore, generalize to individuals taken one at a time—is also a strength in that people happen to live in groups (families, offices, sports clubs, etc.) and their opinions are shaped and anchored in these social and stratified contexts. It would be worth investing in methodological study of the focus group, comparing individual with group decodings, as well as the interaction of natural groups versus purposively constructed ones. More, the dynamics of interaction in such groups—the assumption of roles, the differentiation according to status, sex, etc.—need careful study. Kaboolian and Gamson (1983) and Morley (1980) are two of several sociologists who have used this method, which we find to have great potential.

3. We found that television viewers operate in the critical frame to varying extent and in different modes, and we feel the need to learn more about the conditions that qualify viewers to relate critically to such matters as genre, dramatic construction, mimesis, messages, ideology, and the like. We have speculated that these modes of relating may be engendered by education, familiarity with a medium or a genre, familiarity with other media and genres, a literary tradition, or a tradition of critical thought connected to oral or written texts. Our study did not allow us to go deeply into the processes of socialization that contribute to the critical framings that inhere in the different groups; nor did we examine more than the several communities that were accessible to us.

4. It is obvious that studies such as ours need validation in a much wider gamut of cultural settings. We found groups to vary not just in terms of critical framings but also in terms of referential decodings. We noted differences in the extent of moral opposition to *Dallas*—the more traditional groups specialized in this. Indeed, we suggested that the survival of traditional cultures in the context of modernity may be based on elaborate socialization to just such confrontations (Fried, 1957; Ruth Katz, 1985). For all these reasons, we urge the extension of the study of decodings of television fiction—and news and other genres as well—to a more comprehensive sample of cultures and communities.

5. The inclusion of additional cultures would also permit a more convincing test of our finding that everybody understands the basic story. Perhaps this is not the case in communities of extreme illiteracy. Or, might it be that, even there, the processes of mutual aid would operate to build a coherent story, perhaps even the correct story or some local version of it? What are the mechanisms with which such groups cope with television news and fiction? Some starts have been made in this direction, beginning with the classic study of Lerner (1955). And what about children? How do they cope—individually and in groups—with their premature exposure not only to modernity but also to adulthood (Meyrowitz, 1985; Postman, 1982; Dorr, 1986)? Differences in under-

standing and processing of TV stories by groups from different cultures can be studied through comparing their framings and their retellings of the story in the categories we have developed.

6. Such framings and retellings of television fiction by different groups may serve the further function of giving insight into otherwise inaccessible cultures. In applying our method to the Japanese groups, we sensed that we were getting a glimpse of their own view of themselves and of their cognitive styles. The more a culture is coherent, the more a method of this kind may be fruitful. This method of studying culture at a distance is related, of course, to the wartime work of Mead (1953) and Benedict (1947), except that while they immersed themselves in alien texts and films, we immersed ourselves in texts that are familiar to us but alien to the group being studied.

7. Why do such programs so easily traverse the world? We have proposed that programs like *Dallas* invite several different types of involvement, which are enhanced by the universality of their themes (primordiality) and the structure of their presentation (seriality). But we cannot be certain that such is the case unless we (1) compare the success of soap operas like *Dallas* to other worldwide hits, and (2) understand why *Dallas* failed in certain countries, such as Japan or Brazil. A comparative study of best-selling television programs is clearly called for, using a sample of different cultures; a start in this direction has been made by Silj (1988) and by Hjort (1986) in their comparison of domestic and imported television programs.

8. We have suggested that referential readings—because they give standing to a program, even when accompanied by moral or political opposition—are a wedge through which the values of a program may enter the culture, however confrontationally. This hypothesis as well as the vulnerability of other forms of defense obviously deserve operationalization.

9. Research should be conducted on the transferability of critical ability in television to critical ability in other arts with which the TV viewer is unacquainted and feels less at home. If viewers trained in television can be made aware of their ability and made to feel that it is generalizable, the audiences for the arts may be enhanced thereby.

APPENDIX ONE

Focus Guidelines for Interview

We are conducting research about *Dallas*. We are trying to understand why the program manages to interest people all over the world.

5 MIN   1. What happened in the episode we have just been watching? "How will you tell it tomorrow morning to someone who has not seen it?"
IT IS IMPORTANT TO SUMMARIZE AND CONTINUE PROBING UNTIL SOME FORM OF ANSWER HAS BEEN GIVEN TO THIS QUESTION.
PROBE: "So if I understand you, the story is so and so . . . "
INVITE CORRECTIONS.

        2. ASK TO RANK THE THREE MOST IMPORTANT CHARACTERS IN ORDER OF IMPORTANCE. TRY TO ACHIEVE CONSENSUS OR ESTABLISH CLEAR OPPOSING VIEWS. THEN PROCEED TO ASK ABOUT THE FIRST CHARACTER.

5 MIN.   Who is the most important character in this episode?
* Who is she/he? What do you know about him/her? (Try to get at family and other connections.)
* What motivates the character? What does (s)he believe in?
* Does (s)he get what (s)he wants? How?
* What things get in the way?
* Do you like him/her? (Try clarifying differences of opinion.)

3–5 MIN.   3. Who is the next most important character?
PROBE AS IN QUESTION TWO.

3–5 MIN.   4. Who is the third most important character?
PROBE AS IN QUESTION TWO.

3–5 MIN.   5. Is *Dallas* about real people?
IF YES: What kind of people is it about?

IF NO: How are the *Dallas* people different from real people?
PROBE: Do you know any people like the *Dallas* people?

6. Why do the people on *Dallas* have problems?
7. How would you describe family relations on *Dallas*?
8. Why all the commotion about babies?
   PROBE FOR ADDITIONAL ANSWERS: "Is there another reason?"
9. How would you describe business relations on *Dallas*?
10. What conflicts/value problems come up on *Dallas*?
11. Does the program take a stand? Is there a moral, a lesson, a message in *Dallas*? Are they trying to tell us something?
    PROBE: "Any other messages?"
12. What is *Dallas* saying about American society?
    PROBE: "What does *Dallas* say about American society to viewers in other countries? What is the image of America presented on *Dallas*?"
13. If you were the scriptwriter and had to end the series, what would happen in the last episode?
14. What does *Dallas* do for you? Why do you watch it?

DIRECTIONS FOR OBSERVERS

a. Make sure to mark all documents and questionnaires with group number and date.
b. Map the seating arrangements of participants by first names only and give a copy of the map to the interviewer before discussion begins. Mark (by arrow) who is married to whom.
c. While watching the program, write remarks, reactions, laughter, etc., and note what triggers it.
d. Note first words spoken by each participant and note his name. This will enable us to identify the voices in the cassette.
e. While the discussion goes on, write reactions, nonverbal interactions, etc., and simultaneous speeches which can be missed by the recording. Also, note major differences of opinion among participants, keying these to the number of appropriate question in the interview guide.

Individual Questionnaire

NAME

Here are a few questions we would like you to answer. Please take your time. All responses are completely confidential. Thank you for your help.

1. Before tonight, when was the last time you watched an episode of *Dallas*? Was it . . . (CHECK ONE)

   ( ) in the past month
   ( ) in the past six months
   ( ) more than six months
   ( ) never

   a) How many times have you seen *Dallas* in the last month? (CHECK ONE)

   ( ) one time
   ( ) two times
   ( ) three times
   ( ) four times

2. In the current season, would you
    say you . . . (CHECK ONE)
    ( ) watch *Dallas* regularly
    ( ) watch *Dallas* occasionally
    ( ) hardly ever watch *Dallas*
    ( ) never watch

3. Think about your viewing of *Dallas*
    in previous seasons. Would you
    say that . . . (CHECK ONE)
    ( ) your viewing has not changed
    ( ) you watch *Dallas* more often
        now than in the past
    ( ) you watch *Dallas* less often
        now than in the past
    ( ) never watch

4. What about your viewing of
    Dallas? Do you usually . . .
    (CHECK ONE)
    ( ) watch by yourself
    ( ) watch with one other
        person
    ( ) watch with several other
        people
    ( ) don't watch television in the
        evening

    a) Are these usually the same
       people from night to night, or
       do you watch with whoever is
       around?
       ( ) same people
       ( ) whoever is around

    b) Please tell us your relationship
       to those people.

    _____

    _____

    _____

5. Now, regardless of how you view
    Dallas, let's think about your tele-
    vision viewing in the evening. In
    general do you:
    ( ) watch by yourself
    ( ) watch with one other
        person
    ( ) watch with several other
        people
    ( ) don't watch television in the
        evening

    a) Are these usually the same
       people from night to night, or
       do you watch with whoever is
       around?
       ( ) same people
       ( ) whoever is around

b) Please tell us your relationship
   to those people.

_____

_____

_____

_____

6.a) With whom do you discuss *Dallas*? (CHECK EACH ONE)

Spouse   Yes _____   No _____

Other family members at   Yes _____   No _____
home

Other family members outside   Yes _____   No _____
the home

Friends at work   Yes _____   No _____

Other friends   Yes _____   No _____

6.b)   How often? (CHECK ONE)   ( ) Each time I watch
                                          ( ) Sometimes
                                          ( ) Rarely
                                          ( ) Never

7.   Indicate . . .   ( ) Male
                                          ( ) Female

8.   What is your age?   _____

9.   Are you . . .   ( ) single
                                          ( ) married
                                          ( ) divorced/separated
                                          ( ) widowed

10.   How many people including your-   _____
       self, currently live in your house-
       hold?   number of adults

                                          _____

                                              number of children

       a) What are their ages?   _____

                                                  adults

                                          _____

                                                 children

11.   How many people in your house-   _____
       hold including yourself, currently
       work outside the house?   number work part-time

                                          _____

                                            number work full-time

12.   How many years of formal school-
       ing have you completed?   ( ) less than high school
                                          ( ) high school graduate
                                          ( ) some college
                                          ( ) college graduate

13. Who is the primary wage earner in
     your household?   ( ) myself
                                              ( ) someone else

14. What is your total household $_____
     income?

THANK YOU

APPENDIX TWO

Coding Instructions for "Commuting" Statements from Story to Life, and from Story to Metalinguistic (critical)

1–2	card number (2 commute statements per card)
3–4	focus-group number

Commute No. 1   5–6   AREA OF QUESTIONNAIRE in which commute appears: (1) *Narrative*, (2) *character A*, (3) *character B*, (4) *character C*, (5) *is story real?*, (6) *problems*, (7) *family*, (8) *business*, (9) *babies*, (10) *conflict*, (11) *messages*, (12) *America*, (13) *endings*, (14) *gratifications, reasons for viewing* (see Appendix 1).

7–8   TYPE OF COMMUTE: (1) *referential, story-to-life* (not just statement about life; statement must originate with story), (2) *mimetic*, is story realistic or not? (aesthetic evaluation of program using criterion of realism. It is aesthetically good/bad because it is realistic/unrealistic, exaggerated/not exaggerated, i.e., "the serial is bad because it's not realistic," "it's good because it represents reality," "it's good because it simplifies reality," etc.), (3) *critical*: story-to-metastory, aesthetic criticism analyzing story syntax, story type, or dramatic function of character, (4) *(1) plus (2) or (1) plus (3)*, (5) no commute: *cliché*, (6) *critical statement plus cliché*.

9–10   TYPE OF REFERENTIAL (STORY-TO-LIFE) STATEMENT: (1) *interpretation* (including "life is like *Dallas*," and "*Dallas* is like life"): an explicit analogy between life and the program, excluding evaluation; (2) *evaluation*: evaluation of the story and characters in terms of norms taken from life, applying a norm from life to story (when an interpretation is evaluative, CODE: evaluation), (3) *personal association*: talking about life as stimulated by the story, but not in order to interpret it, (4) *identification*: personal identification with a

164

character, but only when accompanied by explanation why (including ludic/subjunctive statements such as "if I were J.R.'s mother."); (5) *interpretation plus association*, when the association is used to interpret story; (6) *evaluation plus association*.

11	CLICHÉ: (1) *yes*, (2) *no* ("No smoke without fire")
12	PRONOUNS: (1) *abstract* ("they", "businessmen," "women"); (2) *personal* ("I", "we").
Commute No. 2 13–20	as in columns 9–12.

APPENDIX THREE

Table *A.1*. Educational Distribution of Focus-Group Members by Ethnicity (in percent)

	American	Israeli Moroccan	Israeli Arabs*	Israeli Russians	Israeli Kibbutz
Less than secondary school	11	29	24	2	7
Completed secondary school	29	65	56	22	50
Some University	52	4	15	15	7
University graduates	5	1	—	62	17
Unknown	3	—	5	—	19
Total number	(63)	(84)	(34)	(55)	(30)

*These data refer to six of the ten Arab groups. Personal questionnaires were not completed in four groups, which were nevertheless retained in the sample.

Table *A.2*. Educational Distribution by Ethnicity, Ages 30–50, Nationwide* (in percent)

	Moroccan (1st and 2nd generation**)	Arabs	Russians (1st generation)	Kibbutz
Less than secondary school	69	21	40	11
Completed secondary school	19	36	10	45
Some University	5	21	10	18
University graduates	6	4	15	25
Unknown	1	18	34	1

*Estimate based on Manpower Survey, Central Bureau of Statistics, Government of Israel, 1982, for those groups represented in *Dallas* study.

**First generation is born abroad; second generation is born in Israel, parent is born abroad.

NOTES

CHAPTER 1

1. We will complicate this statement in Chapters 7 and 8, where we propose that moral objections to the values of the program may, nevertheless, belong to a hegemonic reading, insofar as the program is being taken as real enough to be worth arguing against.

CHAPTER 2

1. Ironically, there is another similarity between Europe of the moment and the Third World of ten years ago. Confronted with an explosion in the number of hours of broadcasting as a result both of the deregulation of national broadcasting systems and of new media technology, European broadcasting appears to be going in several different directions at once. The Italians—at least in the first phase of deregulation—were scrambling to import whatever lurid reruns they could find, exactly as the Third World nations did when they realized they were committed to broadcasting many more hours than they could produce. The French, on the other hand, more constrained by an ethic of authenticity, are resolved to produce for themselves, but their most famous self-production so far is the intentional imitation of *Dallas*. Based on careful research into the organization, content, and audience reactions to *Dallas*, the French have imported not an American program but an American concept for a program, along with the American way of manufacturing it. This is what the Chianciano Television Festival of 1983 admiringly entitled "Europe Fights Back."

2. It is likely that both Danes and Americans are right. The Danish program reflects a specific social and historical period, whereas *Dallas* is more of an invention. Michael Arlen (1980) argues that the show is carefully stripped of any clues to the constraints of an "outside world," resembling the "smooth pebbles" of fairy tales.

CHAPTER 3

1. The official data on education by ethnicity (Appendix Three, Table A.2., p. 166) show the Russians to have more university graduates than most Israelis, and it is not

surprising, therefore, that the field staff produced Russian groups of higher education than we intended. The Moroccan groups tended to be of slightly lower education than our norm, but well in line with the census data. When we realized that the overlap between education and ethnicity was such that the one might confound the other in explanation-making, we decided to divide all groups by high and low education in order to permit intercultural comparisons while holding education constant. Moreover, during the course of the field work, we decided to add additional Moroccan groups of lower education to enable a stricter test—with a larger number of groups—of the influence of education *within* an ethnic group. We also included four Arab groups without complete background data. See Appendix Three.

2. Excepting the Japanese, of course, who were invited to view the first episode.
3. We apologize for our overuse of the word ethnicity, especially in relationship to the kibbutz. But, for most purposes, the kibbutz community is probably representative of second-generation Europeans in Israel.
4. Recruitment of participants in Israel was organized by us, recruitment in Los Angeles was done by a professional market-research agency that reported considerable difficulty in persuading and convening potential participants, even though honoraria were offered to the hosts. Some of the Japanese groups were convened in a community center because of the inconvenience and unusualness of home meetings.
5. Unlike the Russians, the kibbutz members talk willingly about *Dallas* in the group discussions.
6. Studies of reactions to televised political broadcasts—presidential debates, for example—show that more people have opinions after some time has elapsed, presumably because they have had time to talk over their reactions with others.
7. Of course, the very interaction between interviewer and interviewee is itself a discussion which might crystallize views which had previously been amorphous and unformulated or, perhaps, altogether absent.
8. One might argue that the advantage of the individual interview is precisely in the unnaturalness of the privacy that it guarantees.
9. The detailed analysis of messages made possible by this coding is reported only partially in this book. For further detail, see Liebes (1986).

CHAPTER 5

1. Barthes (1975b) distinguishes between the syntagmatic and the paradigmatic levels in the structure of narrative. The syntagmatic consists of narrative functions, defined as the smallest units of meaning out of which the story is constructed. There are two types of functions: the distributive, which are functions in Propp's sense and correspond to our linear model, and the indexical, which operate at the level of characters' attributes and the general atmosphere of the story. These indexes of personality and atmosphere make their appearance, repeatedly, in the segments of parallel and intersected subplots, which describe the segmented model out of which *Dallas* is constructed.
2. The Japanese groups were not included in the coding of retellings. We wish to thank Mr. Nahum Gelber for his coding.
3. The first digit of the two-digit identification code for the focus groups indicates ethnicity (i.e., Arab groups begin with 4, kibbutz groups begin with 8, etc). Thus, groups are not numbered serially from 1 to 66.
4. We thank Professor Dmitri Segal of the Hebrew University for this interpretation.

CHAPTER 6

1. We will deal with the concept "oppositional" in Chapter 8.
2. In his analysis of public opinion in Soviet Russia, Inkeles (1950) also discusses the decoding skills of Russian newspaper readers.
3. We are here illustrating the metaphoric use of the characters. Such poetic, liminal, and ludic uses of group understandings of the story are also the subject of fantasy games (pp. 97–99).
4. The referential is the subject of Chapter Seven, fn. 4.
5. She described a typical dialogue between an Algerian and his 78-year-old grandmother, who views *Dallas* along with the others: "Do you remember, grandma, those evenings around the *cahoun*? You would delight in telling us *kabil* stories and legends. We would talk among ourselves. Today you are in front of the television set from four o'clock." This Algerian grandmother has lost both her expertise and her special status. Meyrowitz (1985) says that the process of homogenization is characteristic not only of various cultures but also of differences between the sexes and between children and grown-ups. We are not so sure, but—as we shall see later—it is an argument worth considering. If so, one should add that the replacement of grandmother and her stories by the TV set and its stories is a questionable exchange, insofar as the television heroes are more short-lived than the grandmother's heroes and will end their careers without leaving much trace. J. R. and Bobby are very poor recyclings of Esau and Jacob. The homogenization of grandmother is a further cost, both in geriatrics and cultural continuity. Television interpretation gives status to different kinds of people; Ahmed (1983) makes this point in her observations on the role of young people as TV interpreters in the family culture of Pakistan. Cecile, of Moroccan group 20, is our best example.

CHAPTER 7

1. Within each type of involvement, of course, one can speak of more or less. Having decided, after much thought, to treat the critical and the cool as patterns of involvement—no less involved, potentially, than the referential and the hot—we remain without an adequate measure of degree.
2. Note that we are not following McLuhan's usage. McLuhan's cool and hot are attributes of the technology of the media. Our usage has to do with responses of the audience.
3. The Japanese groups are omitted here since this coding was done long before the extension of our study to Japan. Also—as noted in Chapters 8 and 9—the Japanese groups, largely unacquainted with the program, make very few referential statements.
4. Neuman (1982) would disagree. His findings suggest that less-educated viewers make as high a score on both analytic and interpretive statements as more-educated ones and, indeed, may even do better than the more educated in dealing with programs of popular fiction.
5. These data were coded yet again for a close analysis of critical statements, as noted at the conclusion of Chapter 3. Although this recoding dwarfed the proportion of referential statements for reasons explained there, the critical statements of Russians and Americans were approximately equal (slightly in favor of the Russians, as in the present chapter), and the Japanese far exceeded both.

6. The subjects of the referential and critical statements were coded twice—once as abstracted statements, and again as subjects of interaction within the group. We refer to the latter coding in this paper. For details, see the Ph.D. dissertation of Tamar Liebes, the Communications Institute, Hebrew University of Jerusalem.

7. These keyings are applicable also to the critical frame. One can speak of genre, for example, seriously or playfully. One of our respondents defined *Dallas*, poetically, as "Big House on the Prairie," alluding to another popular American soap (see Chapter 8).

8. This is not quite Hall's (1985) oppositional reading in that the message is decoded as intended, even if disagreement follows (see Chapter 8).

9. Statements keyed as play are omitted. They may be assumed to be value-free, and their inclusion does not affect the analysis.

10. The columns have been arranged to display the scalar patterns. A more "logical" order, of course, would show "Frame" as the first column, since it makes the major distinction between referential and critical.

11. Since the majority of all groups spoke in "they" statements, we drop the more universal "they" and compute the ratio of "we" to "I." Thus, a high proportion of "we" will be labelled 1, and a high proportion of "I," 2 in the *Referent* Column.

12. Schramm et al. (1961) say the same thing about viewers of TV news, who may frame their viewing either by the "reality principle" or the "pleasure principle."

CHAPTER 8

1. Instead of coding whole statements and chunks of interaction as referential and metalinguistic (as we do throughout most of Chapters 7 and 8), we coded every reply to the question, "Why all the fuss about babies?" in terms of types of babies (story, real, dramatic) and types of functions (inheritors, pleasure-givers, tension creators, etc.), paraphrasing statements or parts of statements in the form of codeable nuclear sentences. Thus, the response, "There are a lot of problems around babies in such a family: the real identity of the baby, sicknesses, kidnapping. Therefore around them there is a lot of scope for the writer to build up a plot" is coded: *drama babies* function *for producers* as *conflict*. The average group provided some ten codeable replies. Japanese groups could not be expected to answer questions about babies since they viewed only the first episode, where the problem of babies does not yet exist.

2. As in the following example (American group 4):

DONNA: Kids don't play an important *part*. The only time when you ever see them is when the maid is carrying the baby off.

SANDI: The babies play important *roles* only because of what revolves around them.

3. Empirical observations lead us to this conclusion, which reinforces the idea that sophistication may be defined as observation of one's more naive self. Eco (1985), in our opinion, makes too sharp a distinction between the naive and the sophisticated (see Chapter 9 for a fuller discussion).

4. *Dallas* failed in Japan, it will be recalled. For details about Japanese viewers, see Chapters 3 and 9.

5. We omit here the pragmatic domain because our original coding was based only on the semantic and syntactic.

6. The semantic statements are hotter and sometimes include negative evaluations of the ideology of the theme or message, paralleling the statements of normative opposition to the Ewings in the referential. The former qualify as critical because of their explicit recognition that the program has a theme or message.

7. For an analysis of these dimensions from the viewer's perspective, see Livingstone (1987a).

8. We coded all statements beginning with "the program/the story teaches us" or "they—the writers/producers—are trying to show/tell us" as messages and marked whether these messages were manipulative or not.

9. "They (the producers) are trying to show a family; a family needs a strong father image. Some of the programs they show today, so many today, are without fathers anymore. That is not good for family entertainment, we need a strong father figure holding everyone together" (American group 16). "Maybe they are trying to relate to the young people of today, who many of them don't want children because it interferes with their selfish lives, to put across that it is OK to want children, to say that you can care about yourself and be selfish, but you can have a child also" (American group 3).

10. See Chapter 10 for biblical themes in the *Dallas* stories.

11. "*Dynasty*, which I watch a lot of now, moves a little bit slower. You know, with this one, if you really miss an episode you've got to try and figure out what happened in between—unless you're able to talk to someone else, 'cause there always is something going on, and *Dynasty* in comparison the show moves a lot slower . . ." (American group 4).

12. As *Dallas* is not shown in Japan, our Japanese participants were shown the first episode of the series in which Bobby brings Pamela to Southfork after having married her in secret. The new wife happens to be the daughter of the Barnes family, the enemies of the Ewings.

13. "They seem to have certain shows that are preliminary to other shows. I guess they save the better shows until rating time." (American group 16)

14. The Russians are literate. They read the title of the episode, for example, and ask whether it is a good name for the story.

15. As Kyooku puts it, "it might be the difference between meat-eating people (animals?) and grass-eating people. Europeans and Americans are warlike."

16. Because the emphasis was on expanding the critical categories and using a smaller coding unit, the number of critical statements in Table 8.4 far exceeds that of Table 8.2. Moreover, the referential is dwarfed in this coding (as the critical may have been in the previous coding), inasmuch as it was treated as a residual category (not reported in table 8.4). In this new coding, therefore, the proportion of critical exceeds that of the referential. Nevertheless, we remain convinced that Table 8.2 presents a more faithful picture of the referential/critical ratio, because using other expressions of amount of space or length of time, the referential far exceeds the critical in our estimation.

17. Except for messages, which we decided to include, belatedly, among the critical categories. But, as we have noted, the coding permits us to distinguish between messages supplied in answer to our explicit query and those volunteered prior to our asking this question.

18. We note again that we are discussing statements, not people. Almost everybody who makes oppositional statements in the critical frame also makes referential ones.

19. Morley makes the point that his focus-group discussions of a newsmagazine accept-

ed the ideology of *Nationwide* even while they were critical of its aesthetics. Others opposed the ideology while remaining uncritical of the construction. Morley was surprised to learn that critical readings do not necessarily constitute a defense against ideology.

CHAPTER 9

1. One focus-group member explicitly referred to the lateness of the hour. In an effort to save the program, it was moved to an earlier time slot by the station, but to no avail. Of course, it is possible that it would have made a difference had this been done at the outset.
2. Moreover, the medium of television is beginning to lose its charm in Japan. For many years, the Japanese have been the most avid television viewers in the world; recently however, a decline has been noted in the extent of television viewing, and the expression "weaning" is often heard in this connection.
3. The proportion of imported programs has also been dropping in recent years. In 1977, imported programs constituted 16 percent of the dramatic programs broadcasting in Tokyo between 5:00 and 11:00 P.M. by the five major networks; the comparable figure in 1986 was 3 percent.
4. This is an interesting possibility for a cross-cultural methodology, i.e., comparing readings of a standard story from an alien culture. The Bible would be a good example; Laura Bohanan's (1966) study, "Shakespeare in the Bush" is another. The studies of culture at a distance by Benedict, Rhoda Metraux, and Margaret Mead are based on researchers' readings of native texts, whereas our proposal is to study natives' readings of an alien text.
5. In fact, one group was mixed. It did not behave any differently than the others—so our intuitive decision may have been unnecessary—except that there seem to be longer periods of silence. In general, Japanese men are less interested in television drama; they favor sports and news.

CHAPTER 10

1. Whether this is true of the whole world, we cannot say. Specifically, we do not know whether illiterate communities who do not have access to dubbing can make any sense of the pictures, although we have seen examples of the operation of mutual aid even under such a circumstance. The universal connoisseurship of the intricacies of kinship also helps, but that leaves out business and other aspects of the story.
2. Professor Arnold Band of the University of California, Los Angeles, points out that the God of Genesis intervenes subtly (gynecologically, says Daniel Dayan), while the God of Exodus intervenes thunderously. These types of intervention remind one, in turn, of Leo Braudy's (1982) distinction between "soap-opera time" and "catastrophic time."
3. This is quite different, obviously, from the linear model of Proppian (1968) narrative. The classical fairy tale, according to Propp, begins with a problem (lack) and ends with a coronation or a wedding. The typical serial episode—having to end in suspense (lack)—moves from harmony to tension rather than vice versa (Liebes, 1986).
4. This also explains the well-known problem of serial actors who cannot play any other role because they are so heavily identified (even by themselves) with their characters. Thus, an American group member, even while insisting that she is not the kind of

referential viewer who writes letters to soap-opera characters, says, nevertheless, that she would slap Larry Hagman if she met him at the airport.
5. The case of *Dallas* may be even a better fit for the serial structure than the soap opera itself if Michael Arlen (1980) is correct in distinguishing between the strict morality of classical soap opera and the improvisatory morality of *Dallas*. Obviously, improvisation and flexible personalities and values makes the story even more never-ending.

REFERENCES

Ahmed, Duree. 1983. "Television in Pakistan: An Ethnographic Study." Ph.D. diss., Teachers College, Columbia Univ.

Allen, Robert C. 1983. "On Reading Soaps: A Semiotic Primer." In E. Ann Kaplan (ed.), *Regarding Television*. Frederick, Md.: Univ. Publications of America, Inc.

Allen, Robert C. 1985. *Speaking of Soap Opera*. Chapel Hill: Univ. of North Carolina Press.

Alter, Robert. 1981. *The Art of Biblical Narrative*. New York: Basic Books

Ang, Ien. 1985. *Watching* Dallas. London and New York: Methuen.

Arlen, Michael. 1980. *Camera Age: Essays on Television*, 38–50. New York: Farrar, Strauss and Giroux.

Arnheim, Rudolf. 1943. "The World of Daytime Serial." In P. Lazarsfeld and F. Stanton (eds.), *Radio Research*. New York: Duell, Sloan, and Pearce.

Banfield, Edward C. 1958. *The Moral Basis of a Backward Society*. Glencoe: Free Press.

Barthes, Roland. 1975a. *S/Z*. New York: Hill and Wang.

Barthes, Roland. 1975b. *Image, Music, Text*. New York: Hill and Wang.

BBC Audience Research. 1972. *Violence on Television: Program Content and Viewer Perception*. London.

Bechtel, R. B., C. Achelpohl, and R. Akers. 1971. "Correlates Between Observed Behavior and Questionnaire Response on Television Viewing." In Eli A. Rubenstein et al. (eds.), *Television and Social Behavior*. Vol. 4, *Television in Day to Day Life*. Rockville, Md.: National Institute of Mental Health.

Benedict, Ruth. 1947. *The Chrysanthemum and the Sword*. Boston: Houghton Mifflin.

Bennet, A. 1978. "Interruptions and the Interpretation of Conversation." In Proceedings of the 4th Annual Meeting of the Berkeley Linguistics Society. Berkeley: The Department of Linguistics, Univ. of California.

Berelson, B. 1952. *Content Analysis in Communication Research*. New York: Free Press.

Berger, Asa A. 1981. *Media Analysis Techniques*. Beverly Hills: Sage.

Bianchi, Jean. 1984. Comment comprendre le succès international des séries de fiction à la television? le cas "Dallas." *Les Etudes*, Lyon: CNRS-IRPEACS.

Blumler, Jay, Michael Gurevitch and Elihu Katz. 1986. *"Reaching Out: A Future for Gratifications Research."* In Karl E. Rosengren, Lawrence A. Wenner, Philip Palmgreen (eds.), *Media Gratifications Research: Current Perspectives*. Newbury Park, Calif.: Sage.

Bohanan, Laura. 1971. "Shakespeare in the Bush." In James Spradley and David McCurdy (eds.), *Conformity and Conflict: Readings in Cultural Anthropology*. Boston: Little, Brown.

Bombardier, Denise. 1985. "Television as an Instrument of Cultural Identity: The Case of Quebec." In Everett Rogers and Francis Balle (eds.), *The Media Revolution in America and Western Europe*. Norwood: Ablex.

Booth, Wayne. 1982. "The Company We Keep: Self-Making in Imaginative Art, Old and New." *Daedelus* 111/4: 33–59.

Braudy, Leo. 1982. "Popular Culture and Personal Time." *The Yale Review* 71 (41): 481–488.

Brown, P., and S. Levinson. 1979. "When Is an Overlap Not an Interruption." In Esther N. Goody (ed.), *Questions and Politeness: Strategies in Social Interaction*. Cambridge and New York: Cambridge Univ. Press.

Browne, Nick. 1984. "Reflections of Desire in 'The Rules of the Game': Reflections on the Theater of History" *Quarterly Review of Film Studies* 7/3: 251–262.

Bryce, Jennifer, and Hope Leichter. 1983. "The Family and Television: Forms of Mediation." *Journal of Family Issues* 4/2: 309–328.

Cantor, Muriel, and Suzanne Pingree. 1983. *The Soap Opera*. Beverly Hills: Sage.

Carey, James A. 1989. *Communication as Culture: Essays on Media and Society*. Boston: Unwin Hyman.

Cassata, Mary B., and Tom Skill. 1983. *Life on Daytime Television*. Norwood, N.J.: Ablex.

Cavell, Stanley. 1982. "The Fact of Television" *Daedalus* 111/4: 75–96.

Csikszentmihalyi, Mihaly, and Robert Kubey. 1981. "Television and the Best of Life: A Systematic Comparison of Subjective Experience." *Public Opinion Quarterly* 45: 317–328.

Curran, James, M. Gurevitch and J. Wollacott. 1977. *Mass Communication and Society*. London: E. Arnold in association with the Open Univ.

Dahlgren, Peter. 1985. "Media, Meaning and Method: A Post Rational Perspective." *The Nordicom Review of Nordic Mass Communication Research*, vol. 2.

Dorfman, Morris, and A. Matelart. 1975. *How to Read Donald Duck: Imperialist Ideology and the Disney Comic*. New York: International General.

Dorr, Aimee. 1986. *Television and Children*. Beverly Hills: Sage.

Eco, Umberto. 1985. "Innovation and Repetition: Between Modern and Post Modern Aesthetics." *Daedalus* 774/4: 161–184.

Eisenstadt, Samuel N. 1956. *From Generation to Generation*. New York: The Free Press.

Elliott, Philip. 1974. "Uses and Gratifications Research: A Critique and a Sociological Alternative." In Jay G. Blumler and Elihu Katz (eds.), *Uses of Mass Communication*. Beverly Hills: Sage.

Fejes, F. 1984. "Critical Mass Communications Research and Media Effects: The Problem of the Disappearing Audience." *Media, Culture and Society* 6: 219–232.

Fiedler, Leslie. 1982. *What Was Literature? Mass Culture and Mass Society*. New York: Simon and Schuster.

Fish, Stanley. 1980. *Is There a Text in This Class? The Authority of Interpretive Communities*. Cambridge: Harvard Univ. Press.

Fiske, John. 1988. *Television Culture*. London and New York: Methuen.

Fiske, John, and John Hartley. 1978. *Reading Television*. Chap. 6, "Bardic Television," 85–100. London and New York: Methuen.

Freud, Sigmund. 1961. *Totem and Tabu*. Frankfurt: Fischer Buecherei.

Fried, Stanley. 1957. "Suggested Type Societies in Acculturation Studies." *American Anthropologist* 59: 55–67.

Fromm, Erich. 1958. *The Forgotten Language*. New York: Grove Press.

Galtung, Johan, and Marie H. Ruge. 1970. "Structure of Foreign News." In Jeremy Tunstall (ed.), *Media Sociology*, 259–298. London: Constable.

Gans, Herbert. 1979. *Deciding What's News*. New York: Pantheon Books.

Gerbner, George, Larry Gross, et al. 1979. "The Demonstration of Power." *Journal of Communication* 29: 177–196.

Gitlin, Todd. 1980. *The Whole World Is Watching*. Berkeley: Univ. of California Press.

Gitlin, Todd. 1983. *Inside Prime Time*. New York: Pantheon Books.

Glasgow University Media Group. 1976. *Bad News*. London: Routledge and Kegan Paul.

Goffman, Erving. 1974. *Frame Analysis: An Essay on the Organization of Experience*. Cambridge, Mass.: Harvard Univ. Press.

Goody, Esther N. 1977. *The Domestication of the Savage Mind*. Cambridge: Cambridge Univ. Press.

Gouldner, Alvin Ward. 1976. *The Dialectic of Ideology and Technology*. New York: Seabury Press.

Graber, Doris. 1984. *Processing the News: How People Tame the Information Tide*. New York: Longman.

Greenberg, Bradley S. 1982. *Life on Television*. Norwood, N.J.: Ablex.

Hall, Stuart. 1985. "Encoding and Decoding." In Stuart Hall, et al. (eds.), *Culture, Media, Language*, 128–138. London: Hutchinson.

Harrison, Tom, and Charles Madge. 1939. *Britain by Observation*. Harmondsworth: Penguin.

Hartley, John. 1982. *Understanding News*. London and New York: Methuen.

Head, Sydney. 1974. *Broadcasting in Africa*. Philadelphia: Temple Univ. Press.

Herzog, Herta. 1941. "On Borrowed Experience—An Analysis of Listening to Daytime Sketches." *Studies in Philosophy and Social Science*. The Institute of Social Research.

Herzog-Massing, Herta. 1986. "Decoding *Dallas*." *Society* 24/1: 74-77.

Himmelweit, Hilde, et al. 1983. "The Audience as Critic." In Percy Tannenbaum (ed.), *Entertainment Functions of Television*, 67–106. New Jersey: Erlbaum.

Hjort, Anne. 1986. *When Women Watch Television. How Danish Women Perceive the American Series Dallas and the Danish Series Daughters of the War*. Copenhagen: Media Research Department, Danish Broadcasting Corporation.

Horton, Donald, and Richard Wohl. 1956. "Mass Communication and ParaSocial Interaction." *Psychiatry* 19/3: 215–229.

Houston, Beverle. 1985. "Viewing Television: The Metapsychology of Endless Consumption." *Quarterly Review of Film Studies* 9: 183–195.

Inkeles, Alex. 1950. *Public Opinion in Soviet Russia*. Cambridge: Harvard Univ. Press.

Iser, Wolfgang. 1978. *The Act of Reading—A Theory of Aesthetic Response*, 191. London: Routledge and Kegan Paul.

Jakobson, Roman. 1972. "Linguistics and Poetics." In Richard T. De George and Fernande M. De George (eds.), *The Structuralists: From Marx to Lévi-Strauss*. New York: Anchor Books.

Kaboolian, Linda, and William Gamson. 1983. "New Strategies for the Uses of Focus Groups for Social Science and Survey Research." Presented at the American Association for Public Opinion Research Meeting, Boston, Mass.

Katz, Elihu. 1971. "Television Comes to the People of the Book." In Irving Louis Horowitz (ed.), *The Use and Abuse of Social Science* (first edition). New Brunswick, N.J.: Transaction Books.

Katz, Elihu. 1980. "Media Events: The Sense of Occasion." *Studies in Visual Anthropology* 6: 84–89.

Katz, Elihu. 1986. "On Conceptualizing Media Effects." In Thelma McCormack (ed.), *Studies in Communication.* Vol. 2. Greenwich, Conn.: JAI Press.

Katz, Elihu, and George Wedell. 1977. *Broadcasting in the Third World.* London: Macmillan.

Katz, Ruth. 1985. "Societal Codes for Responding to Dissent." In Warren G. Bennis et al. (eds.), *The Planning of Change,* 354–367. New York: Holt.

Katzman, Nathan. 1972. "Television Soap Operas: What's Been Going On Anyway?" *Public Opinion Quarterly* 36: 200–212.

Kilgu:, Ann. 1974. "Using Soap Opera as a Therapeutic Tool." *Social Casework* 55: 525–530.

Lang, Kurt, and Gladys Lang. 1968. *Politics and Television.* Chicago: Quadrangle Books.

Lebra, Takie Sugiyama. 1976. *Japanese Patterns of Behavior.* Honolulu: Univ. of Hawaii Press.

Lemish, Dafna. 1982. "The Rules of Viewing Television in Public Places." *Journal of Broadcasting* 26/4: 757–781.

Lerner, Daniel. 1955. *The Passing of Traditional Society.* Glencoe: Free Press.

Lévi-Strauss, Claude. 1983. "Histoire et Ethnologie." *Annales* 38: 1217–1231.

Liebes, Tamar. 1986. "Importing Culture: 'Readings' of an American Program in Various Social Settings." Ph. D. diss., The Hebrew University of Jerusalem.

Liebes, Tamar. 1989. "On the Convergence of Theories of Mass Communication and Literature Regarding the Role of the Viewer." In Brenda Dervin (ed.), *Progress in Communication Sciences.* Norwood, N.J.: Ablex.

Liebes, Tamar, and Elihu Katz. 1988. "*Dallas* and Genesis: Primordiality and Seriality in Popular Culture." In James Carey (ed.), *Media, Myths, and Narratives: Television and the Press,* 113–125. Newbury Park, Calif.: Sage.

Liebes-Plesner, Tamar. 1984. "Shades of Meaning in President Sadat's Knesset Speech." *Semiotica* 48 (3/4): 229–265.

Livingstone, Sonia. 1987a. "The Implicit Representation of Characters in *Dallas*: A Multi-Dimensional Scaling Approach." *Human Communication Research* 13(3): 399–440.

Livingstone, Sonia. 1987b. "Social Knowledge and Programme Structure in the Representation of Television Characters." Ph.D. diss., Oxford Univ.

Lull, James. 1980. "The Social Uses of Television." *Human Communications Research* 6: 197–209.

McLuhan, M. 1964. *Understanding Media: Extensions of Man.* New York: McGraw-Hill.

Mander, Mary. 1983. "*Dallas*: The Mythology of Crime and the Moral Occult." *Journal of Popular Culture* 17: 44–48.

Mead, Margaret, and Rhoda Metraux (eds.). 1953. *The Study of Culture at a Distance.* Chicago: Univ. of Chicago Press.

Merton, Robert K. 1946. *Mass Persuasion.* New York: Harper and Row.

Merton, Robert K. 1987. "The Focussed Interviewer and Focus Groups." *Public Opinion Quarterly* 51: 550–566.

Merton, Robert K., and Patricia Kendall. 1946. "The Focused Interview." *American Journal of Sociology* 51: 541–557.

Meyrowitz, Joshua. 1985. *No Sense of Place.* New York: Oxford Univ. Press.

Modleski, Tania. 1984. *Loving with a Vengeance: Mass Produced Fantasies for Women.* London and New York: Methuen.

Molotch, Harvey, and Marilyn Lester. 1974. "News as Purposive Behavior." *American Sociological Review* 39/1: 101–112.

Morgan, David L., and Margaret T. Spanish. 1984. "Focus Groups: A New Tool for Qualitative Research." *Qualitative Sociology* 7: 253–270.

Morley, Dave. 1980. *The "Nationwide" Audience*. London: British Film Institute.

Morley, David. 1987. *Family Television*. London: Comedia.

Neuman, W. Russell. 1982. "Television and American Culture: The Mass Medium and the Pluralist Audience." *Public Opinion Quarterly* 46: 471–487.

Newcomb, Horace. 1974. *TV, The Most Popular Art*. New York: Anchor Books.

Newcomb, Horace. 1982. "Texas: A Giant State of Mind." In H. Newcomb (ed.), *Television: The Critical View*. New York: Oxford Univ. Press.

Newcomb, Horace. 1984. "On the Dialogic Aspects of Mass Communication." *Critical Studies in Mass Communication* 1: 44–48.

Newcomb, Horace, and Paul M. Hirsch. 1983. "Television as a Cultural Forum: Implications for Research." *Quarterly Review of Film Studies* 8/3: 45–56.

Nir, Rafael. 1984. "Linguistic and Sociolinguistic Problems in the Translation of Imported T.V. Films in Israel." *International Journal of the Sociology of Language* 48: 81–97.

Nir, Yeshayahu. 1984. "JR, the Kennedys and Arik Sharon." *Hotam* (Summer).

Noelle-Neumann, Elisabeth. 1973. "Return to the Concept of Powerful Mass Media." In H. Eguchi and K. Sata (eds.), *Studies of Broadcasting #9*. Tokyo: NHK.

Olson, David R. 1977. "From Utterance to Text: The Bias of Language in Speech and Writing." *Harvard Educational Review*. 47: 251–281.

Ong, Walter J. 1983. *Oralilty and Literacy: The Technologizing of the Word*. London and New York: Methuen.

Parkin, Frank. 1971. *Class Inequality and Political Order*. London: MacGibbon and Kee.

Postman, Neil. 1982. *The Disappearance of Childhood*. New York: Delacorte.

Propp, Vladimir. 1968. *Morphology of the Folk Tale*. Austin: Univ. of Texas Press.

Radway, Janice. 1985. *Reading the Romance. Women, Patriarchy and Popular Culture*. Chapel Hill: Univ. of North Carolina Press.

Robinson, John P., and Mark R. Levy. 1986. *The Main Source: Learning from Television News*. Beverly Hills: Sage.

Rosengren, Karl Eric, et al. (eds.). 1986. *Media Gratifications Research*. Beverly Hills: Sage.

Rothenbuhler, Eric. 1989. "Values and symbols in Orientations to the Olympics." *Critical Studies in Mass Communication* 6/2: 138–157.

Schramm, Wilbuir, et al. 1961. *Television in the Lives of Our Children*. Stanford: Stanford Univ. Press.

Schroder, Kim C. 1987. "Convergence of Antagonistic Traditions? The Case of Audience Research." *European Journal of Communication* 2: 7–32.

Silj, Alessandro. 1988. *A Est di Dallas: Telefilm usa ed Europei a Confronto*. Rome: Rai, Vpt.

Smooha, Sammy. 1984. "Attitudes of Jews and Arabs in Israel towards Western Culture." A Lecture given at the Van Leer Institute, Jerusalem.

Stephenson, William. 1967. *The Play Theory of Mass Communication*. Chicago: Univ. of Chicago Press.

Stolz, Joelle. 1983. "Les Algeriens regardent *Dallas*." *Les Nouvelles Chaines*. Paris: Presse Universitaire de France, and Institut Universitaire d'Etudes du Development.

Swanson, David L. 1977. "The Uses and Misuses of Uses and Gratifications." *Human Communication Research*. 3: 214–221.

Swanson, Gillian. 1982. "*Dallas*." *Framework* 14: 32–35; 15: 81–85.

Tannen, Deborah. 1982. "Spoken and Written Language: Exploring Orality and Literacy." In Jonathan Fine and Roy O. Freedle (eds.), *Advances in Discourse Processes.* Vol. 9. Norwood, N.J.: Ablex.

Thomas, Sari, and Brian P. Callahan. 1982. "Allocating Happiness: TV Families and Social Class." *Journal of Communication* 32/3: 184–190.

Thorburn, David. 1982. "Television Melodrama." In Horace Newcomb (ed.), *Television, The Critical View.* New York: Oxford Univ. Press.

Tracey, Michael. 1985. "The Poisoned Chalice? International Television and the Idea of Dominance." *Daedalus* 114/4: 17–56.

Tracey, Michael. 1988. "Popular Culture and the Economics of the Global Village." *Intermedia* 16/2: 8–25.

Tuchman, Gaye. 1973. "Making News by Doing Work." *American Journal of Sociology* 79/1: 110–131.

Tunstall, Jeremy. 1977. *The Media Are American.* London: Constable.

Turner, Victor. 1985. "Liminality, Kabbalah and the Media." *Religion* 15: 201–203.

Warner, Lloyd W. and William Henry. 1948. "The Radio Daytime Serial: A Symbolic Analysis." *Genetic Psychology Mongraphs* 38: 3–71.

Williams, Raymond. 1974. *Television: Technology and Cultural Forum.* New York: Schocken Books.

Worth, Sol, and Larry Gross. 1974. "Symbolic Strategies." *Journal of Communication* 24/4: 27–39.

NAME INDEX

SUBJECT INDEX